Preparing for La

WITNESSING TOGETHER

Global Anglican Perspectives on Evangelism and Witness

Edited by
MUTHURAJ SWAMY
and
STEPHEN SPENCER

Published by Forward Movement in 2019

www.forwardmovement.org

The Anglican Communion Office
St Andrew's House
16 Tavistock Crescent
London W11 1AP
United Kingdom

ISBN: 978-0-88028-475-2

Printed in the UK by 4edge Limited

Typeset by Manila Typesetting Company

Cover: Art/The Rev. Godson Samuel of Eden Studio, India.

Design/Michelle DeMoss-Phillips

Contents

Contributors

Joanildo Burity is a Brazilian academic and Anglican layperson; he has a PhD from Essex University and has done extensive research on religion and politics in Brazil. He is a leading researcher and professor at the Joaquim Nabuco Foundation, a social research centre, and a postgraduate teaching fellow in sociology and politics at the Federal University of Pernambuco, both in Recife, Brazil. He is an active member of the Anglican Diocese of Recife and has served as provincial representative to the Anglican Consultative Council.

Marianela de la Paz Cot was born in Camagüey, Cuba. She is part of a pastoral family, and her parents have served as priests for many years. Her mother was a suffragan bishop until her death in 2010, and her father continues to serve as an assistant to the Dean of the Cathedral in Havana. She is Priest-in-Charge of San Felipe el Diácono Episcopal Church in Limonar, Matanzas, Cuba, as well as Professor of Practical Theology at the Evangelical Seminary of Theology in Matanzas. She is also coordinator of the lay formation programme of the diocese and President of the Board of Examining Chaplains.

Joseph Galgalo is Vice Chancellor of St Paul's University in Limuru, Kenya, and Associate Professor of Systematic Theology. He earned a PhD in systematic theology from the University of Cambridge. He is an ordained minister in the Anglican Church of Kenya and honorary canon of All Saints Cathedral, Nairobi, Kenya. He has a keen interest in inter-contextual and contextual theologies as well as theological education.

Vicentia Kgabe is an ordained priest in the Anglican Church of Southern Africa with an MA in practical theology and a PhD in practical theology from the University of Pretoria. She has served as a parish priest in eight parishes in the Diocese of Johannesburg and has also held the post of Director of Ordination Process in the Diocese of Johannesburg. She is currently the Rector of the College of Transfiguration Grahamstown, the only residential seminary and training centre in the Anglican Church of Southern Africa. She also lectures on the topics of pastoral care and counselling, youth ministry, and 'Doing Theology with Women of Southern Africa'. She is passionate about issues of social justice and active citizenry and has contributed to numerous theological publications and newspaper articles.

Lydia Mwaniki is the Director of Theology, Family Life, and Gender Justice at the All Africa Conference of Churches (AACC). Before joining the AACC, she was a lecturer at St Paul's University in Limuru, Kenya, where she also acted as the Dean of Students among other responsibilities. Following a BD degree from St Paul's University (1995), she graduated with an MTH in African Christianity from the University of Kawzulu-Natal, South Africa, in 2001, and with a PhD in theology in the field of New Testament and gender from the same university in 2011. She is an ordained minister in the Anglican Church of Kenya (ACK), Diocese of Nairobi, and has served the ACK in various capacities since 1990. She is involved in advocacy work for gender justice through her engagement with church leaders and other religious leaders in Africa.

Samy Fazy Shehata is the Area Bishop for the episcopal area of North Africa in the Diocese of Egypt. He was consecrated bishop in 2017 and is Dean of St Mark's Pro-Cathedral in Alexandria, Egypt. He also serves as Principal of the Alexandria School of Theology, a non-residential Arabic-medium college operating out of three centres for the education and training of students for lay and ordained ministries. He is married to Madlaine, and they have two sons: Rafik, who is an exchange student in the United States, and Ramy, who is in his fifth year at Alexandria Medical School.

Stephen Spencer is Director of Theological Education at the Anglican Communion Office in west London. Previously he was Vice Principal of St Hild College, Mirfield, where he taught Anglican history, theology, and missiology. He was also Link Officer for the companionship link between Leeds Diocese and Mara region in Tanzania. He has been a parish priest in England and Zimbabwe and undertook doctoral studies at Oxford. He is author of books on William Temple, Anglicanism, and Christian mission, including *Growing and Flourishing: The Ecology of Church Growth* (2019).

Muthuraj Swamy is Director of the Cambridge Centre for Christianity Worldwide and a visiting fellow at St John's College, Durham University. He is also manager of the Theological Education for Mission in the Anglican Communion project. Previously he was a theological educator in India, where he hails from, and he has been involved in interfaith activities for several years. He completed a doctorate in religious studies at Edinburgh University and is author of *The Problem with Interreligious Dialogue: Plurality, Conflict and Elitism in Hindu-Christian-Muslim Relationships*

(2016) and *Reconciliation*, the Archbishop of Canterbury's Lent book for 2019.

Albert Sundararaj Walters is a Malaysian national of South Indian (Tamil) background. He has completed doctoral studies and has taught in various theological colleges, including in Bangladesh. He is an ordained priest of the Anglican/Episcopal Church and serves as Vicar-General in the Diocese of Iran.

Jonathan Wong currently serves as priest of the English congregation of the Church of the Good Shepherd in the Diocese of Singapore, which is part of the Church of the Province of South East Asia. Hailing from Singapore, where he was ordained in 1998, he has been involved with church planting and youth ministry for most of his ministry. He is currently a doctoral candidate (ABD) at Wycliffe College, Toronto.

Engin Yildirim was until recently Priest-in-Charge of the Church of the Resurrection in Pera, Istanbul, Turkey. He was born into a Sunni Muslim family in Turkey and came to faith in Christ at the age of twenty. He studied theology at Wycliffe College, Toronto, and Oxford, and was ordained an Anglican priest in 2008.

Respondents

Victor Austin is Theologian-in-Residence of the Episcopal Diocese of Dallas. His books include *Up with Authority*, *Christian Ethics: A Guide for the Perplexed*, and most recently *Losing Susan*.

Jeremy Bergstrom is the Canon for Vocations in the Episcopal Diocese of Dallas. He also serves as Priest-in-Charge of St Christopher's Episcopal Church, Dallas, Texas. He received his PhD in historical theology and patristics from Durham University. He has served as Adjunct Professor at Redeemer Theological Seminary, Dallas, as well as at Nashotah House Theological Seminary, Nashotah, Wisconsin.

Robert Heaney is the Director of the Center for Anglican Communion Studies and Associate Professor of Christian Mission at Virginia Theological Seminary. He oversees Communion-wide opportunities for theological reflection across differences, develops theological resources for Episcopalians and Anglicans, and promotes inter-cultural and inter-religious practices of reconciliation. He completed his PhD in philosophical theology at Dublin's Milltown Institute of Theology and Philosophy and was ordained a priest in the Church of Ireland in 2002. He has been active in parishes in Ireland, England, Tanzania, and the United States.

Isabelle Hamley is Chaplain to the Archbishop of Canterbury. Before moving to work at Lambeth Palace she was Tutor in Biblical Studies at St John's College, Nottingham, and parish priest in Edwalton. She is passionate about the Old Testament, particularly the difficult texts and how they can speak to the church and the world today. Some of her key responsibilities include leading on the Archbishop's priority of prayer and the renewal of the religious life, including the Community of St Anselm; overseeing the Archbishop's publishing commitments and coordinating his involvement in services; and overseeing worship and providing pastoral care for staff and residents at Lambeth Palace.

Jordan Hylden is Canon Theologian in the Episcopal Diocese of Dallas. He also serves as Co-Vicar of St Augustine's Episcopal Church with his wife, the Rev. Emily Hylden. He received his MDiv from Duke University and his AB from Harvard, and is currently writing his doctoral dissertation in theology and ethics at Duke University under Stanley Hauerwas. He is a contributor to *The Living Church*, *First Things*, and *Christianity Today* and has recently taught courses in theology and ethics at Lutheran Southern Theological Seminary in Columbia, South Carolina, and Saint Louis University in St Louis, Missouri.

Elisabeth Kincaid recently received her PhD in moral theology and Christian ethics from the University of Notre Dame, Indiana. Her dissertation was on Francisco Suárez's theories of legal interpretation and resistance. She received her BA from Rice University, a JD from the University of Texas School of Law, and an MTS from Southern Methodist University, Perkins School of Theology. She is also an Episcopal Church foundation fellow and has taught business ethics at Notre Dame.

Graham Kings is the founder of the Mission Theology in the Anglican Communion project and parish priest at St Matthew's-at-the-Elephant Church in London. He is also an honorary assistant bishop in the Diocese of Southwark as well as an honorary fellow in the Department of Theology and Religion at Durham University. He studied at the universities of Oxford, Cambridge, and Utrecht. He is a published poet and has written books on theology of mission, Kenyan liturgies, and theology and art.

George Sumner is the seventh Bishop of the Episcopal Diocese of Dallas. As bishop he oversees administrative needs throughout the diocese and is chief pastor for the clergy, laity, and congregations. Prior to his election as bishop he served as Principal of Wycliffe College in Toronto, where he led a growing seminary and was responsible for strategic planning, encouraging future priests, stewardship, building relationships with bishops, and overseeing the continuing education of clergy. He has previously served as a youth minister, missionary teacher in East Africa, curate at an inner-city Anglo-Catholic parish, vicar on a Native American reservation, and rector in a small town. He has a PhD in theology from Yale University and has written several books.

Christopher Wells is the executive director and editor of the Living Church Foundation and oversees the publishing, budget, fundraising, marketing, and staff of the magazine *The Living Church.* He completed his doctoral studies in historical theology at the University of Notre Dame and has served as a lay leader in the Diocese of Northern Indiana. He is an affiliate professor of historical theology at Nashotah House Theological Seminary, Wisconsin, where he teaches courses on Thomas Aquinas and Anglican ecclesiology.

Foreword

THE MOST REVD JUSTIN WELBY, ARCHBISHOP OF CANTERBURY

As a Lambeth Conference approaches, it would be easy to feel overwhelmed by the challenges facing the global church: the persecution of Christians in many parts of the world; the challenges of war, conflict, displacement and poverty; environmental issues; dual movements of increasing secularization and increasing radicalization; internal conflicts and so much more. And yet we can choose to turn our eyes elsewhere. We can look at the global church and marvel at its vibrancy and at the work God is so clearly doing within it and through it. This book is a shining testimony to what the church can and should be in a broken world. It is a testimony to the power of Christ living in his church and his people and reaching out to those who still haven't heard the good news.

Evangelism and witness are two of my priorities because I know that there is nothing better a human being can do than give his or her life to Jesus. And, sadly, the church in the Global North has often lost its confidence in witnessing boldly. We can feel crushed by narratives of pluralism or by hostility, or we can become all too comfortable and simply forget. But this isn't the whole story. This volume tells a much bigger story. It tells the story of the church in many different corners of the world, including in the Global North. It sheds light on many different contexts and their challenges; it reveals extraordinary creativity in responding to Jesus' Great Commission to make disciples of all nations. Each context is profoundly unique; opening a window on each of these enables the church in each place to share something of God with the church everywhere else. Unless we come together and share like this, our vision of God is small, impoverished. Because each context is unique, the way in which it embodies the good news, and the strategies and priorities each one follows, are different. And yet they all work together towards the glory of God. But because they are different, they also challenge all of us in our practices. What are Christians in this context doing better? Which virtues are they exhibiting? Which types of courage are they modelling? What is the Spirit telling the church elsewhere about what God can do and will do, if we are willing to follow?

I find this book tremendously encouraging, inspiring and challenging; I hope you will, too. I also hope that, like me, you will listen carefully to its different voices and their richness, be open to its challenges and be inspired to join in more fully with proclaiming the good news of Jesus.

How to use this book

This book is not simply a set of pre-prepared conference papers. It is, rather, an account of a set of conversations, which are ongoing. The main chapters come from the main speakers at the Dallas conference, but they have been revised to some extent in response to the conversation at the conference and beyond. Alongside them the book also includes short responses given to each paper by theologians and church leaders from North America and Europe. This format allows the reader to hear from a number of parties within the conversations and gain a sense of where they are leading. However, there is also a broader conversation, of the chapters in the book as a whole with you and me the readers, each with our own outlook and concerns and calling. By collecting the papers together and turning them into a book the intention has been to provoke us, the readers, into asking, 'What are evangelism and witness in our own contexts?' and 'How can we put them into practice?' These chapters offer a rich mine of resources to help us do this. In other words, they are intended to stimulate and encourage us to engage in evangelism and bear witness to Christ in our own neighbourhoods in culturally appropriate and fruitful ways.

Each of the chapters and responses reveals a different point of view on the topic, from a set of vantage points in the Global South and Global North. Clearly some perspectives are not easily transferable to other contexts. So to help with navigation around the book and with choosing which chapters to study it may be helpful to go through some simple steps.

1 Identify the main features and needs of your own context, for example asking if Christianity is a majority or minority faith, whether the culture of your society is generally receptive or hostile to the Gospel message, and whether the church is culturally dominant, or one outlook among a number of others, or under threat of violence and persecution. Answers to these questions will point you to particular sections of the book and particular chapters as being the most relevant. In sub-Saharan Africa, for example, Christians are often in the majority and there is great receptivity to the Gospel message. By contrast, in the Middle East Christians are a tiny minority of the population and in some places in danger of violence and persecution.

2 Then as you read the relevant chapters it will be important to try to think through how their approach to evangelism and witness could be translated to your context. To do this it is often helpful to identify the underlying principles at work in the different methodologies and then imagine how those principles could be embodied in your own context. For example, when one chapter describes how evangelism can use an evocative image from the local culture to describe Christ and his offer of salvation, we can ask what equivalent kind of images could be employed from our own cultures to do the same kind of thing.
3 Finally, we need to consider the practicalities: what would it take to put this approach into practice, who would need to be involved, what kind of preparation would be required, what kind of timescale would be realistic, how could success be measured? Evangelists need an inspiring vision to generate commitment and energy, and they need some general principles to provide a direction of travel, but they also need practical, detailed guidelines to facilitate implementation of an approach.
4 As you take these practical steps surround them with prayer, as Archbishop Justin wrote at the start of the first 'Preparing for Lambeth 2020' volume, 'we are merely joining in the work that God has already begun. God himself holds the threads of every story.'

All of this will take time to fulfil and will need to draw on the wisdom and experience of others from our local churches. So readers of this book are encouraged to recruit others to help with the formulation of a strategy for evangelism and witness. These chapters are offered to help initiate this reflective process. They are not offered as the last word on the subject but as resources to help us take initial steps in a fresh and creative approach to a perennial and fundamental dimension of Christian discipleship.

Acknowledgements

As editors we are grateful to Bishop George Sumner and the Diocese of Dallas for hosting the conference on which the chapters of this book are based. The diocese showed wonderful generosity, both in the time given to the conference by its staff and clergy and in the financial support that allowed speakers from across the world to travel to Dallas and be accommodated at Southern Methodist University. A particular word of thanks is due to Jordan Hylden, who provided calm, efficient, and cheerful oversight of the arrangements.

This is the second of three 'Preparing for Lambeth 2020' volumes to be published by the Anglican Communion Office and based on the Archbishop of Canterbury's three priorities for his archiepiscopate. They were planned and initiated by the Mission Theology in the Anglican Communion project, conceived and launched by Bishop Graham Kings. We are grateful to him for the vision and commitment to get the project off the ground and for helping to facilitate its transfer into the theological education department at the Anglican Communion Office. It is now called the Theological Education for Mission in the Anglican Communion project (TEMAC) and is looking forward to its third conference, to be held in Kenya in 2019, on the renewal of prayer and the religious life. We are also grateful to the Standing Committee of the Anglican Consultative Council, to Archbishop Josiah Idowu-Fearon, the Secretary General of the Anglican Communion, and to colleagues at the Anglican Communion Office for making the transfer possible.

Thanks are also due to SPCK for providing production services for this volume, to Fiona Little for copy-editing its chapters and to Rev Godson Samuel of the Church of South India for the cover.

Finally, gratitude is due to all the contributors, both the authors of the main chapters and the respondents, for providing a rich and diverse tapestry of perspectives on evangelism and witness which, as they show, remains as important as ever to the life of the church and, more importantly, to the coming of the kingdom of God.

Introduction

STEPHEN SPENCER

Jesus Christ is 'the same yesterday and today and for ever' (Heb 13.8). Is not evangelism, the telling of this good news to others, therefore also the same yesterday and today and for ever? At one level this is undeniable: evangelism is always about the communication of Jesus Christ to those who do not know him. But at another level, when we begin to analyse the language that becomes the vehicle of this communication, it is very far from always being the same: words change their meaning over time, depending on changes in the wider culture, and what may seem crystal-clear to one generation becomes obscure to another. One of the best examples of this is the opening of the collect from the ordination services in the 1662 Book of Common Prayer: 'Prevent us, O Lord, in all our doings with thy most gracious favour, and further us with thy continual help . . .' To modern ears this sounds as if ministry and mission are all about being constrained and restrained in its daily practice. But in the sixteenth and seventeenth centuries, when the Book of Common Prayer was being compiled and published, it carried a different meaning: to 'prevent' was all about 'going before' and 'preparing the way'. So the prayer was all about asking the Lord to open up and free the way forward for deacons, priests, and bishops in their ministry, a completely different meaning.

Furthermore, communication does not only take place through words but also through body language and posture, gesture, facial expression, how we are clothed, the accent of our voice, the way in which we arrive and leave, our social status in relation to those we are with, the cultural assumptions behind what we say and how we say it, the power dynamics behind our relationship with the other, and so on. The more that communication is analysed the more complex and subtle it becomes.

All of this means that engaging in evangelism is not always what it might seem, a lesson that many churches have learned in recent decades as they have made evangelism a priority. This has been the case in the Global North, where churches are often facing a decline in Sunday attendance and are increasingly recruiting new membership, and in the Global

South, where young churches are often working hard to add membership and consolidate their fragile place in society. The bishops of the Anglican Communion, at the Lambeth Conference of 1988, declared that the following decade, the closing years of the millennium, were to be a 'Decade of Evangelism'. This was welcomed and embraced in many parts of the Communion and began to shift the outlook of its churches, from one of 'maintenance' to one of 'mission', helping them to deliberately reach out to new people with the good news. In many places, though, the big lesson of the Decade of Evangelism was that the old model of the evangelistic rally, in which a high-profile speaker addressed a mass gathering of the unevangelized and invited them to step forward in faith, was no longer working. Most mission rallies and church meetings came to be filled with those who were already church members, and those on the outside were increasingly unlikely to turn up. In societies filled with different interest groups trying to gain supporters and money from the general public it would take much more than a simple invitation or flyer through a letter box to get outsiders to come to such a meeting.

Instead it was found that local churches must make contact with such people in neutral and unthreatening settings where relationships could be built and friendships developed. Then, in due course, when trust was well established, the invitation to faith could be made. Furthermore, in cultures where a sceptical spirit was dominant it was found to be important that opportunities were provided for questions, dialogue, and the chance to explore what faith means before inviting people to embrace it. Out of this mix of elements a whole new approach to evangelism gradually emerged, one that came to be labelled as 'the nurture course'. In this approach a local church would arrange a series of meetings for a small group of those known to church members who were invited to take part. The meeting would begin with hospitality, usually a meal, and an opportunity for people to talk and get to know each other. This was crucial in building relationships and a sense of trust. A short talk or video showing would then take place, presenting a key element of the Christian faith in an accessible and lively way. Finally there would be a time for questions and discussion, in which no question was ruled out and everyone was encouraged to express their thoughts and feelings. After several of these meetings a longer session or weekend away would be arranged, in which the Holy Spirit would be the focus of teaching and discussion and would then be invited to come into the hearts and lives of those taking part. At this point faith would start to become a living reality for many of those present.

Nurture courses of this kind have become a regular feature in the life of many churches, especially in the Global North. The Alpha Course is the most famous and widespread example, but there are many others, not least courses written by churches for their own context, which are often the most effective of all.[1] Their emergence and eventual domination of forms of evangelism came as a surprise to many. In a short leaflet produced at the end of the decade, summing up the lessons learned about evangelism over the previous ten years, the dominance of the nurture course was clear, as seen in the way it was highlighted right at the start, in 'Lesson 1': 'In ten years, lots has happened. As a direct result of the Decade…many people have come to faith in Christ, or begun a journey to faith, through local church evangelism…Courses like Alpha, Emmaus and Credo have been developed and widely used . . .'[2]

But now at the end of the second decade of the twenty-first century we are a long way from the Decade of Evangelism.[3] Furthermore, the decline of regular church membership in the Global North has not been reversed (though the rate of decline has been reduced), and in the Global South, where populations continue to grow, the overall proportion of Christians is set to reduce while the proportion of Muslims is set to increase. The need for dynamic and expansive evangelism, in which more and more people are invited to take the leap of faith and live their lives in the company of Christ and his people and be empowered by the Holy Spirit, is greater than ever. The grace and peace and joy of the Gospel are available to any who choose to receive it: the church cannot *not* do all in its power to communicate this precious gift far and wide.

But how should it engage in evangelism in the next decade of this century? In a global community that stretches around the world and includes a multitude of languages, cultures, and customs there is clearly not going to be a 'one size fits all' approach. The days of head office, whether in Rome or London or Geneva or New York, in which objectives and strategies are passed down to branches across the continents, are over. The Decade of Evangelism showed that new and fresh initiatives come from the bottom up, from the grass roots, often in surprising and unexpected ways. Different things happen in different places, and the role of head office is not to direct but to support, encourage, and disseminate experience and lessons to others. Head office needs to be renamed the Support Office. Churches have learned that they are nothing if they are not local and, in Pope Francis's evocative phrase, they are nothing if they are not 'communities of missionary disciples'.

Evangelism, then, will be different in different places. The dynamics of communication, described at the start of this Introduction, make this inevitable. Only the people of a specific place can really know how to communicate the Gospel with sensitivity and clarity to their neighbours in that place. They must be the directors of evangelism. However, there is also a role for the outsider, the one who comes into a community and brings something new and different, a foreign body like the grain of sand that becomes implanted in an oyster and around which a pearl can grow. People often respond positively to being constructively challenged in the way they see life and faith, and they can be lifted out of a spiritual rut. The offer of a different and energizing way of viewing the universe and how to approach life can be life-changing. Evangelism should not simply be a local community being confirmed in its assumptions and beliefs but should be about travelling to a new place with new possibilities. The central offices of the church, then, have an important role, whether they be at deanery or diocesan level, or national or international level. They can find out what is happening at local level, in the nooks and crannies of local church life, and see what is especially creative and innovative, so that they can pass on news of this to others across their areas and provoke and stimulate what is happening more widely. There is also a need to appraise what is happening in one place so that it can be transferred to other places, through discerning the underlying principles that can be employed more widely. Critical evaluation is required, in the most positive sense of that phrase, with due regard to Scripture and Christian tradition, along with awareness of the needs and challenges of the different contexts the church finds itself in. Theological reflection, in other words, has a key role in the promotion of evangelism across the church.

The Archbishop of Canterbury is about to host the Lambeth Conference, a once-in-a-decade meeting in which all the bishops of the Anglican Communion are invited to Canterbury. This will take place in July 2020. Most bishops are likely to attend, and it will provide an exceptional opportunity to share experience and wisdom in the practice of evangelism, among other matters. This book and its collection of chapters by different theologians from across the Anglican Communion have been produced to help the bishops and their sending dioceses and people become aware of a number of different perspectives on evangelism and what it means to bear witness to Christ. It is offered to encourage dialogue on this key area of church life in an accessible, well-informed, and theologically acute way. It does not attempt to be comprehensive, as this would be impossible in a volume of this size. It is, though, intended to offer a lively mix of different perspectives in the hope that there will be something here for everyone. It offers points of view from five continents of the world, though it prioritizes voices from the Global South, bringing them to the foreground because they have not had the exposure that voices from the Global North have had at previous Lambeth Conferences. This volume seeks to help correct such a historic imbalance by giving authorship of the main chapters to theologians from Africa, Asia, the Middle East, and Latin America. Voices from the Global North are also present, however, in a set of diverse 'responses' to the main chapters, from theologians and church leaders from North America and Europe.

The book begins with the region of the world that has seen the fastest growth in church life over the last century, sub-Saharan Africa. But these three chapters call on the African church not to rest on its laurels but to open its eyes to some fresh and sharp challenges and respond with a renewed commitment to evangelism and witness. Joseph D. Galgalo in the opening chapter provides a broad overview of the complex and diverse religious landscape in one African context in which this must take place. All is not as it seems in the townships and villages of Kenya, and Galgalo's chapter challenges the church to respond appropriately and robustly to what it finds. Lydia Mwaniki, from the same context, helpfully builds on this by outlining a range of ways in which the church can respond to these challenges. Vicentia Kgabe from South Africa then narrows the focus to one key group, young people and children, who must not be forgotten or excluded but who need the Gospel to be offered in ways that address their specific needs and tremendous potential.

In the next section a very different region is considered, one in which the church must live alongside other faiths as neighbours, showing respect while still honouring the great commission of Matthew 28. How is this to be done? Albert Sundararaj Walters, writing out of the multi-religious context of Malaysia, offers some culturally embedded and evocative images that can help attract newcomers to the faith while not pressurizing them in ways that would seem to others to be aggressive. Jonathan Wong from Singapore builds on this with his strong emphasis on gentleness and respect within evangelism. Muthuraj Swamy from the Church of South

India digs deep into Scripture and especially Jesus' dialogue with the disciples in Acts 1.6–8 to uncover some guiding principles for witnessing to the risen Christ in the Asian context.

But what about bearing witness in contexts where Christianity is on the margins of society and sometimes being persecuted? Bishop Samy Fazy Shehata of Egypt writes out of such a context where Islam is dominant and Christian churches must be very careful not to attract violence from extremists. His description of three ways in which the Anglican Church has engaged in mission in Egypt is instructive and fascinating. Engin Yildirim from Turkey writes from an equally challenging context and, after some useful biblical exposition, builds on Shehata's approach in thoughtful ways.

In the final section Joanildo Burity from Brazil presents a broadly based and critical description of the culture of his society and of the shifting place of different Christian churches within it. He presents the challenges of Pentecostalization, the de-institutionalization of religious affiliation, and the rise of social and cultural pluralism. Then Marianela de la Paz Cot from Cuba describes what evangelism and witness can mean for the local church where pastoral contact and care can make all the difference. Her chapter, based on a reading of the story of Naaman and Elisha from 2 Kings 5, allows the book to return to the realities, joys, and challenges of the local church as it reaches out to friends and neighbours.

These chapters began life as papers at a Mission Theology in the Anglican Communion conference in Dallas, Texas, at the end of May 2018. The mix and balance of the chapters reflect the mix and balance of the papers at the conference, which were not designed to be fully representative of global Anglicanism but simply to show some of the wonderfully diverse and creative outlooks present within it.

Notes

1 See Mike Booker and Mark Ireland, *Evangelism—Which Way Now?* (London: Church House Publishing, 2003), p. 56.

2 Churches Together in England Group for Evangelisation, '20 from 10: Twenty Insights from a Decade of Evangelism' (2000).

3 Though the Anglican Church of Melanesia has just committed itself to another Decade of Evangelism across its parishes.

Section 1

AFRICAN PERSPECTIVES

1

Africa's ethno-Christianity: a foothold for syncretism

JOSEPH D. GALGALO (KENYA)

The term 'African Christianity' can be misleading.[1] Christianity as practised in Africa presents a rich mosaic of traditions. Differences in traditions span vast periods of time, and in some cases show sharp theological and doctrinal variances. The most ancient of these traditions include the Coptic Church in Egypt, the Ethiopian Orthodox Tewahedo Church, and the Eritrean Orthodox Tewahedo Church. Multiplicity of denominations is typical of African Christianity. Whereas the oldest of these go back to the beginning of Christianity itself, there are new denominations that are hardly known beyond their immediate localities.[2] The plurality of African Christianity notwithstanding, the exponential numerical growth of the church over the last hundred years has earned African Christianity such impressive acclaims as 'a major component of contemporary representative Christianity, the standard Christianity of the present age, a demonstration model of its character'.[3] Those who search for quality beyond the impressive numbers lament that far from being 'the standard Christianity of the present age', 'Christian faith has become a second-rate religion in comparison with African traditional religions'.[4]

The reason for such a rating is understandable. There is a certain disturbing superficial acceptance of a form of Christianity without much commitment to the corresponding moral and ethical demands of the Gospel. This was true in 1986, when Mafico first penned these words, and the same is true today, as nothing much has changed. Mafico hazards a guess as to why such deficiency prevails. 'The majority of Christians who throng the churches on Sundays do so out of tradition, habit and perhaps the search for status.'[5] The reason is perhaps more complex. Evidently, it is puzzling that the impressive numerical growth is not matched by an equal measure of quality of faith and attendant social impact. Christianity has taken on a distinctive ethnic identity where its theology is coloured by ethno-spirituality and ethno-politics. In this sense, ethno-Christianity has become a powerful vehicle for social mobilization, and, fuelled by ethnic moral vision, is providing an external garb for a religion that at its core is a thoroughly 'African traditional religion'.

African Christianity is generally vibrant, strong, and growing, but it is also in part threatened by materialism, stealthy secularism, and perverse syncretism. The phenomenal growth of the African church inspires hope and a sense of satisfaction, but it also spells a measure of uncertainty and exasperation at the same time. A prominent feature of African Christianity, although one hardly recognized, is the ethnic composition of most church denominations and congregations, which largely draw their membership from specific ethnic groups. In practice, the majority of the churches are congregational and are either completely autonomous or semi-autonomous. Even those which for historical reasons find themselves within highly evolved structures, such as the episcopalian one, only loosely maintain allegiances or affiliations to the other ethno-congregations within that structure, despite sharing a common denominational identity. I seek to answer how 'ethno-Christianity' may be re-evangelized, but first, some background issues need to be highlighted to help us understand the nature of Africa's ethno-Christianity.

Africa's ethno-Christianity

The beginnings of Christian missionary work in sub-Saharan Africa go back to the middle centuries of the second millennium. Amid toil and much sacrifice, Portuguese missionaries planted churches in most parts of West and Central Africa and in the coastal regions of East Africa. This phase of African Christianity grew and flourished among the indigenous populations for a span of about 200 years, but with time slowly faded away. The reason for this demise is not hard to guess. There was an obvious lack of indigenous leadership. In the absence of home-grown personnel, the unsteady supply of missionaries could not guarantee a sustained growth. A deficient method of evangelization was also used. The missionaries targeted whole communities, capitalizing on 'mass conversions'.[6] This method succeeded only in planting the Christian faith superficially on a solid bedrock of African traditional religion.[7] Today, a Christianity which was reborn in sub-Saharan Africa from about the mid-nineteenth century is standing tall, but precariously so, on a foundation not of her own. With time, as was the case with the earlier phase, the current phase may too be supplanted by traditional religion. Workable methods of evangelism need to be explored and employed. In order to succeed in this regard, a critical examination of the current status of African Christianity is imperative.

African traditional religion, the solid foundation on which African Christianity stands, is a double-edged sword. It is an indispensable vehicle for enculturation but at the same time a hotbed of syncretism. I concur with George Peters that 'In sub-Saharan Africa the masses…are drifting towards a form of Christianity…, [and that] syncretism and nativism are becoming the greatest danger. A new evangelical strategy is needed if Christianity in a pure form is to dominate.'[8] Peters identifies two major issues with African Christianity, 'syncretism and nativism'. The latter is what I shall here call 'ethno-Christianity'. This is the current dominant form of Christianity in sub-Saharan Africa. In both belief and practice, this form of African Christianity is an admixture of both Christian doctrines and African traditional religions. Whereas the Bible is undoubtedly at its centre, faithful adherence to its ethical and moral teachings often comes a poor second to the sanctions of African traditional religion. In these circumstances, syncretism has become the sacrosanct pillar on which ethno-Christianity stands. Interestingly, this has not occurred by design but as a result of unguided and spontaneous inculturation of the Gospel, a process by which African traditional religion has domesticated Christianity, borrowing from it as much as it gives.

In the early days, Africans accepted Jesus but on their own terms. Where Christianity was accommodated or embraced, attaining benefits such as access to gunpowder, literacy, and the need to align the tribe with powerful allies was always in view. The case of Sechele I of Bakwena (1812–1892), David Livingstone's first and perhaps only convert, is a good example. He loved the Bible and accepted baptism in the name of Jesus, but still found a place for African beliefs and practices accommodating rainmaking, the use of charms, polygamy, and a host of other traditional rituals. Such a dual loyalty is characteristic of African Christianity, and although as such it may be judged a credible indigenous form of Christianity, most early missionaries saw it as 'half Christian and half heathen'.[9]

Today, we see more and more overt promotion of traditional religious practices by professing Christians. This is particularly the case with rites and rituals pertaining to initiations, marriage ceremonies, and funeral rites, as well as emphases on ethnic identity, exorcisms, and responses to witchcraft, misfortunes, and matters to do with childlessness, chronic illnesses, poverty, and necromancy or ancestor veneration. There is a lot in the traditional religious values that is consistent with the biblical teaching; the problem is that there is also a lot that goes on in the name of Christ but is not easily compatible with Christianity. Embracing both of these worlds, African Christians often put up with dualism, a sort of double loyalty that has become a common feature of ethno-Christianity.[10] Nominal adherence to Christianity has continued to support the growth in numbers, but has also continued to provide a strong foothold for syncretism. Most of these 'Christians' are followers of some form of Christianity but are at the same deeply steeped in a world of traditional-cultural beliefs. A kind of openness to religious pluralism, which for a long time has been an integral part of their social landscape, makes the prevailing dualism possible.[11]

Ethno-Christianity is a direct result of missionary evangelistic enterprise in sub-Saharan Africa. Missionary methods were typically similar in all parts of Africa, and all presented a strong social face of Christianity. Missionaries befriended local leaders, and often proselytized them in the hope that they would influence the whole community to ultimately embrace Christianity.[12] None of the methods seems also to have come without some form of benefit. Bible translations, for example, helped promote literacy, a skill strongly desired by Africans, as it aided social mobility and status.[13] For the same reasons missionaries were motivated to build schools and hospitals, and they used such social services to attract Africans to their denominational churches. As Nathan Nunn observes, 'Missionaries soon realized that Africans were most successfully converted when along with conversion came benefits, most notably Western education, but also health care and other forms of training.' He adds the pertinent point that 'These benefits, rather than the word of God alone, were the most effective means of conversion.'[14] Social alleviation in itself is an action not devoid of intrinsic Gospel value. Most missionaries, for example, would agree with David Livingstone, who said, 'In the glow of love which Christianity inspires, I soon resolved to devote my life to the alleviation of human misery.'[15] The approach created genuine converts, but also many who 'converted' not least in order to adapt to the changing social landscape. Conversions, therefore, did not always take place out of any theological or spiritual conviction. This situation gave birth to a social Christianity, which in its typical nominal thrust is often functional, self-serving, and in sync with the socio-political dynamics and interests of the larger community.

One inevitable result of this approach, often overlooked, is ethnic mobilization, the social cradle into which ethno-Christianity is born. A social psyche and communal bonds pull the tribe almost en masse into

Christianity, which becomes a vehicle for social self-expression and not necessarily a spiritual home. The movement into Christianity is not always consciously seen as a conversion from one faith to another, but as a social-religious adaptation where the individual's religious sphere of existence within the broader social confines of the society is enlarged. For most, the movement often happens without deliberate or critical questioning of what it means to accept Christianity while at the same time enjoying the spiritual 'homeliness' of the traditional religion. Whereas some beliefs and practices are left behind, some become part of the new religious terrain. The resultant moral haze is navigated mostly through implicit 'negotiations' between Christianity and the traditional beliefs. The general pattern is that what the Bible does not explicitly condemn may be practised. Some traditional beliefs, which may call for inter-cultural sensitivity, may be upheld but only covertly. An even more subtle reconciliation of varied world-views takes place through creative interpretations of the Bible. Here religious ideas may be mixed and recast, one in light of the other, or held simultaneously even where the resulting dual loyalty may be contradictory. For example, as John Lonsdale observes, such an idea as 'Dread of the Devil has been added to fears of witchcraft to organize the world of the occult into a new hierarchy of [religious] imagination.'[16] The moral universe is informed equally by the Bible and traditional beliefs, even though the heuristic tool that determines the ethics to negotiate the material world—marriage, sexual morality, food taboos, wealth, business, power, ethnic relations and identity, politics, conflict, civil obedience, leadership, church and state relations, and so on —is one provided by the traditional moral universe.

To avoid an over-generalization, we must mention that there are cases of genuine conversion and movement away from the old into the new. In the early missionary period, some converts had to literally move away from their homes to avoid social conflict or for fear of reverting to traditional religious practices that they had denounced.[17] In present-day Kenya, Christianity is a majority religion. Most Kenyans would identify themselves as Christian, but only for historical or social reasons. According to the 2009 population census by the government of Kenya, a total of 83 per cent of the population identified themselves as Christian at that time.[18] This number is projected to grow year by year in proportion to the national growth, even though only a tiny fraction of this number are actively practising Christians. A survey by Daystar University in the late 1980s showed that:

> Although over 80 percent of the city's population identified themselves as Christians, just 27 per cent of Nairobi's population were church members. The figure for regular church attendance was significantly lower, at less than 12 per cent of the total population. Only 8 per cent of Nairobi's population reported attending church every week, and 20 per cent attended once per month.[19]

This means that Kenyan Christianity is largely unchurched. The rest of the 83 per cent are 'Christians' because they so identify themselves. Whereas some among this large number may never attend any church service, some will occasionally do so for social occasions such as a wedding service, funeral, children's baptism, special thanksgiving involving family members, or such functions as the ordination or consecration of someone close to them. Such large numbers of 'unchurched' Christians provide a fertile ground for secularism, syncretism, and openness to religious pluralism. The large number of 'unchurched' Christians only serve to bolster adherence to ethno-Christianity.

Why would most Kenyans identify themselves as Christians even when they are loyal to both Christianity and the traditional religion? The answer lies in the ethnic nature of African Christianity. The composition of most churches has never been anything but ethnic. For example, various denominations in Kenya are largely dominated by particular ethnic groups. As Lonsdale observes, 'The Presbyterian Church of East Africa (PCEA) is almost entirely Kikuyu, and the Anglican Church of Kenya (ACK) is predominantly Kikuyu and Luo.'[20] The same is true for the Methodist Church in Kenya (MCK), which is largely Meru. The Reformed Church of East Africa (RCEA) and the Africa Inland Church (AIC) are largely Kalenjin. The African Brotherhood Church (ABC) is almost entirely Kamba, and the Seventh Day Adventist (SDA) church is dominated by the Kisii. These examples can be multiplied. Even the newer denominations are not spared. The choice of denomination by these different groups is largely due to how the early missionaries demarcated missionary spheres of influence, but also to the language and general cultural affinity that the ethnic face of Christianity presents. Today, denominational fault lines follow patterns of language preference, social interaction (particularly among the youth), and economic class: some churches draw their membership exclusively from certain social group, such as the emerging middle class.

The collective ethnic sense of belonging is also heightened where the church may be seen as a useful vehicle for social, economic, and political progress. Ethno-Christianity influences not only social belonging but also political choices. Responses to the demands of ethnicity are never strictly about individual choices but about a collective moral project.[21] Religion, by way of professing, may take on a 'form of Christianity', but the moral compass and the social vision of ethno-Christianity are shaped by the traditional religious world-view. It is in this regard that syncretism has become a key pillar of ethno-Christianity.

The dangers of syncretism cannot be overemphasized. Where syncretism abounds, 'there is a misleading, deceiving, opposing, immunizing, and resisting force at work which adopts and absorbs Christian elements'[22] yet undermines meaningful Christ-centred life that can effect ethical and moral change. Violent conflicts are common between Christians of different ethnic groups, and divisions are always along ethnic lines, having little to do with doctrinal differences. Ethno-politics reigns, and theology and biblical interpretations and applications are shaped by ethnic morality. In Kenya, for example, following a disputed presidential election result in 2007, terrible violence engulfed most parts of the country. Mwaura and Martinon make this perceptive analysis:

> The events of December 2007 through to February 2008 shook the entire Christian community of Kenya to its foundations and has haunted it ever since. The crisis prompted some congregations to splinter, especially in urban areas with multi-ethnic congregations. Christians and clergy were both victims and perpetrators of the violence. The Kenya Human Rights Commission Report documents that clergy participated in ethnic violence and mobilized their followers to do the same. Writing about needed urgent changes in the Church in Kenya, Henry Makori, a *Daily Nation* columnist, wrote, 'As professed followers of the Prince of Peace, whose law is love, Christians turned on their neighbors with demonic barbarity. They killed, maimed, looted, and raped, torched and evicted. They fuelled hate through telephone and email messages and laughed at their ethnicity. They became agents of evil.'[23]

Kenya is not alone in this. Longman points out that

> Rwanda is overwhelmingly Christian country, with just under 90 percent of the population in a 1991 census claiming membership in a Catholic, Protestant, or Seventh Day Adventist church. [Yet in the 1994 genocide,] Not only were the vast majority of those who participated in the killings Christians, but the church buildings themselves also served as Rwanda's primary killing fields.[24]

Ethno-Christian identity is so acquiescent to politics of ethnic morality that when it comes to Christian ethics of love and hospitality versus violence against the other, the latter is inversely interpreted as a moral duty to the tribe. Although ethno-Christianity readily embraces Christianity for social benefit, it does not equally appreciate the theological, doctrinal, and even ethical aspects of Christianity. It has become possible to identify oneself as a Christian without having to confess faith in Christ. This explains why Africa's most celebrated Christianity is impotent in the face of unbridled greed, corruption, violence, cultism, materialism, tribalism, and generally 'having a form of godliness but denying its power' (2 Tim 3.5, NIV). A syncretic religion that identifies itself as Christian, but which orders its world according to ethnic morality, has taken deep root in sub-Saharan Africa. It is likely that biblical Christianity maybe supplanted by a form of indigenous Christianity whose moral compass is that of the traditional religion. This calls for an urgent Christian response with effective strategies to re-evangelize 'Christian' Africa.

Responses: how do we re-evangelize 'Christian' Africa?

A lot can be learned from the old models—'mass conversions', Bible translations, social work, and charitable support for hospitals and schools. A lot also needs to be changed or applied differently. I argue here for strengthening of the basics—catechism, liturgy, discipleship, and theological education—but also for the need to re-envision a new ecclesial reality. There is need for a church that can rise above ethno-Christianity and can shape a new social and theological vision. With regard to the latter, I will draw substantially on the works of Emmanuel Katongole, but first a word about catechism, liturgy, and theological education as tools for evangelization.

Catechism should be the compass for moral knowledge and adherence to biblical truth and the tenets of Christian faith. Most churches sadly ignore the practice of catechetical teaching. The teaching of a set catechism, even in churches where this is a tradition, has been left to lowly evangelists with limited or no theological training. In these circumstances, systematic teaching of doctrines is neglected. Churches typically specialize in popular preaching where personal testimonies abound and exposition of the Scripture is at best weak. Noisy entertainment, dancing, extempore prayers, and singing of popular choruses, often with questionable theology, are common in most churches. Contemporary issues and social ills such as corruption, tribalism, violence, cultism, and questionable ethnic morality are either ignored or subsumed under vague notions of sin and the need for repentance. Sermons typically major on matters of personal aspirations, and often 'inspirational talks' are preferred to sound biblical or doctrinal teachings. To strengthen its evangelism, the church needs to rediscover and reclaim the practice of catechism. A church grounded in a sound catechistical practice is able to contend for the faith and can stand the tide of ethno-Christianity.

Theological education can be an effective tool of evangelism if, as it should be, theological formation is given a central place in the life of the church. As it is, theological education is never a priority for most churches. Self-made pastors are often ardent critics of theological education, seeing it as a foothold for the devil to plant seeds of doubt and believing that the Spirit, would, after all, give the gift of teaching to those so called, and lead them into all truth. The reality is that such 'teachers' will not be able to 'to preach with sound doctrine and to refute those who contradict it' (Titus 1.9). No meaningful evangelization can happen unless there is sound theological education.

Pentecostalism and charismatic forms of Christianity are influencing the older missionary churches in many ways. The most visible of such impacts is in worship and liturgy. The 'newer' churches have, through spontaneous contextualization, evolved a 'conversational model' that effectively relates the Gospel to the African traditional spirituality.[25] Pentecostal theology generally straddles the world of the Bible and the whole length and breadth of the African moral universe—ancestors, the spirit world, physical and spiritual wellness, wealth and health, fate and destiny, relationships and identity.[26] For example, Anderson points out Pentecostals' emphasis on healing. In African cultures, he writes, 'the religious specialist or "person of God" has power to heal the sick and ward off evil spirits and sorcery. This holistic function, which does not separate the "physical" from the "spiritual", is restored in Pentecostalism, and indigenous peoples see it as a "powerful" religion to meet human needs.'[27] There is a need to tap into this spontaneous process of contextualization for the evangelistic project of the whole church.

Pentecostals are also passionate in evangelism and the work of growing 'mega-churches'. Their aggressive approach to mission is characterized by a spirit of confidence and outward display of success and a victorious, Spirit-led life. Their membership is largely drawn from a certain economic class of society, and churches are less ethnic in composition than the more established ethno-churches. Their 'free' worship and oral liturgy afford the unhindered participation of all, and their entertaining services are equally attractive.

The effectiveness of this approach is evident in the growing 'Pentecostalization' of the 'older' churches. Almost all Kenyan churches now follow a particular pattern of Sunday worship. Most conspicuous in this pattern are the preference for informal, non-liturgical services and the 'praise and worship' segments with choruses and extempore prayers. A more theological influence is seen in the emphasis on the need for revivalism and the desire for personal conversion, where members are encouraged to share their experience of faith, the lordship of Jesus Christ, and their special identity as a 'child of God' with benefits—protected, guided, taught, preserved from sin, sustained in salvation, and inspired with hope of eternal life. 'Healing services' are also becoming common. The 'older' churches can learn from the Pentecostals' approach to evangelism. De-emphasizing ethnicity as primary identity-marker and emphasizing personal salvation and commitment can limit the negative aspects of ethno-Christianity and the tendency to syncretize.

De-ethnicizing Africa's ethno-Christianity should be prioritized by the church in Africa. If evangelism can focus on building strong communities of faith, it is possible to create viable alternatives to the ways in which ethnic morality envisions identity and social belonging. What is needed is a strategy for 'New Evangelization'.[28] Emmanuel Katongole writes extensively on how this could be done.[29] He pins 'the context, possibilities, and urgency for the New Evangelization'[30] against the background of Africa's social and political history of suffering, beset by excess greed and exploitation, ethnic conflict, political oppression, wars, poverty, diseases, and endless cycles of violence and argues for the need of a new social imagination, which should provide an alternative context for 'New Evangelization'. Katongole's thesis is summarized in his own words as follows:

> The faith crisis in Africa is neither primarily nor predominantly cultural, but political. More specifically it has to do with the ongoing phenomenon of political violence, which is traceable to the colonial heritage and imagination of Africa's modernity. Given this foundational story, the missiological and theological challenge has to do with the search for a fresh vision—a different, nonviolent story as the basis of a new African society.[31]

Katongole draws on stories of 'nonviolent activism' and Christian individual actors in Congo, Uganda, Sudan, and Rwanda to illustrate possible models for re-envisioning a church that can midwife a new social reality and ecclesial communities of faith. In both *The Sacrifice of Africa* and *Born from Lament*, he describes stories of selected Christian leaders and their projects that have been born out of enduring resilience and 'innovative, diverse, and far-reaching civic engagement'.[32] The stories of Angelina Atyam, Paride Taban, Maggy Barankitse, Christopher Munzihirwa and David Kasali, Emmanuel Kataliko, and Rosemary Nyirumbe form a rich composition in a vision of a possible world, ordered according to 'a different foundational narrative' of forgiveness and reconciliation.[33] Katongole contends, 'For a new future to take shape in Africa, the wanton sacrificing of African lives would have to be confronted—no, interrupted—by a different story.'[34] 'The church community', he adds, 'is uniquely suited for the task of the social re-imagination of Africa.'[35] Katongole makes a compelling case for ecclesial models and 'nonviolent, political interventions' as a way of strengthening and re-orienting Christianity in order to enable it to champion new communities of faith unfazed by ethnic and political divides. We suggest that 'the search for a fresh vision' should not only weave 'a new narrative' and guide new ways of social formation, but also undertake the urgent theological task of intentionally deconstructing the ethnic moral universe that so pervades Christianity and weakens it from within. 'New Evangelization' should take the form of 'nonviolent activism' and promote formation of alternative ecclesial communities. The ultimate goal should be to separate genuine Christian faith from the popular ethno-Christian religiosity and also to devise effective strategies to transform it. To inform pertinent responses, a theological study of how the ethnic moral universe impacts moral and ethical choices, and the congruence between ethnic morality and Christian doctrines, is imperative.

Conclusion

Christianity has been domesticated as an indigenous religion through a mixture of Bible teachings and African traditional religion. In sub-Saharan Africa, it has largely remained an outward wrapping for most adherents, who seem to have uncritically appropriated the name 'Christianity' for a religion that in every other sense is an African traditional religion impregnated with Christian ideas. Christianity here is, largely by historical provenance, ethnically based, and in spite of massive Christian influence, the moral universe of the majority of the adherents seems to be ordered according to their ethnic morality. The biggest problem with ethno-Christianity is its inability to live above the world in ways enlivened, inspired, and shaped by values espoused by the Gospel. This has created a 'crisis of faith', in which most 'believers' would choose the tribe over the church to solve serious social and political issues, and sometimes even by means of violence, if the tribe so chooses. These two worlds are so entangled that faithfulness to Gospel imperatives is lost in the ethnic moral maze. The church needs to be re-evangelized and empowered through effective theological education, catechistical training, models of new narratives, and successful inter-ethnic projects with a vision to form new ecclesial communities of faith that are able to shape 'fresh social imaginations'.

Response

GEORGE SUMNER (UNITED STATES)

There is a bumper sticker I used to see in the United States that says 'My karma ran over your dogma.' You might reinterpret that motto to represent the constant battle, running through all of church history, between the ethnic culture of a place and unique claims of the Christian faith. The latter always has to express itself in the former, but what if things get turned around and it is the culture expressing itself through the so-called church? Since the day on the mount of ascension when Jesus sent his disciples out to convert and baptize, the nations, the struggle has been there.

I want to thank Galgalo for his chapter, which highlights this struggle in the particular context of Africa. Its form of faith is ethno-Christianity, where the traditional religion out of which it has grown has actually come to dominate the faith. Churches are in each denomination and region tribally defined. There may always be a problem, but it is flagrantly so in the tribal tensions of Kenya in the past decade, or in the genocide of Rwanda late in the past century. I have seven questions for Galaglo, each somehow or other growing out of this perennial struggle and its particular instance in contemporary Africa.

1 He speaks of 'African traditional religion', and it does still exist and still exerts its power. But we live in a time when modernity also sweeps over Africa: cellphones in villages, China and the global marketplace, urbanization. How has all this affected what African traditional religion looks like and how and when it exerts its influence?
2 In his book of half a century ago, *Christian Ministry in Africa*, Bengt Sundkler said that the key factor in inculturation was actually the local pastor, what he called 'the middle man' (now man or woman), who stood between the old life and the new. What changes make him optimistic or pessimistic of the readiness of the pastor to fulfil this role?
3 A related question has to do with Galgalo's appeal to more earnest catechism. He is undoubtedly right. I have been listening to theologians in this continent say the same thing. But seeing the antidote and applying it are different. We never seem to get to it! What might that look like, what would be its forms, in the African context? What roles, for example, do the system of bush Bible schools and the catechist-evangelist still play?
4 In the history of Africa, and in particular among evangelical Anglicans in East Africa, as he well knows, the classic form of response to this challenge of ethno-Christianity was the East African revival, beginning

in the 1930s in Rwanda and then in Uganda. It sought to address precisely this factor of the resurgence of traditional culture, and wanted to provide a bridge to the new life. In other words, ninety or so years ago people were seeing things similarly, and here we are. What lesson does the revival have vis-à-vis his argument?

5 Connected to this historical chapter is the suggestion that more influence of the Pentecostal/charismatic stream would help revive contemporary African Christianity. This is a medicine helpful in limited doses. Missiologists used to talk about 'functional substitutes', the communion of the saints, say, for the ancestors, or a fellowship group for clan members, prayer for healing for the exorcism of a shaman, an *mchawi*. Would he see the remedies he mentions as functional substitutes, and how so?

6 All of this is playing itself out in a time of protracted intra-communion strife. This is perhaps relevant to the argument. The late Church of South India bishop and missiologist Lesslie Newbigin believed that a communion of churches should function to critique churches about their inappropriate adaptations to local culture. They were to tell one another whether what they saw was a true leading of the Spirit. It does not always work—for example, the missionaries at first could not see the work of the Spirit in the revival but came to see it better. Now if the problem of excessive inculturation is endemic, then we might say that ethno-Christianity also is a way of describing the struggle of the church in North America. We have been conformed to the norms of the marketplace and the consumer, of emotivism and postmodern self-creation. Galgalo's diagnosis would work for us too, only it looks different. Can he imagine a way in which a healthy communion of churches would help?

7 It has been almost a generation since many have recognized that the centre of gravity of global Christianity has shifted, that we are in what Philip Jenkins called 'the next Christendom', that the median Anglican is young, black, and in an evangelical church. I still think all of that is true. But I do not know what the assumption has done to how churches see themselves and their problems. Is it distant from ordinary church life? Is it a burden? How does it affect, or not affect, that kind of help which African churches would welcome, and how they see the task before them?

Notes

1 As Joel Carpenter observes, 'African Christianity, like Africa itself, is a huge generalization'; see 'Preface', in Lamin Sanneh and Joel A. Carpenter (eds.), *The Changing Face of Christianity: Africa, the West, and the World* (Oxford: Oxford University Press, 2005), p. viii.

2 See 'Ecclesiastical Cartography and the Invisible Continent', in *The Dictionary of African Christian Biography*, http://www.dacb.org/xnmaps.htm.

3 Andrew Walls, *The Cross-Cultural Process in Christian History* (Maryknoll, NY: Orbis Books, 2002), p. 119.

4 Temba L. J. Mafico, 'The Old Testament and Effective Evangelism in Africa', *International Review of Mission*, c75/300 (Oct. 1986), 400.

5 Ibid.

6 The best analysis is perhaps one provided by Adrian Hastings, *The Church in Africa 1450–1950* (Oxford: Clarendon Press, 2004), pp. 451–3.

7 See Bengt Sundkler and Christopher Steed, *A History of the Church in Africa* (Cambridge: Cambridge University Press, 2000), p. 55.

8 George W. Peters, 'Missions in Historical Perspective', in Roy B. Zuck (ed.), *Vital Missions Issues: Examining Challenges and Changes in the World Evangelism* (Eugene, OR: Wipf and Stock, 1998), pp. 21–30 at 30.

9 Stephen Tomkins, *David Livingstone: The Unexplored Story* (Oxford: Lion Hudson, 2013).

10 For a helpful exposition of this idea, see, for example, Aylward Shorter, 'African Traditional Religion: Its Relevance in the Contemporary World', *Cross Currents*, 28/4 (Winter 1978–9), 421–31, and M. J. S. Masango, 'African Spirituality that Shapes the Concept of Ubuntu', *Verbum et Ecclesia*, 27/3 (2006), 934.

11 As I was preparing this chapter a heated debated arose following the Presbyterian Church's banning of a traditional ritual, *mburi cia kiama*, which involves blood sacrifice. Most of these Christians do not seem to see any inconsistency between this practice and being a communicant.

12 Pioneer missionaries, like David Livingstone, found leaders to be the natural stepping stones for reaching out to the tribe; see, for example, Tomkins, *David Livingstone*.

13 For example P. T. Mgadla, observes: 'For the missionaries to achieve their goal of Christianizing their hosts, they had first to teach them rudiments of literacy, reading and writing. These skills were meant, hopefully, to enhance the reading and understanding the message of the Bible. Western education in most areas in which missionaries operated was introduced...to facilitate conversion to the Christian religion . . .'. 'Missionary Wives, Women and Education: The Development of Literacy among the Batswana 1840–1937', *PULA Journal of African Studies*, 11/1 (1997), 70–81 at 70. See also Patrick Harries, 'Missionaries, Marxists and Magic: Power and the Politics of Literacy in South-East Africa', *Journal of Southern African Studies*, 27/3, special issue for Shula Marks (Sept. 2001), 405–27. John Karanja states that 'Mission education offered access to

the "white man's magic" of literacy'; see his 'The Role of Kikuyu Christians in Developing a Self-Consciously African Anglicanism', in Kevin Ward and Brian Stanley (eds.), *The Church Mission Society and World Christianity, 1799–1999* (Grand Rapids, MI, Cambridge, and Richmond: Eerdmans, 2000), pp. 254–82, cited in Donald M Lewis (ed.), *Christianity Reborn: The Global Expansion of Evangelicalism in the Twentieth Century* (Grand Rapids, MI, and Cambridge: Eerdmans, 2004), p. 59.

14 Nathan Nunn, 'Religious Conversion in Colonial Africa', *American Economic Review: Papers & Proceedings*, 100/2 (May 2010), 147–52, http://www.aeaweb.org/articles.php?doi=10.1257/aer.100.2.147. For general discussion of missionaries' use of education as a means of evangelistic enterprise, see Edward H. Berman, 'African Responses to Christian Mission Education', *African Studies Review*, 17/3 (1974), 527–40; Felicity Jensz, 'Missionaries and Indigenous Education in the 19th Century British Empire, Part I: Church–State Relations and Indigenous Actions and Reactions', *History Compass*, 10/4 (2012), 294–305; and Terence Ranger, 'African Attempts to Control Education in East and Central Africa 1900–1939', *Past & Present*, 32 (1965), 57–85.

15 Quoted in Tomkins, *David Livingstone*, p. 11.

16 John Lonsdale, 'Kikuyu Christianities: A History of Intimate Diversity', in David Maxwell with Ingrid Lawrie (eds.), *Christianity and the African Imagination: Essays in Honour of Adrian Hastings* (Leiden: Brill, 2001), pp. 157–95 at 181.

17 John Karanja, *Founding an African Faith: Kikuyu Anglican Christianity 1900–1945* (Nairobi: Uzima Press, 1999).

18 See http://www.kenya-information-guide.com/kenya-population.html.

19 Ian J. Shaw, 'What has Glasgow to do with Nairobi? The Churches and Rapid Urban Growth in Twentieth-Century Nairobi: A Comparison with Nineteenth-Century Glasgow', *Studies in World Christianity*, 20/2 (2014), 166–86 at 172–3.

20 'Kikuyu Christianities: A History of Intimate Diversity', p. 186.

21 John Lonsdale, 'Kikuyu Christianities', *Journal of Religion in Africa*, 29/2 (1999), 206–29.

22 George W. Peters, 'Missions in a Religiously Pluralistic World', in Roy B. Zuck (ed.), *Vital Missions Issues: Examining Challenges and Changes in the World Evangelism* (Eugene, OR: Wipf and Stock, 1998), pp. 42–53 at 50.

23 Philomena Njeri Mwaura and Constansia Mumma Martinon, 'Political Violence in Kenya and Local Churches' Responses: The Case of the 2007 Post-Election Crisis', *Review of Faith & International Affairs*, 8/1 (2010), 39–46, https://www.tandfonline.com/doi/full/10.1080/15570271003707812?src=recsys.

24 Timothy Longman, *Christianity and Genocide in Rwanda* (Cambridge: Cambridge University Press, 2009), p. 4.

25 Ogbu Kalu, *African Pentecostalism* (New York: Oxford University Press, 2008), p. 86.

26 For a helpful exposition, see Allan Anderson, *Evangelism and Pentecostal Growth in Africa* (Selly Oak, Birmingham: Centre for Missiology and World Christianity, University of Birmingham, 2000), and Allan Anderson. *African*

Pentecostals in South Africa (Pretoria: University of South Africa, 1992); see also David Maxwell, 'Delivered from the Spirit of Poverty: Pentecostalism, Prosperity and Modernity in Zimbabwe', *Journal of Religion in Africa*, 28/3 (1998), 350–73, and 'Christianity without Frontiers: Shona Missionaries and Transnational and Pentecostalism in Africa', in David Maxwell with Ingrid Lawrie (eds.), *Christianity and the African Imagination: Essays in Honour of Adrian Hastings* (Leiden: Brill, 2002), pp. 295–332.

27 Anderson, *Evangelism and Pentecostal Growth in Africa*, p. 2.

28 First coined by Pope John Paul II; the need for 'New Evangelization' is outlined as a call to counter 'religious indifference, secularism, and atheism'. See Emmanuel Katongole, 'The Gospel as Politics in Africa', *Theological Studies*, 77/3 (2016), 704–20 at 705.

29 Katongole is Associate Professor of Theology and Peace Studies at the University of Notre Dame, Indiana, and a Catholic priest of the Archdiocese of Kampala, Uganda. For the purpose of writing this piece, I have consulted three of his writings that expound his project of a 'new social vision for Africa': *Born from Lament: The Theology and Politics of Hope in Africa* (Grand Rapids, MI: Eerdmans, 2017); *The Sacrifice of Africa: A Political Theology for Africa* (Grand Rapids, MI: Eerdmans, 2010); and 'The Gospel as Politics in Africa'.

30 Katongole, 'The Gospel as Politics in Africa', p. 705.

31 Ibid.

32 Katongole, *Born from Lament*, p. xv.

33 Katongole, *The Sacrifice of Africa*, p. 83.

34 Ibid., p. 17.

35 Ibid., p. 84.

2

Re-envisioning evangelism and witness in Africa: challenges as opportunities for the church

LYDIA MWANIKI (KENYA)

This is a call for the church in Africa to articulate evangelism and witness in response to the current realities in the continent.

The theme of the 2018 Mission Theology in the Anglican Communion conference, 'Evangelism and Witness', could not have been explored at a better time than this in Africa. It has come soon after the Conference on World Mission and Evangelism was held in Arusha, Tanzania, on 8–13 March 2018, exactly sixty years after Africa last hosted the World Mission Conference in 1958 in Achimota, Ghana. The Arusha conference, whose theme was 'Moving in the Spirit: Called to Transforming Discipleship', was meant to evoke 'the consciousness that as African Christians we are *called*, set apart, and commissioned to engage in discipleship that is empowering, transforming, and healing', and to show that, though surrounded by many dark forces, 'Africa is not a continent of despair but of great hope and resilience.'[1]

Besides, Africa as the venue of the conference was of historic significance in that, according to Agnes Abuom, the moderator of the World Council of Churches (WCC) Central Committee,

> The venue provides space to engage with the current realities of African stories of pain, anger, and celebration, including the challenges of ecumenical mission today...Africa must once again revisit the drawing board of the faith in Christ and ask whether the type of discipleship expressed is empowering, transforming lives of people across the globe, or whether it continues to subjugate some.[2]

These words, and the focus of the entire Arusha conference in which I was a participant, inspire and inform the theme of this chapter. I concur with Abuom that there is a need for more innovative, contextual, and transforming approaches to evangelism and witness, without which the church will be irrelevant in the continent.

The imperative need for the church to be contextual and relevant has been expressed from the beginning. Jesus for example did not only teach about the kingdom of God, but also demonstrated what it really is, by feeding the hungry, healing the sick, raising the dead, and addressing many other social needs. Following this integral approach, Vatican II coined the phrase 'human and integral'.[3] African theologians have emphasized this holistic approach to theology and mission. Jesse Mugambi, for example, argues that theology cannot be done in a vacuum, but must address the context in which it is done because theology is 'The systematic articulation of human response to revelation in a particular situation and context.'[4] Likewise, Steve de Gruchy appeals to the church to *connect back from mission to social development*'.[5]

My chapter responds to the call of Abuom and other (African) theologians to the church in Africa to *remain relevant* in the continent by 'once again *revisiting* the drawing board of our faith in Christ' (Abuom). It singles out evangelism and witness as the two components of mission which should be *re-envisioned* by the church in Africa, a theological process that needs to be informed by the new experiences, challenges, and opportunities.

The chapter begins by defining important terms. It then presents an overview of some of the Western missionary approaches to evangelism and witness, followed by the contemporary African context in which evangelism and witness are done, and some of the evangelistic approaches therein. It then proposes some ways in which evangelism and witness can be re-envisioned in the light of the context.

Definition of terms

Evangelism and witness: These terms mean different things. The term 'evangelism' comes from the Greek word *euangelion*, which means to proclaim the good news of Jesus Christ. According to the Archbishop of Canterbury, Justin Welby,

> Evangelism is joining in the work of God to bring redemption to this world. It's proclaiming the revolution of love that has rescued God's world from darkness to light...There is no greater privilege in life than to see God at work in changing lives.[6]

Welby continues to define witness and distinguishes it from evangelism:

> Not every Christian is an evangelist. However every Christian is a witness. A witness is someone who simply says what they have experienced – what they have seen and heard for themselves. And they give testimony to this when they are asked . . .[7]

In this case, while evangelism is proclamation of the good news, witness is giving testimony.

Re-envisioning evangelism and witness: In this chapter, to 're-envision' means to renew, re-think, or develop new approaches to evangelism and witness that are appropriate and relevant for the new contextual experiences, changes, and challenges in the continent. It is going back to the drawing board and searching for the new opportunities to do evangelism and witness.

Transforming discipleship: The Greek term *mathētēs* was used in Jesus' time in Hellenistic terms to refer to a 'learner', or adherent (follower) of a master or great thinker. In this chapter, 'disciple' refers to a follower of Christ. 'Transforming discipleship' refers to life-changing discipleship or learning, in which, through evangelism and witness, the disciple becomes more and more Christ-like and in return transforms the church and the world to conform to Christ.

Integral mission: Integral mission or holistic mission is the proclamation of the Gospel (evangelism) and the demonstration of it. Demonstration involves engaging in people's social needs as a way of demonstrating God's love to the world, as exemplified by the holistic mission of Jesus.[8] In this chapter, 'integral mission' refers to holistic evangelism and witness, which seeks not only spiritual transformation for eternal life, *but also to transform conditions that deny Africans the fullness of life on earth* which Jesus has proclaimed in John 10.10.

Brief overview of missionary methods of evangelism and witness in Africa: the 'three Cs formula'

The year 1884 is regarded as marking the beginnings of colonization in Africa, when it was partitioned by the West. Western mission had preceded this process and had already made great contributions to the development of Africa. The missionaries' main focus was on the religious and cultural landscape and value system, while the colonizers focused on economic and political life of Africans.[9]

Nevertheless, the missionaries' approach to evangelism was heavily indebted to the colonial enterprise, in such a way that the collaboration between the two left no clear demarcation between their distinctive roles. Consequently, missionaries were seen to have prepared the ground for Africa to be governable. Since the missionaries followed their flag mainly for protection, they were able to engage in the political and economic dimension as approaches to evangelism, besides their focus on religious and cultural aspects. As early as 1849, for example, when David Livingstone, a missionary and an explorer, toured Africa, he denounced the evils of the slave trade and recommended Christianity, commerce, and civilization as a better alternative. This was regarded as the *three Cs formula.*

Later missionaries in Africa saw themselves as agents of this formula. The initial motive of the formula was to intensify the anti-slavery measures throughout East Africa, and to bring greater opportunity for economic development, peace, and constitutional rule so as to enable them to preach the Gospel in a peaceful environment.[10] This is one of the indicators that Western missionaries, right from the beginning, had a holistic or integral approach to mission. Nevertheless, their social intervention against the slave trade was unfortunately the major excuse used by the colonial governments to colonize many African states and partition Africa, since many missionaries invited their governments to intervene. Consequently, it turned out that the West's motivation for abolishing the slave trade was mainly an economic one, for its own benefit, rather than a wish to promote African dignity.

The other respects in which the missionaries' approach to evangelism was holistic, besides their efforts to abolish the slave trade, lay in their establishment of schools and health centres, and their work in feeding and clothing the needy. Education was the major tool for evangelism. Schools served as centres for teaching the Catechism, and Christians were also taught the art of reading and writing. Such education required the converts to detach themselves from their traditional way of life. It was therefore a means of civilization, and missionaries were praised by colonial administrators for being agents of civilization.[11]

Missionaries in Africa therefore embraced holistic ministry as a means of evangelism and witness in their endeavour to execute the three Cs formula. While their motive was good, their role as agents of the oppressive colonial agenda for Africans contradicted their initial calling of evangelism and witness, since they had to comply with the government's agenda.

Secondly, some Africans embraced Christianity simply for its material benefits rather than spiritual transformation.

Moreover, embracing Christianity called on Africans to be Europeans first, before they became Christians, by obliging them to abandon their culture. African culture, including its religious customs, was loathed by the missionaries as demonic and backward, in contrast to the European way of life, which they deemed civilized. In their resistance to this, Africans established their own African schools and churches, through which they could identify with God in their own culture and hear God speak in their African languages.[12]

Evangelism and witness are not meant to uproot people from their cultures, but rather to turn them to Christ, who through the Holy Spirit helps the individual to be transformed from aspects of culture that are not in line with the Gospel and to grow into Christ's likeness.

The contemporary African context and approaches to evangelism and witness

The contemporary African context in which evangelism and witness take place presents various realities. These include the rapid growth of Christianity, which exists simultaneously with ungodliness, the population increase, especially among the youth, religious pluralism, and several other challenges. Each has profound implications for evangelism and witness in Africa, though this list is far from being exhaustive. This section focuses on some of these contextual realities and challenges, which prompt a re-envisioning of evangelism and witness in the continent.

The rapid growth of Christianity in Africa

Several sources bear witness to the rapid growth of African Christianity. Statistical data from the *Atlas of World Christianity*, for example, show that in 1910, the population of Africa was less than 10 per cent Christian; but that this proportion increased to 50 per cent by 2010, with sub-Saharan Africa well over 70 per cent Christian.[13] Thus, according to the Pew Research Center, Christianity is growing faster in Africa than anywhere else in the world.[14] It is estimated that by 2060, more than four out of every ten Christians will live in Africa.[15]

Examples of the factors leading to the rapid growth of Christianity in Africa, some of *which also serve as approaches to evangelism and witness*, are well captured by John Mbiti as described below.[16]

The shift from Western Christianity to African Christianity

The latter part of the twentieth century was marked by a change in Christian dynamics, characterized by the rise of churches in the Global South in terms of their numerical growth as well as their engagement with African socio-cultural contexts. This engagement was instrumental in the shift from Western Christianity, which was planted by missionaries, to African Christianity, with which Africans could identify. According to John Mbiti, 'By the beginning of the 21st century, Christianity in Africa had taken shape and established roots in all areas of African reality. It has come to stay.'[17]

African religiosity

Africans are by nature religious. Their religiosity serves as a fertile ground for Christianity and any other religion to germinate and grow. African Christian theologians argue that missionaries did not bring God to Africa because the God of the Bible is the same God who was worshipped by African communities before the missionaries came.

Oral theology

The emergence of African Christianity mentioned above led to an oral theology, in which Africans could understand and retell Bible passages orally through their own languages expressed in songs, prayers, dance, fellowship, and sermons. Written theology came later, and by the twenty-first century, African theology had literally burst out in articles, books, conferences, research, symposia and college and university courses, both in Africa and in other continents. This sense of identity and ownership has no doubt attracted more Africans to Christianity.

Bible translation

Translation of the Bible into different African languages is a very significant factor. Mbiti indicates that by the end of 2014, the languages numbered close to 800. Hearing the Word of God in one's own language adds value to the Gospel, because people appreciate the fact that God understands and values their own language. It leads to ownership of the Bible as 'our Bible'.

Africans' own initiative to evangelize

African Christians themselves have taken the initiative to evangelize both formally and informally. They use radio, television, films, social media, open-air meetings, pastoral visitations, Bible studies, testimonies, and normal conversations, to mention just a few.

The rapid growth of Christianity, therefore, is an opportunity for the church to permeate the continent as its salt and light, as Jesus commanded the church in Matthew 5.13–14. Since Africa is like a *porous rock* in matters of religion, in that religion permeates it with much ease: it is not difficult to transform and strengthen the faith of Africans through proper evangelism and witness, under the guidance of the Holy Spirit. Nevertheless, Christians have not always lived out their faith for what it is, as evidenced by the huge dichotomy between faith and action. This dichotomy is well captured by Philomena Mwaura:

> Africa is a context that tells or depicts two stories that are diametrically opposed. One is a story of frustration and cry of children, women and men who are tired of unending debt, poverty, unlimited exploitation of their natural and human resources and who desperately seek to end the misery caused by civil wars, ethnic conflicts, inept and unaccountable leadership, mismanagement of national affairs and resources, debilitating disease including Ebola, Malaria and HIV and AIDS.
>
> The other story is one of a vibrant Christianity, a rich spirituality that engenders hope and sustains her in the midst of this apparent chaos... *It is as if night and day exist simultaneously in modern Africa.*[18]

This disconnect between faith and action raises a pertinent question about the quality of the Christian faith and models of evangelism and witness, thus prompting the need to re-envision evangelism and witness in the continent.

Ecumenism

Christianity in Africa includes various Christian identities such as Roman Catholic, Orthodox, Protestants, Pentecostals, Evangelicals, and African-instituted churches. Ecumenism is an effort to bring together all the different denominations to work for the common good of proclaiming the Gospel. Efforts to deepen ecumenical relations have been made since the first World Mission Conference in New York in 1900, which brought together various mission organizations working in Africa in order to find ways of coordinating their activities. The second World Mission Conference, in Edinburgh in 1910, also focused on Africa. The World Council of Churches (WCC, founded in 1948), the All Africa Conference of Churches (AACC, 1963),[19] and the national councils of churches and Pentecostal national ecumenical associations, among others, all represent efforts to bring churches together in order to seek theological solutions to the challenges facing the continent with a common voice.[20]

Religious pluralism

Africa is a multi-religious continent. Among the most popular religions are Christianity, Islam, traditional African religions, Hinduism, Bahá'i faith, Buddhism, and Judaism; Christianity and Islam remain the most dominant and the fastest-growing.[21] The relationship between Islam and Christianity has differed from place to place. In some countries where large Christian populations exist alongside a Muslim majority, such as Nigeria, Sudan (before the independence of South Sudan in 2011), and Egypt, there have been religious and political conflicts, while in a place like Senegal, where Islam is the dominant religion, the two religions have amicable relationships.

The rise of Islamic militant groups in Africa has however continued to strain the relationships between Christians and Muslims. The two main ones are the Al-Shabaab militants, whose headquarters are in Somalia, and the Boko Haram Islamists in north-eastern Nigeria, whose aim is to impose sharia law in the region. Olupona argues that the two have close connections.[22] Nevertheless, Boko Haram has targeted not only Christians in Nigeria but also fellow Muslims whom it considers to be state agents.

Efforts to promote peaceful co-existence between Christians and Muslims include dialogue on the issue of violent extremism, holding joint conferences, and advocacy workshops to address issues of peace and security, gender-based violence (GBV), HIV, and various other issues affecting the continent and individual nations.[23] In Kenya, for example, the Interreligious Council of Kenya (IRCK), a national coalition of all faith communities,[24] has been instrumental in promoting dialogue among political actors to ensure peaceful elections and other activities.

Therefore, since religion plays an important role in providing the ethical standards that can shape cultural, social, economic, and political norms, evangelistic approaches should aim not only to convert people of other religions to Christianity, but also to *promote peaceful co-existence* among religions. This in return raises the question of the moral authority, integrity, and unity of religious leaders to address the challenges in the continent.

Challenges and ungodliness in Africa

We have seen that while Christianity is growing rapidly in Africa, this growth is marred by much ungodliness. Some of this ungodliness, which calls for a re-envisioning of evangelism and witness, has been discussed by Abuom and Mwaura among other scholars, as mentioned above. This section elaborates on some of the most burning issues.

Gender-based violence (GBV)

GBV is an umbrella term for any kind of discrimination or harmful behaviour which is directed against a person on the basis of their gender. It can be physical, sexual, psychological, economic, or socio-cultural.

Although GBV affects all human beings including men, women, youth, and children, research shows that prevalence of GBV is mostly among women and among young people, especially girls. Forms of GBV in Africa include, but are not limited to, wife battering, wife inheritance, widowhood rites, female genital mutilation (FGM), rape (especially in war-torn countries and conflict areas), early marriage for girls, and child labour, many of which deny the girl-child a chance to pursue education, hence blocking opportunities for a meaningful future career. Other situations that undermine women's dignity are lack of access to and control of resources, and limited participation of women in leadership and decision-making processes in the religious, political, and societal arena.

GBV in Africa is escalated by cultural norms and religious teachings that relegate women to a state of subservience. This is clear from Joseph D. Galgalo's observation that justification of discrimination against women 'is even sought in religious faith where culturally premised hermeneutics buttress theological positions'.[25]

Conflict and war

Africa is a bleeding continent. In countries such as South Sudan, Burundi, the Democratic Republic of the Congo, and even some parts of Nigeria, peace is very fragile. The main sources of conflict include political wrangles, ethnic skirmishes, fights for natural resources, and personal differences, among others. Other forms of conflict include human trafficking and forced migration, racism and xenophobia, and abject poverty.

Corruption

Corruption involves stealing public funds and bribery. This impoverishes African nations in that it causes many people to be dehumanized, below the poverty line and unable to afford basic needs. Again corruption leads to a culture of *impunity* where evildoing is not punished. Corruption has become a major issue in Africa, to the extent that the African Union's theme for 2018 is 'Winning the Fight Against Corruption: A Sustainable Path to Africa's Transformation'.

The prosperity gospel

The prosperity gospel in Africa is propagated by some Pentecostal churches which promote amassment of resources and wealth and demonize poverty.[26] Its theology is wanting in that it regards earthly wealth as a sign of blessing from God and poverty as a curse. While the Bible does not condemn wealth but rather loathes systems that create poverty, the prosperity gospel is contrary to the theology of the cross, which is characterized by suffering and pain. Further, Biri observes that the prosperity gospel promotes poverty by exploiting its followers economically in the guise of earthly blessings, through corruption, a lack of democratic and accountable structures, abuse of power by leaders, and sometimes by partnering with the government in development projects.[27]

Re-envisioning evangelism and witness in Africa

How can the church in Africa *re-envision* evangelism and witness in the light of the reality in the continent, in order to remain relevant? This section addresses this question, regarding the challenges in Africa not as means of weakening the church, but as *opportunities* to re-envision evangelism and witness. By the power and guidance of the Holy Spirit, this can be done through the following approaches.

Developing transforming discipleship programmes

The disconnect between faith and action mentioned above can partly be attributed to a general lack of seriousness about God, that is, a state of spiritual laxity and a lack of will to obey baptismal and confirmation vows. Thus, intentional discipleship programmes aimed at deepening the faith of church leaders and their followers in the Word of God must be developed in order to eliminate this lukewarmness and equip Christians to transform their society into Christ's likeness. These programmes may include contextual Bible studies, teaching and preaching on topical issues affecting Christians, midweek fellowship, prayer, and seminars and conferences for individual groups in the church, to mention just a few.

The ethical method of developing these programmes of discipleship should be to use Scripture, Gospel proclamation, and, to borrow from Emmanuel Katongole, the development of 'a more deeply entrenched theological practice which can challenge the different histories and politics which tend to obscure…[the] aspiration of African peoples'.[28]

Katongole rightly considers these theological practices to be those embedded within the eucharistic liturgy, especially the act of greeting.[29] Such embedded practices are one source of ethical action which Anglicanism has to offer. In line with the insights from the 'greeting' of peace at the eucharist is the African spirit of *Ubuntu*, of building solidarity among human beings,[30] another ethical practice which should characterize discipleship programmes and the entire Christian life. Father Paulinus Odozor, for example, argues that Christians can retrieve from African traditional religious practices 'lessons about the importance of human solidarity, the maintenance of family cohesion, the sacredness of human life, and the importance of living morally upright lives'.[31]

Since catechesis is crucial in Christian formation, because it contains teachings on the essential truths of the Christian faith and how Christians live those truths, it should be taught properly and seriously by *qualified theologians*. Mwaura warns that:

> Numerical growth of the African church requires to be matched by deep catechesis if it will escape the fate of the North African church which grew numerically but its shallowness could not withstand the onslaught by Islam in the 7th Century.[32]

The emphasis in catechesis, which usually has a question-and-answer method, should not be on intellectual learning of the faith alone, *but on living it*: a catechesis that facilitates a living personal and communal encounter with the Risen Lord. This will promote appropriate moral behaviour and mutual concern and responsibility. Equipping the teachers of the Word with the true Gospel, and urging them to teach faithfully, is a powerful tool to combat heretical teachings including the heresies of the prosperity gospel. We cannot evangelize and witness to others *until we have known God personally and intimately.*

Interpreting gendered biblical texts in liberating ways

Promoting and empowering women's voices is undoubtedly crucial for a full-throated proclamation of the Gospel, as well as contributing to the flourishing of the entire community and the advancement of the common good. Nevertheless, generally speaking, gender issues cut across all Christian denominations in the continent. The main debates are centred on women's ordination to priesthood and consequently their full participation in leadership positions in the church. It is worrying that some churches do not ordain women at all, for example the Roman Catholic, Coptic, and Orthodox Churches. In some churches where the ordination of women has been accepted in principle, for example the Anglican Church in Africa, the pace of women's ordination is still slow compared with that of men,[33] the number of women archdeacons is minimal, and there are only three women bishops, two of them in the Anglican Church of Southern Africa, and there is no woman archbishop.

The main challenge is the way in which the Bible is interpreted to reinforce cultural bias against women. The quest for gender justice and dignity entails that the church, especially church leaders, should make a deliberate effort to interpret and apply the Bible in liberating ways for all. The Bible contains numerous passages which could be used as a basis for gender justice, such as Genesis 1.27, Galatians 3.28, and those describing Jesus' treatment of women, in which he accorded them dignity. Efforts to promote ecumenism should address the question of gender equality as a justice issue.

The Church's engagement with the African Union and United Nations Development Agendas

In her evangelistic work, the church cannot afford to stay aloof from or ignorant of the continental and global development agenda and promotion of human dignity. Besides, as Dietrich Werner rightly says, 'The knowledge about Christianity is needed for governments and the United Nations is "crying out" to work with faith-based organizations (FBOs).'[34] Some of the legal instruments which the church can engage, even in the area of gender justice, include the Sustainable Development Goals (SDGs) and African Union Agenda 2063.

Since the entry point for the church is her Scriptures, the church needs to find biblical and theological foundations for these legal instruments and apply them using a theological critique which results in transformation. This will empower faith actors to use biblical teachings to *reinforce* legal instruments in mission work, and hold governments accountable when human rights are violated. Church leaders need to recognize the authority they have, not only to speak out against policies and practices that are not life-giving, but also to influence policy implementation at the church and governmental level. In so doing, the church will remain relevant to the African church and society, and promote human dignity.

Strengthening ecumenical and interfaith relations for peace-building and reconciliation

Religious, ethnic, and denominational barriers have been a big threat to the efforts of religion to address the overwhelming challenges in Africa. As Mwaura rightly observes, 'Dialogue has not been a common practice in the Church due to fundamentalist currents, and misuse of the power of religion by economic and political vested interests.'[35]

Promoting unity in diversity will break ethnic, denominational, and interreligious barriers, hence creating synergy to address the numerous challenges in Africa, since no single group can overcome these challenges alone. Unity does not mean uniformity; as Karamaga rightly argues, as churches 'We can be quite different, but have the unity of vision and unity of action, translated through working together and moving in the same direction, serving the kingdom of God.'[36]

Prioritizing the ministry to youth

Africa is the most youthful continent in the world. According to Stephen Williams, 'Africa has the fastest-growing and most youthful population in the world. Over 40% are under the age of 15, and 20% are between the ages of 15 and 24. These statistics present a serious challenge.'[37]

The focus of the African Union in 2017 was on youth under the theme 'Harnessing the Demographic Dividend through Investments in Youth: Empowering Young People, Especially Young Women, for Leadership and Civic Participation'. The biggest challenges among youth remain unemployment and minimal inclusion in leadership positions, and these are matters which the government and the church need to address, since youth are an untapped resource in Africa. Besides, as Mwaura notes, the youth department 'is the most under-funded and undervalued in many churches'.[38] If properly nurtured, the high percentage of youth in Africa will *not present a challenge but a great opportunity for the church to flourish.* Young people are energetic and have a great wealth of talent, potential, energy, and all that is necessary to do evangelism and witness for the growth and prosperity of the church in Africa.

Conclusion

The new experiences and challenges in Africa resulting in the dichotomy between faith and action, often reflected in various malpractices in the continent, call for a re-envisioning of evangelism and witness. The church in Africa is slowly falling short of the ethical values of the eucharist and African *ubuntu*, and needs *revival* and *transformation* of both its leaders and other believers by the power of the Holy Spirit. Alongside this need for renewal is the need for the church to renew and intensify its holistic ministry in mission and evangelism in ways that give life and resist life-denying forces. Thus, proclaiming spiritual liberation should always seek to accompany liberation from poverty, injustice, and physical suffering as well. Jesus' application of the description of the liberator in Isaiah 61.1 to himself in Luke 4.18–20 should be understood in terms of spiritual and physical liberation. Only then will the church become the salt of the earth and the light of the world, as mandated by Jesus in Matthew 5.13–14. Then the transformed church will soon transform the challenges and powers of ungodliness into *golden opportunities* to propagate this good news of Jesus Christ, through evangelism and witness.

Response

ELIZABETH KINCAID (UNITED STATES)

Thanks are due to Mwaniki for a clear, detailed, and comprehensive analysis of both the challenges and the opportunities for evangelism in contemporary Africa. Her chapter provides an excellent primer for understanding the challenges for evangelism in the church on this continent and outlines an important agenda going forward. As an ethicist, not a scholar of missiology or of African Christianity, I found her chapter especially useful for orienting me to several fields to which I have had little exposure.

There are two key elements of her proposed agenda which stood out to me as especially valuable. First, Mwaniki reminds her readers that to engage in (or support) evangelism in Africa, we first have to understand the African context, with context understood in an exceptionally broad sense, to include history, politics, praxis, and economics. In setting these parameters, Mwaniki urges those committed to evangelism in Africa to first know the story of Africans and African Christianity. Stanley Hauerwas has written, 'To know our creator, therefore, we are required to learn through God's particular dealings with Israel and Jesus, and through God's continuing faithfulness to the Jews and the ingathering of a people to the church.'[39] Mwaniki would add to this statement that in order to invite Africans into the story of the God of Abraham, Isaac, Jacob, and Jesus, we have to know the story of God's faithfulness in Africa, and how evangelists in Africa have reflected and failed to reflect that faithfulness. Specifically, we have to consider the complicated moral legacy of European and American evangelists in Africa, and the effects of their attempts and failures on Africa today.

Secondly, Mwaniki argues that any form of evangelism must not only include the proclamation of the Gospel, but also transformation according to the Gospel. She does not envision evangelism as impacting people's lives only on a spiritual or supernatural level, but rather as always leading to conversion and then transformation of all facets of human existence. In the words of *Gaudium et Spes*, the effects of evangelism must be integral.[40] To achieve this goal, Mwaniki calls the church in Africa to 're-envision' evangelism in Africa. She argues that evangelism not only is a proclamation of God's love, but demonstrates that love through an intense commitment to meeting people's physical needs and supporting them in their struggles. Those proclaiming spiritual liberation from the power of sin and death should always seek to accompany this liberation with liberation from poverty, injustice, and physical suffering as well. Evangelists should always understand Jesus' appropriation of the title of the liberator in Isaiah 61.1 to himself in terms of spiritual *and* physical liberation (Lk 4.18–19).

Moving beyond describing these primary and crucial planks of her project, I would like to pose a few questions to Mwaniki's chapter which I hope might be helpful for the next stages of her research and project. My questions seek to gain a better theoretical understanding of her academic method and a better practical understanding of her experiences of transformative practices of evangelism on the ground in Africa. I will consider each of her three constructive proposals in turn, and then ask a question related to the engagement between her project and the church in the West.

Mwaniki's first constructive proposal is that evangelism begins with the proclamation of the Gospel, but must always lead to the development of transformative discipleship programmes in which new Christians are equipped for 'a living personal and communal encounter with the Risen Lord' in ways which 'promote appropriate moral behaviour and mutual concern and responsibility'. This is a robust, scripturally grounded mandate. However, given the complexity of the context which Mwaniki has described, I believe an important next step is outlining precisely how the content of these programmes will be determined. The content of moral Christian teaching is not uncontested within Anglicanism. As Emmanuel Katongole points out, Africa itself is subject to the spectre of postmodernism, expressed through even 'celebration of Africa's cultural difference and uniqueness'.[41] What is the ethical content of these programmes which can hold against the postmodern deluge of relativism? Scripture and the Gospel proclamation will undoubtedly take pre-eminence, but what other resources are available? Katongole argues that part of the solution may be the development of 'a more deeply entrenched theological practice which can challenge the different histories and politics which tend to obscure the actual historical struggles, conflicts and aspirations of the African peoples'.[42] In a different essay, Katongole considers such theological practices as those embedded within the eucharistic liturgy, especially the act of greeting.[43] These types of embedded practices within the liturgy, which carry their own ethical significance, are one source of ethical action which Anglicanism may retrieve as well. Perhaps the development of these practices would also call for the retrieval and reclaiming of the African patristic sources which Mwaniki identifies early in her chapter? The Oxford Movement, for example, discovered new insights into scriptural interpretation and application through the retrieval of patristic sources. Might African Christianity as well? Another alternative source may be some areas of African traditional religion which also align with Christian convictions. For example, Paulinus Odozor argues that Christians can retrieve from African traditional religious practices 'lessons about the importance of human solidarity, the maintenance of family cohesion, the sacredness of human life, and the importance of living morally upright lives'.[44]

Mwaniki's second constructive proposal is a call to interpret gendered biblical texts in liberating ways. Promoting and empowering women's voices is undoubtedly crucial both for a full-throated proclamation of the universal message of the Gospel, as well as contributing to the flourishing of the entire community and the advancement of the common good. However, her condemnation of churches where women are not ordained to the priesthood seems to conflict with her fourth constructive claim that ecumenism and even interfaith engagement are essential for this work of transformative evangelism. How much room does Mwaniki's call for gender-neutral interpretation leave for partnership with churches which affirm only male pastoral leadership, such as Roman Catholics and Copts, two churches with a historical and contemporary presence in various parts of Africa?

Mwaniki's third constructive proposal is to engage with the Sustainable Development Goals (SDGs) and African Union Agenda 2063. This proposal is appealing because it provides an objective measure for how churches can work to promote integral human development, as well as useful steps towards this achievement. I agree with Mwaniki's claim that these goals lack a theological foundation, and her constructive suggestion that this may be something which churches are equipped to provide. However, I do not think she goes quite far enough in considering what type of critique should be carried out by the church when appropriating secular goals. In certain cases, there may not only be a need for a theological foundation, but a need for a theological deconstruction and then reconstruction of both the method and the goals. Emmanuel Katongole identifies one example of the need for this type of critique when he discusses how the widespread promotion and distribution of condoms, carried out with the laudable goal of preventing the spread of AIDS, has also resulted in what he refers to as the 'condomization' of Africa—the promotion of a culture promoting disposability, freedom, and pleasure at all costs. In order to react to this type of cultural transformation, the church is called to critique and reconstruct, not simply provide theological justification.[45]

My final question is focused on the needs of the church in the West, not Africa, which is, admittedly, not the subject of Mwaniki's chapter, which focuses on the questions of transformative evangelism within Africa carried out by Africans. This question looks ahead to a potential future project on a related topic. First, what is the appropriate involvement of the churches in the West in this evangelism within Africa? Mwaniki provides a nuanced and careful analysis of the historical gifts of Western missionaries, the flaws in their missionary endeavours, and the negative effects of their failures. In addition to her analysis, a quick review of news stories related to the effects of contemporary Christian humanitarian aid to Africa, intended to promote human flourishing, demonstrates how often these well-meaning attempts promote more harm than good. Given these historical realities, is there anything the Western church can or should be doing to support our brothers and sisters in Africa? Or does the reality of the contextual challenges which she has identified make engaging in this work an almost insurmountable obstacle? This question seems especially important in the context of our own Anglican Communion: what are the limits on that communion imposed by the constraints of these historical failures?

Notes

1 Lesmore Gibson Ezekiel and Jooseop Keum, 'From Achimota 1958 to Arusha 2018: A Journey to and after Arusha', in Lesmore Gibson Ezekiel and Jooseop Keum (eds.), *Conference on World Mission and Evangelism from Achimota to Arusha: An Ecumenical Journey of Mission* in Africa (Nairobi: Acton Publishers and WCC, 2018), p. 10.

2 Agnes Abuom, 'Foreword', in Lesmore Gibson Ezekiel and Jooseop Keum (eds.), *Conference on World Mission and Evangelism from Achimota to Arusha: An Ecumenical Journey of Mission* in Africa (Nairobi: Acton Publishers and WCC, 2018), p. vii.

3 For details on the historical development of integral mission see C. R. Padilla, *Integral Mission and its Historic Development* (2003), http://www.micahnetwork.org/sites/default/files/doc/library/integral_mission_and_its_historical_development_padilla.pdf.

4 Jesse Mugambi, 'The Future of the Church and the Church of the Future in Africa', in The All Africa Conference of Churches Information Desk (eds.), *The Church of Africa: Towards a Theology of Reconstruction* (Nairobi: Motif Creative Arts Ltd, 1991), pp. 40–1.

5 Steve de Gruchy, 'Integrating Mission and Development: Ten Theological Theses', *International Congregational Journal*, 5/1 (2005), 26.

6 Justin Welby, 'Sharing Jesus: The Revolution of God's Love', https://www.archbishopofcanterbury.org/priorities/evangelism-and-witness.

7 Ibid.

8 See also the definition by the Micah Challenge project in de Gruchy, 'Integrating Mission and Development', p. 29.
9 See Chukwudi A. Njoku, 'The Missionary Factor in African Christianity, 1884–1914', in Ogbu U. Kalu (ed.), *African Christianity: An African Story* (Trenton, NJ: Africa World Press, 2007), pp. 218–52.
10 Keith Anderson, *Church History and Theology* (Nairobi: Provincial Board of Theological Education, 1984).
11 A. J. Temu. *British Protestant Missions* (London: Longman, 1972), pp. 90–3.
12 See Lydia M. Mwaniki, 'The Impact of the Church on the Development of the Identity of an African Christian Woman: A Case Study of the Anglican Church of Kenya, Diocese of Kirinyaga 1910–1999', master's dissertation, University of Natal Pietermaritzburg, 2000, pp. 51–3.
13 See Jesse Mugambi, 'The Profile of African Christianity at Home and in the West', in Isabel Apawo Phiri et al. (eds.), *Anthology of African Christianity*, Regnum Studies in Global Christianity (Oxford: WCC, 2016), p. 1.
14 David McClendon, 'Sub-Saharan Africa will be Home to Growing Shares of the World's Christians and Muslims', Pew Research Center (Apr. 2017), http://www.pewforum.org/2017/04/05/the-changing-global-religious-landscape/.
15 See a detailed account of the growth of Christianity in the Global South with reference to its past, present, and future in Phiri et al. (eds.), *Anthology of African Christianity*; cf. a table showing the shift in the demographic centre of Christianity from the northern to southern continents in J. Kwabena Asamoah-Gyadu, 'Growth and Trends in African Christianity in the 21st Century', ibid., p. 65.
16 John S. Mbiti, 'Foreword', in Phiri et al. (eds.), *Anthology of African Christianity*, p. xix.
17 Ibid.
18 Philomena Mwaura, 'The Prophetic Role of the Church in Addressing Challenges of Africa', paper presented during the All Africa Conference of Churches Theological Reflection Meeting, Kigali, Rwanda, 9–12 Oct. 2017, p. 1 (emphasis added).
19 For membership of AACC denominations, see Andre Karamaga, 'The Imperative of Unity of the Church towards a United Africa', paper presented during the All Africa Conference of Churches Theological Reflection Meeting, in Kigali, Rwanda, 9–12 Oct. 2017, p. 1.
20 For more information, see David N. A. Kpobi, 'Evangelicals and African Ecumenism', in Phiri et al. (eds.), *Anthology of African Christianity*, pp. 834–40; Fidelis Nkomazana, 'Pentecostals and African Ecumenism', in Phiri et al. (eds.), *Anthology of African Christianity*, pp. 841–9.
21 Jacob Olupona, 'Muslim–Christian Encounters in Africa', in Phiri et al. (eds.), *Anthology of African Christianity*, p. 100.
22 Ibid., p. 102.
23 As I wrote this chapter, forty Christian and Muslim leaders were meeting at the headquarters of the AACC for a workshop on advocacy training for peace and

conflict resolution (30 Apr.–4 May 2018). In 2017, the AACC organized a two-day interfaith workshop on 22–25 Oct. for advocacy training on legal instruments for gender justice, and input into the African Union Gender Strategy, hence influencing gender justice at the policy level. Other organizations which promote interfaith relations include PROCMURA (Program for Christian–Muslim Relations), the World Council of Churches (WCC), INERELA (an international network of religious leaders living with or personally affected by HIV), the Interreligious Council of Kenya, and the Faith to Action Network, to mention just a few.

24 The mission of IRCK is 'Fostering respect, tolerance, peace and common action among different religions in the pursuit of social and economic well being of all the people of Kenya'. See 'Inter-Religious Council of Kenya (IRCK): Strategic Plan', *Wajibu: A Journal of Social and Religious Concern*, 21 (2006), http://africa.peacelink.org/wajibu/articles/art_7508.html.

25 Joseph D. Galgalo, 'Foreword', in Keumju Jewel Hyun and Diphus C. Chemorion (eds.), *The Quest for Gender Equity in Leadership: Biblical Teachings on Gender Equity and Illustrations of Transformation in Africa* (Eugene, OR: Wipf and Stock, 2016), pp. xv–xvii.

26 Examples of such Pentecostal churches in Africa are the Zimbabwe Assemblies of God Africa, the Redeemed Church of God in Nigeria, and the International Central Gospel Church in Ghana, to mention just a few. For more details of the prosperity gospel in Africa, see Kudzi Biri, 'Neo-Pentecostal Churches in Africa ("Prosperity Churches")', in Phiri et al. (eds.), *Anthology of African Christianity*, p. 415.

27 Ibid., p. 418.

28 Emmanuel Katongole, 'Post-Modern Illusions and the Challenges of African Theology', *Modern Theology*, 16/2 (Apr. 2000), 243.

29 Emmanuel Katongole, 'Greeting: Beyond Racial Reconciliation', in Stanley Hauerwas and Samuel Wells (eds.), *The Blackwell Companion to Christian Ethics* (Oxford: Blackwell, 2004), pp. 70–83.

30 *Ubuntu* is the African philosophy that 'I am who I am because we are'. It is the African communal understanding of relationships, which entails solidarity, building inclusive community, care for one another, accepting what is right for the good of the community, affirming one another, and the understanding that each of us is shaped by the individual contribution to the whole. Ubuntu affirms our deepest connections as human beings.

31 Paulinus Odozor, *Truly African, Truly Christian* (Notre Dame, IN: University of Notre Dame Press, 2014), p. 115.

32 Mwaura, 'The Prophetic Role of the Church in Addressing Challenges of Africa'.

33 According to the 2016 Staff Establishment of the ACK Diocese of Nairobi, where I am an ordained priest, for example, ordained women constituted only 15.6% of all ordained priests in that year, while men constituted 84.4%. See table in Lydia Mwaniki, 'Biblical Gender Equity and Women in Leadership:

An Examination of the Anglican Church of Kenya', in Hyun and Chemorion (eds.), *The Quest for Gender Equity in Leadership*, pp. 14–27.
34 Lawrence Iwuamadi, 'Anthology of African Christianity Highlights the Continent where the Faith is Growing Fastest', https://www.oikoumene.org (16 Feb. 2017).
35 Mwaura, 'The Prophetic Role of the Church in Addressing Challenges of Africa'.
36 Karamaga, 'The Imperative of Unity of the Church towards a United Africa'.
37 Stephen Williams, 'Africa's Youth: The African Development Bank and the Demographic Dividend', https://www.afdb.org/fileadmin/uploads/afdb/Documents/Generic-Documents/AFDB%20youth%20doc.pdf.
38 Mwaura, 'The Prophetic Role of the Church in Addressing Challenges of Africa'.
39 Stanley Hauerwas, *Peaceable Kingdom* (Notre Dame, IN: University of Notre Dame Press, 1993), p. 28.
40 Pope Paul VI, *Gaudium et Spes* (1965), http://www.vatican.va/archive/hist_councils/ii_vatican_council/documents/vat-ii_const_19651207_gaudium-et-spes_en.html.
41 Katongole, 'Post-Modern Illusions and the Challenges of African Theology', p. 243.
42 Ibid.
43 Katongole, 'Greeting: Beyond Racial Reconciliation'.

Bibliography

Abuom, Agnes, 'Foreword', in Lesmore Gibson Ezekiel and Jooseop Keum (eds.), *Conference on World Mission and Evangelism from Achimota to Arusha: An Ecumenical Journey of Mission* in Africa (Nairobi: Acton Publishers and WCC, 2018).

Anderson, Keith, *Church History and Theology* (Nairobi: Provincial Board of Theological Education, 1984).

Asamoah-Gyadu, J. Kwabena, 'Growth and Trends in African Christianity in the 21st Century', in Isabel Phiri, Dietrich Werner, Chammah Kaunda, and Kennedy Owino (eds.), *Anthology of African Christianity*, Regnum Studies in Global Christianity (Oxford: WCC, 2016), pp. 65–75.

Biri, Kudzi, 'Neo-Pentecostal Churches in Africa ("Prosperity Churches")', in Isabel Phiri, Dietrich Werner, Chammah Kaunda, and Kennedy Owino (eds.), *Anthology of African Christianity*, Regnum Studies in Global Christianity (Oxford: WCC, 2016), pp. 415–19.

De Gruchy, Steve, 'Integrating Mission and Development: Ten Theological Theses', *International Congregational Journal*, 5/1 (2005), 27–36.

Galgalo, Joseph D., 'Foreword', in Keumju Jewel Hyun and Diphus C. Chemorion (eds.), *The Quest for Gender Equity in Leadership: Biblical Teachings on Gender*

Equity and Illustrations of Transformation in Africa Chemorion (Eugene, OR: Wipf and Stock, 2016).

Gibson, Lesmore Ezekiel, and Jooseop Keum, 'From Achimota 1958 to Arusha 2018: A Journey to and after Arusha', in Lesmore Gibson Ezekiel and Jooseop Keum (eds.), *Conference on World Mission and Evangelism from Achimota to Arusha: An Ecumenical Journey of Mission* in Africa (Nairobi: Acton Publishers and WCC, 2018), pp. 1–11.

'Inter-Religious Council of Kenya (IRCK): Strategic Plan', *Wajibu: A Journal of Social and Religious Concern*, 21 (2006), http://africa.peacelink.org/wajibu/articles/art_7508.html.

Iwuamadi, Lawrence, 'Anthology of African Christianity Highlights the Continent where the Faith is Growing Fastest', https://www.oikoumene.org (16 Feb. 2017).

Karamaga, Andre, 'The Imperative of Unity of the Church towards a United Africa', paper Presented during the All Africa Conference of Churches Theological Reflection Meeting, Kigali, Rwanda, 9–12 Oct. 2017.

Katongole, Emmanuel, 'Greeting: Beyond Racial Reconciliation', in Stanley Hauerwas and Samuel Wells (eds.), *The Blackwell Companion to Christian Ethics* (Oxford: Blackwell, 2004), pp. 70–83.

Katongole, Emmanuel, 'Post-Modern Illusions and the Challenges of African Theology', *Modern Theology*, 16/2 (Apr. 2000), 237–54.

Kpobi, David N. A., 'Evangelicals and African Ecumenism', in Isabel Phiri, Dietrich Werner, Chammah Kaunda, and Kennedy Owino (eds.), *Anthology of African Christianity*, Regnum Studies in Global Christianity (Oxford: WCC, 2016), pp. 834–40.

Mbiti, John S. 'Foreword', in Isabel Phiri, Dietrich Werner, Chammah Kaunda, and Kennedy Owino (eds.), *Anthology of African Christianity*, Regnum Studies in Global Christianity (Oxford: WCC, 2016).

McClendon, David, 'Sub-Saharan Africa will be Home to Growing Shares of the World's Christians and Muslims', Pew Research Center (Apr. 2017), http://www.pewforum.org/2017/04/05/the-changing-global-religious-landscape/.

Mugambi, Jesse, 'The Future of the Church and the Church of the Future in Africa', in All Africa Conference of Churches Information Desk (eds.), *The Church of Africa: Towards a Theology of Reconstruction* (Nairobi: Motif Creative Arts Ltd, 1991), pp. 40–1.

Mugambi, Jesse, 'The Profile of African Christianity at Home and in the West', in Isabel Apawo Phiri et al. (eds.), *Anthology of African Christianity*, Regnum Studies in Global Christianity (Oxford: WCC, 2016), pp. 105–13.

Mwaniki, Lydia M., 'Biblical Gender Equity and Women in Leadership: An Examination of the Anglican Church of Kenya', in Keumju Jewel Hyun and Diphus C. Chemorion (eds.), *The Quest for Gender Equity in Leadership: Biblical Teachings on Gender Equity and Illustrations of Transformation in Africa* (Eugene, OR: Wipf & Stock, 2016), pp. 14–27.

Mwaniki, Lydia M., 'The Impact of the Church on the Development of the Identity of an African Christian Woman: A Case Study of the Anglican Church of Kenya, Diocese of Kirinyaga 1910–1999', master's dissertation, University of Natal Pietermaritzburg, 2000.

Mwaura, Philomena, 'The Prophetic Role of the Church in Addressing Challenges of Africa', paper presented during the All Africa Conference of Churches Theological Reflection Meeting, Kigali, Rwanda, 9–12 Oct. 2017.

Njoku, Chukwudi A., 'The Missionary Factor in African Christianity, 1884–1914', in Ogbu U. Kalu (ed.), *African Christianity: An African Story* (Trenton, NJ: Africa World Press, 2007), pp. 218–52.

Nkomazana, Fidelis, 'Pentecostals and African Ecumenism', in Isabel Phiri, Dietrich Werner, Chammah Kaunda, and Kennedy Owino (eds.), *Anthology of African Christianity*, Regnum Studies in Global Christianity, (Oxford: WCC, 2016), pp. 841–9.

Odozor, Paulinus, *Truly African, Truly Christian* (Notre Dame, IN: University of Notre Dame Press, 2014).

Olupona, Jacob, 'Muslim-Christian Encounters in Africa', in Isabel Phiri, Dietrich Werner, Chammah Kaunda, and Kennedy Owino (eds.), *Anthology of African Christianity*, Regnum Studies in Global Christianity, (Oxford: WCC, 2016), pp. 99–104.

Padilla, C. R., *Integral Mission and its Historic Development* (2003), http://www.micahnetwork.org/sites/default/files/doc/library/integral_mission_and_its_historical_development_padilla.pdf.

Phiri, Isabel Apawo, Dietrich Werner, Chammah Kaunda, and Kennedy Owino (eds.), *Anthology of African Christianity*, Regnum Studies in Global Christianity (Oxford: WCC, 2016).

Temu, A. J., *British Protestant Missions* (London: Longman, 1972).

Welby, Justin, 'Sharing Jesus: The Revolution of God's Love', https://www.archbishopofcanterbury.org/priorities/evangelism-and-witness.

Williams, Stephen, 'Africa's Youth: The African Development Bank and the Demographic Divided', https://www.afdb.org/fileadmin/uploads/afdb/Documents/Generic-Documents/AFDB%20youth%20doc.pdf.

3

Evangelizing and witnessing in a church where young people and children are not excluded, left behind, or forgotten

VICENTIA KGABE (SOUTH AFRICA)

The starting point of our proclamation is Christ and Christ crucified. At the very heart of the church's vocation in the world is the proclamation of the kingdom of God inaugurated in Jesus Christ crucified and risen, '. . . but we proclaim Christ crucified, a stumbling-block to Jews and foolishness to Gentiles' (1 Cor 1.23).

The words 'evangelism' and 'evangelization' derive from the Greek term *evangelion*, meaning the 'good news'. An old English form of the term is *godspell*, from which our modern word 'Gospel' derives. It also means 'good message' or 'good news'. The idea of 'good news' goes back to the tradition of Isaiah and Psalms, referring to the messianic good news, the glad tidings that God's universal reign has begun: 'How beautiful upon the mountains are the feet of the messenger who announces peace, who brings good news, who announces salvation, who says to Zion, "Your God reigns"' (Isa 52.7).

Evangelization is basically the spreading of the good news about God's kingdom. It is the revelation of God's saving love, and of God's dialogues with humanity—God's mission to the world. That mission took a final shape and orientation in the life, death, and resurrection of Jesus Christ, and subsequently in the mandate which Christ gave to the church, which is the seed and the sign of God's kingdom. The church is therefore by definition associated with the divine mission. However, the divine activity goes beyond the visible limits of the historical church and time.

Whether we talk of evangelization or evangelism, the underlying idea is that the Christian faith has to be shared by means of an active apostolate. The spreading and deepening of the Christian faith depend upon such faith-sharing and the spreading of the good news, which is a reconciling activity that brings individuals, communities, and nations together. The 'great commission' at the end of the Synoptic Gospels explicitly envisages such a process of sharing: 'Go and make disciples of every nation [regardless of gender, ethnicity, race, or age].' Evangelism is the spreading of the good news about God's kingdom and the realization that God's kingdom is not a human one.

Witnesses to the *Missio Dei*

Stromberg writes that 'the mission of the church ensues from the nature of the church as the Body of Christ, sharing in the ministry of Christ as the mediator between God and God's creation. The church manifests God's love for the world in Christ, through word and deed, in identification with all humanity, in loving service and joyful proclamation; the church, in that same identification with all humanity, lifts up to God its pain and suffering, hope and aspiration, joy and thanksgiving in intercessory prayer and Eucharistic worship. Only a church fully aware of how people (and her members) in the world live, think and feel can adequately fulfil its witness and mission. It is at this point that the church recognizes the validity and significance of the ministry of others to the church, in order that the church may better understand and be in closer solidarity with the world, knowing and sharing its pains and yearnings. Only by responding attentively to others can we remove our ignorance and misunderstanding of others and be better able to minister to and with them.'[1] Bosch makes a point about the nature of mission when he writes, 'mission is a multifaceted ministry, in respect of witness, service, justice, healing, reconciliation, liberation, peace, evangelism, fellowship, church planting, contextualization and much more'.[2]

My context: evangelism and young people

In many books that I have read, and in the forums relating to evangelism I have participated in, the target market or focus is adults. But it is not only over the adult members of our worshipping communities that we exercise *cura animarum*—'cure of souls'—and not just the adult members who deserve our full attention and inclusion when we talk about evangelism. Young people and children too need to be taken into consideration. They find themselves growing up in contexts that are challenging socio-politically, economically, spiritually, and in terms of faith. In a world largely shaped by adults, they are silent witnesses whose presence is conveniently ignored, until they leave the church in frustration and/or explode in anger.

I grew up in a context where young people were welcomed to church but reminded very often that young people and children are to be seen and not heard; this statement became a mantra, and it was familiar as it was also used in our homes. At church we were reminded that silence is golden, and to try to make us feel good and valuable we were cheerfully reminded that we were the 'church of tomorrow'.

And this constant reminder caused conflict as we, the young people, felt excluded from the life and mission of the church of today; we were welcomed only to window-dress and entertain, but not valued as partners in the mission of God, witnessing alongside the adults and exploring what a Christ-centred church looks and feels like. Baartman, commenting on young people being told to be seen and not heard, writes, 'teenagers/young people are not just future adults. They are persons, full persons, who feel, see, smell and taste just like any other person. Jesus Christ was a great respecter of human beings. He made people whole at times if not most of the time, [while] we go to teenagers and ask them to be quiet and as if they were empty buckets to be filled with great truths that we [adults] know, we don't give them time to process and think.'[3]

Shorter's take on this matter is that 'through the sacrament of baptism, a person is inserted into the Christian community and accepts the obligation which this community imposes'.[4] Thus, the activity of evangelization should be an integral part of the life of a baptized Christian. Baartman's view on what Shorter says here is that 'the church as an institution is of vital importance for evangelism amongst youth. The Gospel preached is not only words uttered from the pulpit, but the whole church life as an institution must be a living testimony to the presences and action of God in this world...in evangelizing young people, we must not forget the fact that we are asking them to come into a community. This community must also be an authentic community. Young people today are concerned with great themes of the Bible: peace, justice, love, freedom, salvation and creation to name a few. What the church is requested to do is to anchor them in Christ.'[5]

I interpret this to mean that through baptism no one can be left out or left behind or even excluded in ministries that the church is engaged in, especially in the area of witnessing and evangelizing about the good news. Beyers Naudé writes, 'in our struggle for what it means to be church and mission of Christ, we need to ask what is Good News for the poor (economic justice)?—what is Good News for the oppressed and marginalized?—what is Good News for the youth (the excluded)?'[6]

I have seen many young people and young adults, though they love the Anglican Church, leave it for other denominations (and in some cases start their own churches) because they felt unnecessarily restricted and excluded by the adults or felt that their gifts were not appreciated. Some have succeeded in their ministries and some have not. Some young people in our church have questioned why some of our clergy and lay leaders are unhappy when they raise the issues of evangelization and witness. The clergy and lay leaders, they claimed, thought these were un-Anglican and were done only by Pentecostal churches. Vineeth Koshy writes that 'Youth is a state of life and mind when there is a quality of thinking, a predominance of courage and appetite for adventure. However, one of the alarming features of today's youth participation and leadership in the church is that the young generation is in the "exit-phase" and there may be various reasons for justifying the exit. We are forgetting that the gifts of the Holy Spirit are distributed equally and widely in the church. Therefore, it is quite essential that the spiritual experience and expertise of every member must be recognized and drawn into the common spirituality of the local congregation. Thus, the concern for the church must be broad-based involving the youth, women and children.'[7]

Shorter points out that 'evangelization is most effective when it operates through interpersonal relationships. These relationships are to be found ideally in the family or community, through the mutual influence of adults and young people or children'. He notes that in Nairobi, Kenya a pool of young people evangelizers has been set up, and 'meetings are arranged between these young people and members of the parental generation so that they can witness their faith and discover ways of communicating with each other. The influence of peer groups is often stronger than that of family, and young people are more powerfully impressed by them. This explains the influence of Christian students and young professionals movements.'[8]

Acting in the light of Christ

Nel in his work with young people coined a definition of youth ministry in this way: 'youth ministry is *to*, *with* and *through* the young people'.[9] The young people dream of a church fully catering to their needs, a church in the new and evolving context of 'common global culture', as much as they are active participants in the life of a local and global church; the church continues to see and refer to them as the 'church of tomorrow' or the 'church of the future', missing out on the value they add as active participants and partners of the church of today. The *perspectives*, *enthusiasm*, *energy*, and *gifts* they possess are pivotal in the work of evangelism and witness that the wider church is participating in.

The ministry of young people and their instruction on what the church and her mission is have been left to young people themselves or to someone (often a volunteer) who has time for them. And in those parishes that can afford to employ a youth pastor or youth worker, the responsibility falls on them. By doing this the local church abdicates its responsibility and sits back to judge how well the youth pastor or volunteer is doing with the youth ministry. Martinson emphasizes this observation by pointing out that 'youth ministry is the responsibility of the entire congregation through its elected, volunteered or paid representatives, the congregation as a whole, needs to support the life and mission of young people in the church and community. The involvement of the whole church in maturing and supporting young people's ministry will be helpful as young people in our churches come from diverse socio-economic and political situations.'[10]

The Church of England says of its ministry to children and young people, 'We believe that children and young people can follow Jesus and be full members of the church and that discipleship is possible at any age. They are integral to our churches, but we need to make sure there are no obstacles preventing them from getting involved.'[11] One wishes that the 'obstacles' could be unpacked or unmasked so that the church would be able to decisively deal with them. Hannah Barr, a youth worker in Oxford, England, in her article in the *Church Times* titled 'What I Wish the Church Knew about Young People', writes,

> So what do I, as a youth worker, wish the Church knew about youth work and young people? First, the whole Church needs to be involved in the discipleship of young people. Often, people have a specific image in mind when they think about youth workers: they should be young...and they should be cool...But it is the job of the Church collectively to come alongside young people, to invest in them, and to show them what a life lived with Jesus looks like. Young people are not the Church of tomorrow, they are the Church of today. To dismiss them as being just for the youth-work team to deal with sends the message that they are not full participants in the life of the Church. We need to involve them, discern their gifts, and take risks in letting them have a go. They come with a particular way of seeing and expressing things, without the inhibitions of older generations. Yes, it can be unpredictable, but there are gems of wisdom in what they see, say, and do.[12]

One of my colleagues has remarked that young people are marginalized in most church ministries and church proceedings, and that this results in their voices being silenced; she added that without the voice of the young people the trends for the future mission will not be realized soon enough for the church to act in light of the Gospel. Her observation resonates with what Shorter alludes to when he says, 'the gospel of Christ cannot be domesticated. On the contrary, it continues to challenge the Christian community and moreover, this community itself is subjected to profound social and structural changes. Human groupings changes, human groupings can change their identity, can coalesce with one another, or even disappear altogether. They are not static and unchanging.'[13] Baron, in exploring the role of church youth in the transformation agenda of South African cities, writes, 'although the church has a responsibility towards society, it should not exclude the church youth, which forms part of the church participating in God's mission on earth. This is often the case as the youth in the church is at times only good for church activities, through taking part in the Sunday worship and the various ministry departments in the church.' Quoting Nel (2015), Baron writes, 'Nel argues that the church should make young people disciples that will continue making disciples (he explains discipleship as not solely about learning more about God, but how to live one's life to glorify God) and this should be a conscious and intentional process.'[14]

The Anglican Communion's Mission and Evangelism Department, in its 2008 report titled *Holistic Mission: A Profile of Mission and Evangelism in the Anglican Communion*, said the following regarding young people:

> A particular context for mission and evangelism is young people; both as those reached out to and also as those doing mission. Generally, in the West they are being seen as an unchurched generation 'young people are uninterested in the church...yet interested in spirituality and life encouraging values' (Canada). Evangelists are being specifically trained for child evangelism (West Africa) and there are initiatives with street children (Central Africa). Mention is made of ministry with young people (Egypt, Southern Africa and Southern Cone) and of investing much time and money into initiatives with children and young people with the appointment of diocesan youth officers in each diocese (Uganda) as well as many exciting activities for young people.
>
> Elsewhere there are examples of young people being encouraged to take on responsibility within the church: leading services and being appointed to church positions, choir groups etc. (Tanzania) and of the evangelistic role of youth choirs (Central Africa). Young people aged 18 to 22, are gaining

short experiences of mission through a GAP year program (England and Australia) and there are increases in young people offering for ministry (Church of North India).[15]

It will be interesting to revisit the above-mentioned provinces ten years later and evaluate the progress made in the intentional involvement of young people in mission and evangelism, and to hear from young people themselves how they perceive their inclusion. I know for my province that the number of young people who are coming to church has increased, and apart from being members of the altar servers' guilds, Sunday schools, and youth groups, some of them are also members of the St Agnes Guild (females only). Their aims and objectives of the St Agnes Guild are:

- To worship God regularly through prayer;
- To encourage Bible studies among members;
- To build fellowship among members;
- To visit and help those in need; and
- To practise and encourage stewardship among members.

The St Bernard Mizeki Men's Guild, which has also created a junior group (for males only, between the ages of twelve and nineteen), is named after one of the African converts who was killed during the Mashonaland rebellion in Zimbabwe in 1896. Its aims are:

- To promote and encourage the participation and nurturing of men's leadership in the life of the church;
- To proclaim the kingdom of God as manifested in Jesus Christ, by:
  - Encouraging the participation and nurturing of boys in the life of the church;
  - Encouraging Bible studies and faith sharing;
  - Practising stewardship;
  - Doing visitations, seeking out the sick, and practising the ministry of healing;
  - Being involved in the affairs of the community;
  - Promoting fellowship among the people; and
  - Imitating Christ daily.

There is also a newly established Girls and Boys Friendly Society whose objectives are as follows:

- To give praise to God by bringing girls and boys to the true fellowship of the church;

- To help girls and boys in the knowledge and love of our Lord Jesus Christ;
- To help those who, because of little knowledge, find themselves falling under bad influences; and
- To give girls and boys broader knowledge about Holy Scripture.

These organizations pursue their aims and objectives largely on their own, and their plans are not incorporated into parish plans, which can be a source of tension. They are each assigned a chaplain; some of the chaplains are ordained and some are lay people, and they lack a proper or guided plan of what their role is or the intended outcome of what they have agreed to do.

Those young people and children who are not members of any of these groups are left out, but this does not mean that they too would not want or love to be regarded as disciples and carriers of the good news. And the churches' revolving door will continue to operate at high speed as they leave to seek more inclusive and accepting faith communities. Fung, in advocating intentional youth participation in evangelism, recommends that '. . . the church [adults] needs to realize that spending time with youth is more important than haggling with church bureaucrats over youth participation in the established structures',[16] while Bosch talks about the 'All-inclusive mission of Christ',[17] the mission that dissolves alienation and breaking down the walls of hostility, of crossing boundaries between individuals and/or groups.

Pope John Paul VI said in relation to the evangelization of a Christian community, 'one cannot fail to stress the evangelizing action of the family in the evangelizing of the apostolate of the laity. At different moments in the Church's history and also in the Second Vatican Council, the family has well deserved the beautiful name of "domestic church". This means that there should be found in every Christian family the various aspects of the entire church. Furthermore, the family like the church, ought to be a place where the Gospel is transmitted and from which the Gospel radiates. In a family which is conscious of this mission, all the members evangelize and are evangelized. The parents not only communicate the gospel to their children, but from their children, they can themselves receive the same Gospel as deeply lived by them.'[18]

Conclusion

This call to inclusive discipleship that I make in this chapter is both an opportunity and a challenge. It moves us to a point of recognition that

God is already at work, and has been working with and through all races, ages, genders, and ethnicities revealing Godself. As the World Council of Churches puts it, 'the mission of God (*Missio Dei*) is the source of and basis for the mission of the church, the body of Christ. Through Christ in the Holy Spirit, God indwells the church, empowering and energizing its members. Thus, mission becomes for Christians an urgent inner compulsion, even a powerful test and criterion for authentic life in Christ, rooted in the profound demands of Christ love, to invite others to share in the fullness of life Jesus came to bring. Participating in God's mission, therefore, should be natural for all Christians and all churches, not only for particular individuals or specialized groups.'[19]

Response

GRAHAM KINGS (UNITED KINGDOM)

Within a holistic view of mission, Kgabe draws on various works by theologians of mission and gives some contextual examples from South Africa. She provides a perceptive comment concerning her memory of being a young person in church:

> We were welcomed only to window-dress and entertain, but not valued as partners in the mission of God, witnessing alongside the adults and exploring what a Christ-centred church looks and feels like.

Also helpful was the quotation from Vineeth Koshy about young people who have 'a quality of thinking, a predominance of courage and appetite for adventure'.

It was encouraging to hear that the number of young people coming to church in her province has increased. I would have liked to have heard more about the Guilds of St Agnes and of St Bernard Mizeki and the newly established Girls and Boys Friendly Society and how these, as Kgabe longs, could be involved in evangelism as well as church activities. It may be that evangelism and witness among young people and children should be interactive, interrogative, intriguing, and imaginative.

When I served as Bishop of Sherborne in Dorset, England, I led a service celebrating fifty years of the village church primary school building. The previous one had burned down, following a sad accident with an oil heater. I pointed out the irony of the first hymn, 'Give me oil in my lamp, keep me burning'.

As part of the sermon, I took questions from the children, and these, as usual, were a mixture of the personal and profound. The most searching question was: 'What was God doing before he made the world?' I dared not mention Augustine's tongue-in-cheek jest in 397 AD—that he said he would *not* give to such a question: 'He was preparing hell for those who pry into mysteries'[20]—but I did say 'He was loving.' I developed this briefly in mentioning the eternal love between the Father, the Son, and the Holy Spirit.

This taught me the importance of church schools in evangelism and witness, the depth of some children's thinking, their willingness to articulate it, and their delight in asking questions.

Jesus, when he was twelve, was found by Mary and Joseph 'in the temple, sitting among the teachers, listening to them and asking them questions' (Lk 2.46). Perhaps we need to provide opportunities for children and young people to do the same.

In both state and church secondary schools in Dorset I used to take part in 'Grill-a-Bishop' sessions with 16–18-year-olds, where no question was out of bounds. There were so many questions that these would often be followed up with 'Grill-a-Bishop' half-hour sessions, live online on the Diocese of Salisbury website.

For these online sessions, the students, with a teacher, would be in the classroom, and I would be in my study or a café. They would type short questions and I would attempt to answer them and provide hyperlinks to other resources.

One student asked, 'When does life begin?' I replied, 'After the first cup of coffee in the morning', but then went on to discuss the underlying question of abortion. There were sometimes up to thirty questions, and I would manage to give brief answers to ten or twelve in the half hour, and follow up on the others in my own time. I learned theologically and profoundly from these experiences and had to rethink some issues. As usual, the good news bounces back, with joy and challenge, on the person sharing it. The BBC Radio 4 *Today* programme heard about Grill-a-Bishop and on 20 January 2011 broadcast short interviews with some of the sixth-formers, with the title 'Did God Plan the Creation of Nuclear Weapons?'

In retirement, I am serving a multicultural inner-city parish in London, St Matthew's-at-the-Elephant, just south of the River Thames, and we have recently appointed a part-time director of music. He is also a young composer and singing teacher in a school. He has started a children's choir, with fourteen members, and has already written a new Kyrie and Gospel Acclamations, which the children have taught the congregation. The children are encouraging their friends from the council local estate to join them and have distributed leaflets about the church. So the children are involved in teaching and evangelism. After preparation classes, four children were confirmed in April and another four admitted to Holy Communion in May.

In the Anglican Communion, Archbishop Justin's evangelism and witness initiative, 'Thy Kingdom Come', includes young people and children in its focus for prayer between Ascension and Pentecost each year. In England there were Beacon events in thirty-seven cathedrals at Pentecost. The *Church Times* reported on 25 May 2018:

> It was the third instalment of what is now a global, ecumenical prayer movement, which invites Christians to pray throughout Ascension-tide. Several thousand young people in St Albans on Saturday evening listened to Archbishop Welby and the US Presiding Bishop, Michael Curry, fresh from their involvement in the wedding of the Duke and Duchess of Sussex.

Weddings are good news. This royal wedding, at Windsor Castle, was broadcast live to 1.9 billion people around the world. Michael Curry rose to the occasion in his sermon to share the holistic good news of God with so many people.

Kgabe cites a fine quotation from Pope John Paul II, and it may be worth drawing also on Pope Francis's major apostolic exhortation of 2013, *Evangelii Gaudium* (*The Joy of the Gospel*), where a key repeated phrase is 'missionary disciple'. He mentions young people in paragraphs 105 to 108:

> How beautiful it is to see that young people are 'street preachers' (*callejeros de la fe*), joyfully bringing Jesus to every street, every town square and every corner of the earth! (§ 106)

> Young people call us to renewed and expansive hope, for they represent new directions for humanity and open us up to the future, lest we cling to a nostalgia for structures and customs which are no longer life-giving in today's world. (§ 108)[21]

Pope Francis also wrote about the vocation of theologians:

> I call on theologians to carry out this service as part of the Church's saving mission. In doing so, however, they must always remember that the Church and theology exist to evangelize, and not be content with a desk-bound theology. Universities are outstanding environments for articulating and developing this evangelizing commitment in an interdisciplinary and integrated way. (§ 134)

To draw on earlier ages concerning the possibility of witness, it may be worth contrasting Plato, the philosopher in Athens, with John Chrysostom, the bishop in Constantinople. Plato (d. 347 BC), in his *Timaeus*, wrote: 'But the father and maker of all this universe is past finding out; and even if we found him, to tell of him to all men would be impossible.'[22] John Chrysostom (d. 407 AD), in his sermon on Acts 9.10–12 about Ananias, who prayed for Saul in Damascus, preached:

> Say not, 'it is impossible for me to induce others (to become Christians)'—for if thou art a Christian, it is impossible but that it should be so. For as the natural properties of things cannot be gainsaid, so it is here: the thing is part of the very nature of the Christian. Do not insult God. To say, the sun cannot shine, would be to insult Him: to say that a Christian cannot do good, is to insult God and call him a liar. For it is easier for the sun not to give heat, nor to shine, than for a Christian not send forth light: it is easier for the light to be darkness, than for this to be so.[23]

So evangelism and witness involve living and articulating the good news of the kingdom, in the power of the Spirit, to a world in need, by a church in love. In particular, we are called to help children and young people realize that they matter to God because they matter to us.

Notes

1 Jean Stromberg, *Mission and Evangelism: An Ecumenical Affirmation*, WCC Mission Series (Geneva: WCC, 1983), p. 11.

2 David J. Bosch, *Transforming Mission: Paradigm Shifts in Theology of Mission* (Maryknoll, NY: Orbis Books, 1991), p. 524.

3 Michael Cassidy (ed.), *I Will Heal their Land: Papers of the South African Congress on Mission and Evangelism, Durban, 1973* (Maseru: Morija Printing Works, 1973), p. 172.

4 Aylward Shorter, *Evangelization and Culture* (London: Geoffrey Chapman, 1994), p. 57.

5 Cassidy (ed.), *I Will Heal their Land*, p. 172.

6 Mark Hestenes, Johan Botha, Bongani Mazibuko, and Andrew Josias (eds.), *The Relevance of Evangelism in South Africa Today* (Johannesburg: South African Council of Churches, 1986), p. 124.

7 Vineeth Koshy, 'Youth Envisaging Ecumenical Mission: Shifting Ecumenical Mission Paradigms for Witnessing Christ Today', in Petros Vassiliadis (ed.), *Orthodox Perspectives on Mission*, Regnum Edinburgh Centenary Series, 17 (Oxford: Regnum, 2013), p. 233.

8 Shorter, *Evangelization and Culture*, p. 143.

9 Malan Nel, *Youth Ministry: An Inclusive Congregational Approach* (Pretoria: Jeugbediening Publishers, 2000), p. 65.

10 Roland Martinson, *Effective Youth Ministry: A Congregational Approach* (Minneapolis: Augsburg Publishing House, 1988), p. 11.

11 'Children and Young People', Church of England, https://www.churchofengland.org/more/children-and-young-people.

12 Hannah Barr, 'What I Wish the Church Knew about Young People', *Church Times* (19 Jan. 2018), https://www.churchtimes.co.uk/articles/2018/19-january/features/features/what-i-wish-the-church-knew-about-young-people.

13 E. Baron, 'The Role of Church Youth in the Transformation Agenda of South African Cities', *HTS Teologiese Studies/Theological Studies*, 73/3 (2017), 4, a4771, https://doi.org/ 10.4102/hts.v73i3.4771.

14 Ibid.

15 *Holistic Mission: A Profile of Mission and Evangelism in the Anglican Communion* (2008), p. 5, Anglican Communion Mission and Evangelism Department, https://www.anglicancommunion.org/media/143024/holistic_mission.pdf.

16 Raymond Fung, *Evangelistically Yours: Ecumenical Letters on Contemporary Evangelism* (Geneva: WCC, 1992), p. 20.

17 Bosch, *Transforming Mission*, p. 20.
18 *Evangelii Nuntiandi*, §71.
19 *Come Holy Spirit—Heal and Reconcile* (2005), World Council of Churches, www.wcc-coe.org/wcc/what/mission/m-e-in-unity.pdf.
20 St Augustine, *Confessions*, trans. J. G. Pilkinton, ed. J. Lovill (London: The Folio Society, 1993), book 11, chap. 12, p. 216.
21 Pope Francis, *Evangelii Gaudium* (2013), https://w2.vatican.va/content/francesco/en/apost_exhortations/documents/papa-francesco_esortazione-ap_20131124_evangelii-gaudium.html.
22 Plato, *Timaeus* 28 C, in *The Dialogues of Plato*, trans. Benjamin Jowett, ed. R. M. Hare and D. A. Russell, vol. III: *Timaeus and Other Dialogues* (London: Sphere Books Ltd, 1970). p. 234.
23 John Chrysostom, *Homily XX*, in Philip Schaff (ed.), *A Select Library of the Nicene and Post-Nicene Fathers of the Christian Church*, vol XI: *Saint Chrysostom, Homilies on the Acts of the Apostles and the Epistle to the Romans* (Grand Rapids, MI: Eerdmans, 1989), p. 134.

Bibliography

Baron, E., 'The Role of Church Youth in the Transformation Agenda of South African Cities', *HTS Teologiese Studies/Theological Studies*, 73/3 (2017), 4, a4771, https://doi.org/ 10.4102/hts.v73i3.4771.

Barr, Hannah, 'What I Wish the Church Knew about Young People', *Church Times* (19 Jan. 2018), https://www.churchtimes.co.uk/articles/2018/19-january/features/features/what-i-wish-the-church-knew-about-young-people.

Bosch, David J., *Transforming Mission: Paradigm Shifts in Theology of Mission* (New York: Orbis Books, 1991).

Cassidy, Michael (ed.), *I Will Heal their Land: Papers of the South African Congress on Mission and Evangelism, Durban, 1973* (Maseru: Morija Printing Works, 1973).

'Children and Young People', Church of England, https://www.churchofengland.org/more/children-and-young-people.

Come Holy Spirit—Heal and Reconcile (2005), World Council of Churches, www.wcc-coe.org/wcc/what/mission/m-e-in-unity.pdf

Fung, Raymond, *Evangelistically Yours: Ecumenical Letters on Contemporary Evangelism* (Geneva: WCC, 1992).

Hestenes, Mark, Johan Botha, Bongani Mazibuko, and Andrew Josias (eds.), *The Relevance of Evangelism in South Africa Today* (Johannesburg: South African Council of Churches, 1986).

Holistic Mission: A Profile of Mission and Evangelism in the Anglican Communion, Anglican Communion Mission and Evangelism Department (2008), https://www.anglicancommunion.org/media/143024/holistic_mission.pdf.

Koshy, Vineeth, 'Youth Envisaging Ecumenical Mission: Shifting Ecumenical Mission Paradigms for Witnessing Christ Today', in Petros Vassiliadis (ed.), *Orthodox Perspectives on Mission*, Regnum Edinburgh Centenary Series, 17 (Oxford: Regnum, 2013), pp. 233–41.

Martinson, Roland D., *Effective Youth Ministry: A Congregational Approach* (Minneapolis: Augsburg Publishing House, 1988).

Nel, Malan, *Youth Ministry: An Inclusive Congregational Approach* (Pretoria: Jeugbediening Publishers, 2000).

Pope John Paul VI, *Evangelii Nuntiandi.*

Shorter, Aylward, *Evangelization and Culture* (London: Geoffrey Chapman, 1994).

Stromberg, Jean, *Mission and Evangelism: An Ecumenical Affirmation*, WCC Mission Series (Geneva: WCC, 1983).

Section 2

ASIAN PERSPECTIVES

4

Evangelism and witnessing in multi-religious Malaysia: towards a fresh approach

ALBERT SUNDARARAJ WALTERS (MALAYSIA)

Introduction

Ethnic Malays make up a large part of the population in Malaysia. In recent years many Christians and missionaries have been reaching out to them through evangelism, though the dangers and risks are numerous and multi-faceted. All Malays are legally bound by the federal constitution, which requires them to profess the Islamic faith.

Apostasy is a crime in Malaysia, and it carries the death penalty in at least two states. Individuals accused of apostasy can spend up to thirty-six months in isolated rehabilitation centres. Any Malay who rejects Islam is seen as betraying the Malay race, culture, and community. Ethnicity and religion are intricately intertwined so much that the term *masuk Melayu* ('to become Malay') describes conversion to Islam.

About 60 per cent of the nation's multi-racial, multi-religious population identify themselves with Islam, Malaysia's official religion. Witnessing to Malays is illegal, and so Islamic religious officials keep a close watch on churches, Christian schools, and private social events. Islamic groups portray Christianity as a symbol of encroaching Western imperialism that erodes Malay-Muslim culture and values, further stoking religious and ethnic tensions.

Besides Islam, there has been a noticeable resurgence in Hinduism and Buddhism, and these religions have recently been recharged with a strong sense of mission. They are committed to the ideal of propaganda. Christian evangelism has to contend with much opposition and resistance.

In such a context how do we as Christians practise evangelism, and how can we honestly witness to our faith and belief? How can we fulfil Jesus' mandate to 'make disciples' in Malaysia while taking into account the sensitivities of a multi-ethnic, multi-religious society? Can there be a fresh approach to evangelism and witnessing despite the many challenges and restrictions placed on the church and Christians in general?

In this chapter, I will try to answer some of the questions raised above. The chapter will focus on a new and fresh approach to evangelism and witnessing in a predominantly Islamic context. To elucidate and understand the topic at hand, it is pertinent that the Malaysian context in which Christians live and carry out the church's mission be considered. The many challenges facing evangelization and its implications will be examined. Taking into account various contextual hurdles and opportunities, a new way forward will be explored. It is envisaged that this work will stimulate further research regarding the issue of evangelism and witnessing in a largely Islamic context.

Key issues affecting Christian mission in Malaysia

Kelly James Clark with the help of Rupert Shortt makes a telling point about the state of Christianity in the world today:

> In early November [2012],German Chancellor Angela Merkel declared that Christianity is 'the most persecuted religion in the world.' Although met with predictable criticism, Rupert Short[t]'s recent research report for Civitas UK confirms Merkel's claim—we may not want to hear it, but Christianity is in peril, like no other religion. While this is a contest no one wants to win, Short[t] shows that 'Christians are targeted more than any other body of believers.' Short[t] is the author of the recently published *Christianophobia: A Faith Under Attack*. He is concerned that '200 million Christians (10 percent of the global total) are socially disadvantaged, harassed or actively oppressed for their beliefs.'[1]

In his report, Rupert Shortt highlighted the plight of Christians and the declining state of Christianity in the Middle East. He finds that between a half and two thirds of Christians in the Middle East have departed or been killed over the past century. Shortt attributes the intolerance and violence towards Christians to rising Islamization in Middle Eastern countries. Some of the oppression is government-sanctioned and some government-permitted; most is government-ignored. The situation that he describes is not very dissimilar from the situation in Malaysia.

Malaysia is a democratic secular federation with Islam as its official religion. However, over the last four to five decades, this unique model of tolerance and accommodation has been undergoing astonishing developments politically, socially, and economically. Intense intra-Muslim struggles coupled with increased state-mobilized Islamizing efforts have produced disturbing knock-on effects on non-Muslim minorities, especially Christians.[2]

While the Malaysian constitution recognizes the government's obligation towards Islam, it also pledges to uphold freedom of worship and to allow non-Muslims to practise their own religions.[3] The constitution, however, allows for the restriction of the propagation of religions other than Islam to the Muslim community. The issue of religious freedom and the position of Islam in Malaysia provides for a most pertinent and interesting illustration of the interaction between religion, politics, and socio-economic factors in the modern world.'

With Islamization have come greater restrictions imposed upon non-Muslim minorities with regard to the practice of their religion. One of the concerns expressed by affected non-Muslim communities is marginalization and discrimination. Besides that, Christians in Malaysia are troubled by specific statements and actions that seem to undermine their position within the country. In 1981, a federal-level statute was introduced banning the possession and circulation of the Indonesian-language Bible, the *Alkitab*. The *Alkitab* was restricted because it was deemed to be prejudicial to national interests and the security of the country. A year later the ban was amended to allow Christians to possess copies for their personal and liturgical use. In 1991, limitations were placed on the use of four terms regarded as Islamic: *Allah, Kaabah, Baitullah, and Solat.*[4] This move was particularly significant for Christians, since the term *Allah* had been in regular use to refer to God in Christian worship and liturgy. In April 2003, the *Bup Kudus* (Iban-language Bible) was banned because it used the phrase *Allah Tala*, which was said to be similar to *Allah ta'ala*, meaning 'Almighty God' in Islamic usage. In addition, Christian literature is required by law to carry a caption 'for non-Muslims only'. Furthermore, there is control in the distribution of land, building of non-Muslim places of worship, and allocation of land for non-Muslim cemeteries.

The question of religious conversion and apostasy is often a very controversial and contentious issue in Malaysia. In 1987, one of the incidents that greatly impacted the Malaysian church was the arrest and detention of more than 100 persons under the Internal Security Act. They were accused of subversion, violence, and threat to national security. Among those arrested for propagating Christianity to Malay Muslims was Jamaluddin bin Othman (also known as Yeshua Jamaluddin), a convert to Christianity. Another outstanding case related to the issue of apostasy was that of Lina

Joy, a Malay-Muslim who converted to Christianity in 1998. Malay citizens who convert out of Islam are no longer considered Malay under the law because Article 160 defines a Malay as one who is born to a Malaysian citizen, professes to be a Muslim, habitually speaks the Malay language, adheres to Malay customs, and is domiciled in Malaysia. These and many other cases regarding conversion and apostasy beg the question, especially for non-Muslim minorities, of whether the way of life guaranteed under the constitution is still available to them.

High-handed activities against the Christian community went further than official authoritative restrictions with the torching of church buildings. This occurred in a number of states in Peninsular Malaysia in July and October 2001 and was another clear indication of deteriorating community relations in the country. Again in January 2010, churches were attacked after the Kuala Lumpur High Court struck down the three-year-old ban on non-Muslims using of the word *Allah*. This destructive action left five churches severely damaged or ruined. Though these incidents may have been caused by some disgruntled anti-government extremist groups or over-zealous bureaucrats, they raise major concerns in the Christian community regarding progress towards harmonious interreligious relations.

Issues related to religion, particularly Islam, are ultra-sensitive in multiracial Malaysia, especially with politicians ready to exploit religious sentiments. One of the most thorny challenges Christians face is the objection made by certain religious communities regarding the use of unethical means in their mission and evangelism. In June last year, there was a suggestion that Christian evangelism should be banned. An essay published in a Malay daily and written by the Centre for Human Rights Research and Advocacy chief executive Azril Mohd Amin called for 'anti-evangelicalism laws' outlawing Christian evangelism in the country. The author claimed that evangelicalism, which he described as having 'exhibited new religious tendencies towards positivism, unfettered freedom and a tendency to uncontrolled openness', was seriously threatening Malaysia's religious harmony. The call for an anti-evangelical law follows claims by conservative Muslim figures that some Christian groups were conspiring to 'Christianize' Muslim-majority Malaysia, which restricts propagation of any faith other than Islam to Muslims.[5] Generally, it has been the practice of the church in Malaysia to not actively proselytize the Muslim community.

Conversion is a sensitive issue in Malaysia. Tension between Christians and Hindus has risen over allegations of mass conversions of Hindus to Christianity, particularly among Hindus in rural plantations. According to estimates compiled by a respectable Hindu organization, about 130,000 Malaysian Hindus have converted to Christianity over a period of about thirty years.[6] As a result, Hindus have appealed to all religions to abandon evangelism as a policy in the context of Malaysia. There are therefore religious, social, political, and ethnic factors that appear to militate against conversion from one religion to another.[7]

With intense and aggressive Islamization policies coupled with resurgence in other religions, there is grave concern among Christians about the prospects of evangelism and witnessing in Malaysia. In such a context, how do Christians boldly proclaim the Gospel of Jesus Christ?

Evangelism and witnessing in Malaysia: some challenges and concerns

Ever since the Day of Pentecost, Christians and Christianity have encountered various challenges in its attempts to proclaim the Gospel in obedience to Jesus' command to go and make disciples of all the nations (Mt 28.19). The Christian church has a unique identity and God-given task in the world to witness to Christ. Christian witness has to join in the work of the Christ-like Spirit of God, who blows to re-create and sanctify the whole creation. And so the most important issues for the church in Malaysia are mission and evangelism, especially in a country where about 90 per cent of the population do not profess to be Christians.

Furthermore, globalization and its processes of rapid transmission of information, knowledge, and personal contact have not only affected the socio-cultural, economic, and political situation of Malaysia. They have also meant the globalization of missions. Many short-term programmes and efforts that have been packaged in the West are being exported to Asia. Numerous churches in Malaysia have adopted such methods in 'reaching the unreached'. Missions are now guided by market-driven values such as 'least sacrifice, cheapest possible, fastest result, and greatest return on investment'. As is the case in the West, Malaysia faces similar currents towards pragmatism and managerial framework when evangelism is packaged to manufacture as many 'new babes' as possible.

Related to the above concern is the tendency among many Christians in Malaysia to duplicate methods employed in the West. Evangelism training seems to focus mainly on simply learning techniques. But techniques do not motivate us at a deeper level. Nor are they effective in building authentic relationships. This is not to diminish the importance of offering practical help. But the practical must be framed within a deeper theological understanding. Our effectiveness in witnessing does not come from learning new methods but from understanding the message. Our freedom to witness comes from understanding the author of the message, God himself! In other words, our theology must impact our methodology. Understanding the character of God will be the deepest motivation possible for witness. Knowing Christ well drives us to want to make him well known.

As I mentioned earlier, it is undeniable that in Malaysia racial and religious tensions have been heightened in the last couple of decades. As a result, there are numerous challenges and concerns among Malaysian Christians with regard to evangelism and witnessing. There is first of all the challenge to a wider and deeper understanding of mission and evangelism. Christian mission is a movement of the People of God in their context. When there is a crisis in their context, the mission of God is to recognize, engage, and address it and thus witness Christ in and through their words, lives, and action. Equally challenging is how to motivate those in the pews each Sunday. How do we encourage the 'unfaithful faithful' to share the good news of Jesus? How can we equip our churches to become inwardly strong yet outwardly focused with people who are ablaze with the love of Jesus?

Furthermore, there is an urgent need for a serious effort to understand Islam and other Asian religions. Of all the world religions, it is perhaps Islam that poses the biggest challenge to Christianity. There are several reasons for this. But the more important one is its missionary outlook. And so there has never been a more pressing need for Christians to study Asian religions and make an informed, compassionate, and confident response. Mission and evangelization can hardly be relevant and meaningful in a multi-religious context unless Christians in Malaysia formulate a contextualized and relevant 'theology of religions'. The church in Malaysia must become a truly 'Malaysianized' church whose character is distinctly Malaysian and whose loyalty to the nation and the people is unquestionable.

Evangelism and witnessing: towards a fresh approach

Having considered the challenges and concerns among Christians, there is a need to rethink mission in Malaysia. But then again Christians and especially Anglicans have often become very uptight particularly about evangelism. Sometimes it is called 'the e-word', as if 'evangelism' is an unspeakable swear word. Personal evangelism is generally not a regular discipline among believers in mainline churches. There are many reasons why Christians choose not to talk about their faith. Many don't want to participate in high-pressure tactics or in the kinds of emotional manipulation seen on television. They don't want their friends to think they are foolish or simple-minded. Nor do they want to be seen as being confrontational or disrespectful of others' deeply held religious beliefs. And yet anyone who has joined a church has made a commitment to be a witness for Jesus Christ. The Bible says, 'in your hearts sanctify Christ as Lord. Always be ready to make your defence to anyone who demands from you an account of the hope that is in you; yet do it with gentleness and reverence' (1 Pet 3.15–16).

What is evangelism and how can it be practised in Malaysia with 'gentleness and reverence'? The term 'evangelism' stems from the New Testament Greek word *euangelion*, meaning 'good news'. Evangelism is the sharing of the life-giving Gospel of Jesus Christ in word (proclamation) and deed (actions). And so as Anglicans/Episcopalians

> we are called to participate in God's mission in the world, by embracing respectful evangelism, loving service and prophetic witness. As we do so in all our varied contexts, we bear witness to and follow Jesus Christ, the crucified and risen Saviour.[8]

The Anglican Communion's Five Marks of Mission express a common commitment to, and understanding of, God's holistic and integral mission.[9] The first Mark of Mission, identified with personal evangelism, is a summary of what all mission is about, because it is based on Jesus' own summary of his mission.

As Christians, and as the church of Jesus Christ, we are called by our Lord to 'Go…and make disciples' (Mt 28.19). The call to bear witness is part of God's plan to bring the kingdom of God on earth as it is in heaven. Yet many of the evangelistic 'magic bullets' that worked in the past are now not as effective in many parts of the world. Is there a way to approach evangelism that is biblically sound yet culturally relevant? Are there principles we can glean from Scripture that are effective in a predominantly Islamic context like Malaysia? Sharing the Gospel is something that all Christians can and should do. The question is, 'How well and how effectively do we do it?' In a diverse, multi-religious, multicultural country like Malaysia, where so many faiths exist simultaneously with Islam, how do we communicate the absolute uniqueness of Christ? Our evangelism and witnessing, our lives should be so filled with Christ that they create a thirst for the Gospel in the 'other'.

In the Malaysian context evangelism and witnessing can be based on two common images familiar to the people and integral to the cultural environment. The first is friendship, which relates to God's friendship with humankind through Jesus. The second image is that of a fruit-bearing banana tree symbolizing a fruit-bearing and self-giving Christian in the community. Both these metaphors give people's experiences of the divine considerable significance.

Friendship evangelism

The Edinburgh 2010 conference issued a 'Common Call' which states:

> Remembering Christ's sacrifice on the Cross and his resurrection for the world's salvation, and empowered by the Holy Spirit, we are called to authentic dialogue, respectful engagement and humble witness among people of other faiths—and no faith—to the uniqueness of Christ. Our approach is marked with bold confidence in the gospel message; it builds friendship, seeks reconciliation and practises hospitality.[10]

One of the common images familiar to Malaysians and integral to the cultural environment is hospitality and friendship. Hospitality and friendship are two admirable qualities found among most Malaysians, in fact most Asians. Christians extend friendship because God came to be their friend in Jesus Christ.[11] Jesus acts as a bridge in drawing Christians into a living relationship with the one God in whom they profess to believe.

In the Christian tradition, human community is a reflection of the divine community, the Trinitarian reality of God, in which love is the supreme value. Thus relational witnessing is based on the Trinitarian model of interconnectedness. A Christian's life finds meaning as he/she participates in the life of God, in God's way of being as Trinity. Through life in the body of Christ, through us coming to live as Trinitarian persons, we relate to the Beyond All. We relate to the incarnate Son in our neighbours. And then we relate to the Spirit who Jesus Christ says is within us. And so we grow and relate as Trinitarian beings. Christian negotiation and relations with other people of faith are not possible outside a Trinitarian dynamic.

Trinity is a way of being and it is central to living the Christian faith. It is our way of being in the world that matters most, and this stance or 'way of being' has to do with the theological foundation we stand on when we engage in evangelism. An element that is often missing from most discussions of evangelism is our understanding of the triune nature of God. The Trinity teaches Christians vital truths about human relationships, both as individuals and in community. The relationship between the persons of the Trinity provides a recipe for the best sort of human relationships. And so Christians in a pluralistic context like Malaysia should reconsider, re-express, and contextualize the Trinity employing categories and concepts more familiar to ordinary people of faith. Christians are called to interpret the doctrine from within their own specific historical context. In a religiously plural context, how do Anglicans believing in the doctrine of the Trinity relate to one another and with other people of faith? How are we to live and relate to others so as to be more Christ-like? What sort of Trinitarian theology should the church project?

As a response to a religiously pluralistic situation, Christians should recognize friendship with people of other religions as a theological virtue.[12] Christians are called to present Christ in 'neighbourological' terms (to use Kosuke Koyama's term). The basic purpose of this relational approach is to encourage Christians to engage honestly with people of other faiths at the grass-roots. I would call this a 'pragmatic approach' which takes the context of Christians and people of other faiths seriously and enables them to relate to each other in new ways. Building relationship, recognizing each other's dignity, and creating a space for freedom are part and parcel of Christian mission.

The way to the soul of a person is through his/her heart. Kindness, care, interest in the person as an individual opens his/her heart. Then, when a genuine confidence has been built up, getting across eternal thoughts becomes natural. Therefore the best way of reaching the other is through personal contact.[13] While reaching out to other people of faith, Christians need to be real friends. Muslims and others may be suspicious of Christians and have a very negative view of 'missionaries', who are often seen as resorting to deceitful tactics in order to win converts. It is crucial that Christians are seen to be real people with real concern for their friends, and not just as out to convert them by any means.

Our call as Christians is to win others to the love of God and the grace that has been revealed to us in Jesus Christ. Our motive as Christian witnesses of the grace of God as it is revealed in God's Son must be 'that the sharing of your faith may become effective when you perceive all the good that we may do for Christ' (Philem 1.6). What is needed, primarily, is a desire to win their confidence—to build up a spirit of mutual trust and a bond of true friendship. Our aim should be to develop pure and genuine friendships, based solely on a desire to express the love of Jesus as we have come to experience it.

When people of other religions experience such love they will be all the more willing to share their lives with Christians and grow in confidence and trust towards us. When we learn to so love them, they will sense a greater depth of compassion and sincerity in us. And because 'God's love has been poured into our hearts through the Holy Spirit that has been given to us' (Rom 5.5), we will begin to communicate. The development of personal relationships is one of the most vital ingredients in effective evangelism among people of other religions.

In the life and ministry of Jesus Christ the concern for friendship was developed in a unique fashion. Jesus was always surrounded by the *ochlos*, the crowd, which consisted mainly of the poor, the discriminated-against, whom the Pharisees referred to as 'tax collectors and sinners'. Jesus cultivated companionship among young and old, rich and poor, men and women, those who were marginalized and down-trodden. This finally cost him his life. He initiated a new type of friendliness manifested in Jesus' commandment: 'love one another as I have loved you.... I have called you friends' (Jn 15.12–17).

Sharing one's life, even to death, is the true mark of friendship and solidarity with others. As friends of Jesus, Christians become friends of God. For Christians, friendship—both divine and human—is biblically based. God is a friend. God initiated relationships. Abraham, the man of faith, is also called God's friend (2 Chr 20.7; Isa 41.8). Wisdom is said to make people friends of God (Wis 7.27). Moses was a special friend because God spoke to him face to face (Ex 33.11).

Relational or friendship evangelism is the ideal form of evangelism as it is the outward expression of selfless love towards other people of faith. This is ultimately the greatest of all Christian virtues and the one most likely to make a lasting impact on others.

Incarnational witness

Evangelism is a highly contextual activity. As Christians, we are called to know how to share the apostolic message of salvation through Jesus Christ. But we are also called to share that message in a way that enables people to understand and receive it. This is the incarnational act of evangelism: bringing the Gospel to each time, place, culture, and subculture, and demonstrating that Jesus is just as powerful to effect salvation there as he was in first-century Palestine.[14] It is important that we as Christians understand and prepare ourselves to be Jesus among the people we live. Jesus is the Word who became flesh for us (Jn 1.14), but our calling is to be flesh that portrays the Word. Being an incarnational witness means that Jesus is paramount and not peripheral to our preaching, sharing, and witnessing.

Since incarnation was fundamental to God's mission in the world, so incarnation is essential to the church's mission in the world. In the words of *Ad Gentes* of Vatican II:

> The Church, in order to be able to offer all men the mystery of salvation and the life brought by God, must implant herself into these groups for the same motive which led Christ to bind Himself, in virtue of His Incarnation, to certain social and cultural conditions of those human beings among whom He dwelt.[15]

The point being made here is that mission is incarnational in that it must relate deeply and thoughtfully with its host culture.

Evangelism is also grounded in God's self-sacrifice on the cross. At the core of faith is self-giving love, both manifested on the cross and demanded by it. It is this self-giving core that grounds our way of being in the world. It is this self-giving love which opens us up and makes us able and willing to give ourselves for others. This self-giving relationship is exemplified fully in the imagery of the banana tree. It symbolizes a fruit-bearing and self-sacrificing Christian in the community. The image of the banana tree is closely linked to the Trinity, and it is a symbol of the fullness of life.

For the Christian, the banana tree symbolizes being rooted in the earth, which means being rooted in our identities—religious, cultural, social, linguistic, and national identities. We need to be rooted in our Christian faith and tradition and whatever we have inherited. Our Christian mission becomes meaningless unless we are rooted in Christ. Our faith is in Christ and we are witnesses for Christ.

In the Tamil culture, the banana tree is called the 'tree of unending life', and it has unique utility value. Every part of the tree can either be eaten or be used meaningfully. The leaf can be used like a plate for eating, for packing food, and as an umbrella in times of rain. The flower is edible as a fruit or vegetable. The banana fruit is edible as a fruit or vegetable and a wholemeal staple food for millions around the world. Banana is often offered in worship and cultural ceremonies. The inner stem of the tree is cooked and is edible as a vegetable. The withered outer bark can be converted into fibre to make a durable string or rope. The whole tree with fruits and flower intact is a very meaningful decoration in houses and Hindu temples. It is also used in public areas during religious and social festivals and at funerals, especially by people of Indian cultural background.

The flower has the shape of the 'heart'. As the flower unfolds, the fruits appear in combs from under the unfolding petals. The fruits have no other function except to be fruits. They can never be planted to become trees. The tree endures severe pruning (slaughter) about two feet from its base a few times in its young life, only to survive to be stronger and ultimately to bring forth a larger bunch of fruits. It is destined to die as soon as the fruits ripen on it. It bears fruit only once, and having lived a full fruitful life it dies. The very nature of the tree continues to live by producing on-going life in shoots that sprout from its base.

The analogy of the banana tree has a number of parallels with the quality of human life that each Christian is called to demonstrate in his/her lifetime. A person is called to be of full and complete utility as a being in every aspect of his/her life. Charity and love-in-action flow abundantly when one opens one's heart exhibiting fruits of the Spirit. Christians are urged to allow our good deeds to remain so. Good deeds should not become an obligation to the beneficiary, demanding gratitude or servitude, but should simply allow the fruits to be fruits.

The human being needs to endure much pain and loss through pruning to become stronger and more fruitful. The process of becoming fruitful includes pain, loss, and even ultimate death, so that others may thrive at our expense. The capacity to give away all of life with the assurance of generating new life is entrenched in human nature. The celebration of offering one's own life in total reproduces one's own life in others whom one leaves behind.

The person and life of Jesus are well epitomized in the banana tree. The characteristics of the banana tree's intrinsic nature, through the ages, can be summed-up as pointing to the beauty and fullness of life. The banana tree thrives throughout the year as a common reminder in pointing to the truth that in God, being is sustained in being given away.

Incarnational witnessing is about integrating the salvation event of Jesus' death and resurrection in our daily life and work. The purpose of incarnational witness is 'so that grace, as it extends to more and more people, may increase thanksgiving, to the glory of God' (2 Cor 4.15).

Conclusion

This chapter has attempted to describe the particular emphases on evangelism and witnessing in the largely Islamic context of Malaysia. Evangelism is more than dialogue, more than being a friend, more than walking alongside someone in their spiritual journey, more than caring for the poor. It has to do with sharing in the life of the Trinity and the offering of oneself as a living sacrifice to God. The two metaphors of hospitality and friendship and that of the banana tree, though emerging from a particular context, may not be well thought out and articulated. But they provide meaningful and hopeful pointers to people of faith living in challenging circumstances.

Other people of faith will be impressed with the words of Christians only if they experience genuine friendship and see Christians living consistent moral lives. And Christianity is not merely a religious message which they must believe, but a *life* to be received in the person of the Lord Jesus.[16] One's testimony must be matched by one's lifestyle. And so we need to heed the words of St Paul, who reminds us: 'only, live your life in a manner worthy of the gospel of Christ' (Phil 1.27).

Response

JEREMY BERGSTROM (UNITED STATES)

In spite of the vast differences between the contexts where Walters and I live—Malaysia and Texas—it seems from his chapter that we have everything in common: a love for Christ, a strong desire for evangelism and witness, and a desire to put flesh and blood on the love of God given to us in Jesus Christ, bearing witness to our Lord through the testimony of our lives wherever our Lord may have called us to serve.

Walters's proposal is a welcome one: 'a new and fresh approach to evangelism and witnessing in a predominantly Islamic context', which he hopes will produce 'a truly "Malaysianized" church whose character is distinctly Malaysian and whose loyalty to the nation and the people is unquestionable'. And as he has taught us, the preservation of Malaysian identity is especially important in a place where the relationship between the government, the Muslim faith, and Malay ethnicity is so jealously guarded, and where Christian proselytization is seen as an invasion of Western culture.

Before discussing his two important strategies of friendship and the incorporation of the image of a banana tree as a properly Malay symbol, I would like to begin with a couple of questions:

1 How do the strategies he has proposed help avoid the potentially severe penalties for proselytization? If conversion to Islam is what makes one Malay, won't any conversion to another religion (especially Christianity) cross the authorities, no matter how properly 'Malay' the flavour of Christianity may actually be? And how were those slick Western programmes he mentions able to succeed in this environment, however shallow their converts might have been?

2 At the beginning of his chapter Walters says, 'the most important issues for the church in Malaysia are mission and evangelism, especially in a country where about 90 per cent of the population do not profess to be Christians'. Yet he goes on to describe lots of pre-packaged evangelistic programmes from the West which have nearly exclusive focus on producing 'new babes' at greatest efficiency and lowest cost, seeking not to make disciples, but to get greatest return on investment, presumably through mere professions of faith and baptisms. If they are mass-producing Christians through shallow, nominal conversions, and the need is for deeper understanding, rather than immediate evangelization, it seems to me that the urgent and greatest need is for a two-step process: discipleship of the Christians you already have, *leading to*

quality growth. Indeed, it seems to me that Walters is saying as much when he calls for their methods to 'be framed within a deeper theological understanding', 'understanding the message', and how 'our theology must impact our methodology'. As Walters so beautifully says, 'Understanding the character of God will be the deepest motivation possible for witness.' Amen!

If I have read him rightly, it seems his two proposals of (1) friendship evangelism and (2) incarnational witness through incorporation of the traditionally meaningful symbolism of the banana tree would be particularly effective in his goal of discipleship leading to quality growth.

Friendship evangelism

First, a word on friendship. I must confess, along with several theologians I find the recent discussions of human community as a reflection of the divine community to be less than convincing. This view of Christian society was virtually non-existent in the Christian tradition until the work of Jürgen Moltmann, John Zizioulas, and Colin Gunton in the early 1980s. I realize this view will not make me popular, especially since we are still in the afterglow of so many Trinity Sunday sermons on just this theme. But I stand with Professor Karen Kilby,[17] among others, in believing that this leads to a dangerous tendency to project our own grand ideals about human community onto the divine, and then turn around and project this view back onto the world God has made, saying that this is in fact what is *important* about the doctrine, and is thus descriptive and normative for our relationships with one another.

We are on safer ground when we take a more apophatic approach towards the godhead, and restrict ourselves to the language that Christ himself gives us when he talks about friendship and Christian unity, which is of course found in solidarity and union with the man Jesus Christ. The dominant biblical models given to describe this relationship involve the union of husband and wife, of head to body, of many members united to one head, of many branches grafted into one vine. This has the added advantage of keeping in view that which brings about such unity, and that is, the cross of our Lord. Social Trinitarian models end up having little real need for the cross, and lend themselves to dangerous claims of an almost gnostic immediacy to the divine via the Holy Spirit, among other problems. What could be more Anglican in its love of the incarnation of our Lord than a strong focus on the flesh of Christ and the scriptural language of our union with him?

As Walters himself writes, 'Christians extend friendship because God came to be their friend in Jesus Christ. Jesus acts as a bridge in drawing Christians into a living relationship with the one God in whom they profess to believe.' Yes indeed, 'God is love.' And if we would listen to St John fully, we must go on reading:

> God's love was revealed among us in this way: God sent his only Son into the world so that we might live through him. In this is love, not that we loved God but that he loved us and sent his Son to be the atoning sacrifice for our sins. Beloved, since God loved us so much, we also ought to love one another. (1 Jn 4.9–11)

Indeed, as St John tells us in chapter 3, 'We know love by this, that he laid down his life for us—and we ought to lay down our lives for one another' (3.16). So I propose that our love and friendship is not so much Trinitarian as it is cruciform, bound up in the broken body of Jesus and his blood shed on his cross, to whose body we find ourselves united as living members the more we participate in the love of God given through him. This is what it means to be 'incarnational', and is what allows us to sanctify all the gritty realities of Malay, Iranian, English, and even American culture.

Augustine of Hippo follows this pattern given in 1 John, and is perhaps best on this cruciform, incarnate friendship; he looks always to the cross and the work of the Holy Spirit in uniting us embodied creatures to the incarnate Son. The power of seeing such love on display is powerfully moving, and produces a powerful desire to reciprocate the same love: 'For there is no mightier invitation to love than to anticipate in loving; and that soul is over hard which, supposing it unwilling indeed to give love, is unwilling also to give the return of love' (*On the Catechising of the Uninstructed*, 4.7).[18] So it is that true friendship is found in sharing the love of God given to us in Jesus Christ:

> If, therefore, it was mainly for this purpose that Christ came, to wit, that man might learn how much God loves him; and that he might learn this, to the intent that he might be kindled to the love of Him by whom he was first loved, and might also love his neighbor at the command and showing of Him who became our neighbor, in that He loved man when, instead of being a neighbor to Him, he was sojourning far apart…(4.8)

Aelred of Rievaulx is perhaps the most famous proponent of this Augustinian notion of friendship, and he provides three types of friendship which we can perhaps consider as a sound strategy for evangelization through friendship. He outlines three types of friendship, which I believe could be used as a ladder: carnal, worldly, and spiritual. The goal would be the old Ciceronian definition of friendship: true 'agreement in things human and divine, with good will and charity' (*Spiritual Friendship*, I.31–46).[19]

We might not want to engage in carnal friendship, which Aelred defines as 'conspiracy in vice'. But the worldly friendship he describes is a solid beginning, for it involves people coming together for 'hope of gain'. This would involve many very practical partnerships involving food and shelter, coming together for shared labour and business, and perhaps even more intimate things like helping with childcare and even sharing a meal. Though such a relationship would be 'worldly' in its character, within these everyday practical encounters there are innumerable opportunities to show forth the love of Christ; as Aelred says at one point, the love given to us in Christ brings perfection to our charity through sacrificial diligence, even giving us the strength to befriend 'many who are a burden and a bore to us' (II.19). He continues, 'In friendship, then, we join honesty with kindness, truth with joy, sweetness with good will, and affection with kind action. All this begins with Christ, is advanced through Christ, and is perfected in Christ' (II.20). This is what he has in mind when he talks about that which alone is properly called friendship.

As Augustine says frequently, such love cannot be resisted by many before it begins to be reciprocated. Aelred thus can talk easily of how human friendship readily ascends to the source of friendship, which is God himself (III.87), who 'himself acts to channel so much friendship and charity between himself and the creatures he sustains...that in this way each one may love another as himself' (III.79). So the inner, innate human desire for friendship with God through Christ is awakened and encouraged by means of Christian friendship, which refers the newly-beloved to Christ himself. And in Aelred's lofty conclusion, he even reflects on the way Christians themselves grow in their own friendship with God through their prayers for their earthly friends.

> Praying to Christ for a friend and desiring to be heard by Christ for a friend, we focus on Christ with love and longing. Then sometimes suddenly, imperceptibly, affection melts into affection, and somehow touching the sweetness of Christ nearby, one begins to taste how dear he is and experience how sweet he is. Thus rising from that holy love with which a friend embraces a friend to that with which a friend embraces Christ, one may take the spiritual fruit of friendship fully and joyfully into the mouth, while looking forward to all abundance in the life to come...then with the beginning of relief from care we shall rejoice in the supreme and eternal good, when the friendship to

> which on earth we admit but few will pour out over all and flow back to God from all, for God will be all in all (1 Cor 15). (III.133–34)

Incarnational witness

This section offers a few reflections and ideas on the use of the central Malay devotion to the banana tree. Walters mentions the long history of the banana tree in Malay culture, especially the common presence of banana trees in Hindu temples. This is full of possibilities but also raises a sense of caution, for fear of the very real possibility of the introduction of theological ambiguity or perhaps even syncretism were the banana tree symbolism to be introduced wholesale into Christian life without some sort of visible, Christian distinctiveness. Such was the difficulty we see in Paul's Corinthian correspondence on what Christians are to do with meat sacrificed to idols (1 Cor 8), or the incompatibility of pagan cultic rites with the Christian mysteries (1 Cor 10). This concern may resonate with Walters, given his stated desire to proclaim the unique quality of Christ when compared with other faiths.

To avoid resurrecting yet another instance of the Corinthian controversy in a Malaysian context, I wonder whether it might be possible to incorporate elements of the banana tree into existing ancient Christian iconography involving trees, such as a banana version of the old Byzantine Tree of Life, with Christ imposed in the centre and the Apostles hanging off the branches like so many pieces of fruit; or what about the Jesse Tree, where the lineage of Christ through David springs from Jesse, and various members of the family are, again, presented as an abundance of fruit, with Christ himself in the canopy? One could easily employ Christian imagery imposed over a tree, even providing a kind of banana cosmos, with angels as the canopy of leaves. It could also be lovely to have the image of the vine enhanced with banana-like features, an incorporation and even merging of the Malay culture into the imagery of Scripture, like some sort of scriptural genetic hybrid. And perhaps the most obvious of all, a cross could quite easily be portrayed with banana features, its roots planted deeply in Malaysian soil, drinking deeply from the river of the water of life flowing from the heavenly throne of God, laden with fruit, whether those fruits be various Christian virtues, or the Apostles and saints themselves.

Conclusion

The purpose in this response is to strengthen the incorporation of the incarnation of Christ into Walters's evangelism initiatives. After all, there is no hope for the sanctification of Malay culture (or any other human culture) apart from the cross of Jesus Christ. Such initiatives will be all about making friends for Christ, a ministry that will be sacrificial and therefore fruitful wherever it finds you, whether that involves bananas, pomegranates, or some of other fruit suitable for the mission field.

Notes

1 Kelly James Clark, 'The Most Persecuted Religion in the World', *The Blog* (6Mar.2013),https://www.huffingtonpost.com/kelly-james-clark/christianity-most-persecuted-religion_b_2402644.html.

2 See A. S. Walters, 'Issues in Christian–Muslim Relations: A Malaysian Christian Perspective', *Islam and Christian–Muslim Relations*, 18 (Jan. 2007), 67–83.

3 See Tun Mohammad Suffian bin Hashim, *An Introduction to the Constitution of Malaysia* (Kuala Lumpur: Government Printer, 1976), pp. 218–19.

4 *Allah* is Arabic for 'God'; the *Kaabah* is a building located inside the mosque known as Masjid al-Haram in Mecca; *Baitullah* is from the Arabic *bayt Allah*, 'House of God', and *Solat*, from the Arabic *salat*, is commonly used to refer to the five daily prayers in Islam.

5 Syed Jaymal Zahiid, '"Anti-Evangelism Laws" Not for Malaysia, Deputy Home Minister says', *The Malay Mail Online* (17 June 2017), http://www.themalaymailonline.com/malaysia/article/anti-evangelism-laws-not-for-malaysia-deputy-home-minister-says#ZIDrxCqWTelhMxZY.97.

6 '160,000 Convert Out of Hinduism in Malaysia', *Hinduism Today*, web edn (Feb. 1992), https://www.hinduismtoday.com/modules/smartsection/item.php?itemid=900.

7 S. Batumalai, 'A Malaysian Neighbourology (To Know Malaysia is to Love Malaysia): A Prophetic Christology for Neighbourology', *Asia Journal of Theology*, 5/2 (1991),119, 123.

8 'The Anglican Way: Signposts on a Common Journey', Report from the Singapore Consultation of the Theological Education in the Anglican Communion (TEAC) Working Party of the Anglican Primates (2007), https://www.anglicancommunion.org/media/109378/The-Anglican-Way-Signposts-on-a-Common-Journey_en.pdf.

9 The Anglican Communion, 'Marks of Mission', http://www.anglicancommunion.org/mission/marks-of-mission.aspx. The Five Marks of Mission are (1) to proclaim the good news of the Kingdom; (2) to teach, baptize, and nurture new believers; (3) to respond to human need by loving service; (4) to

transform unjust structures of society, to challenge violence of every kind, and pursue peace and reconciliation; and (5) to strive to safeguard the integrity of creation, and sustain and renew the life of the earth.

10 Lalsangkima Pachuau and Knud Jorgensen, 'Witnessing to Christ in a Pluralistic World: Christian Mission among Other Faiths' (2011), p. 6, http://digitalshowcase.oru.edu/re2010series/13.

11 See S. Batumalai (ed.), *Vision 2020: A Malaysian Christian Response* (Kuala Lumpur: S. Batumalai, 1992), pp. 175–6.

12 Cf. James L. Fredericks, 'Interreligious Friendship: A New Theological Virtue', *Journal of Ecumenical Studies*, 35/2 (Spring 1998), 159–74.

13 Gerhard Nehls, *The Great Commission: You and the Muslim* (Bellville: SIM International, 1988), p. 25.

14 Mark R. Teasdale, 'Preface', *Witness: The Journal of the Academy for Evangelism in Theological Education*, 31 (2017), http://journals.sfu.ca/witness/index.php/witness.

15 Vatican II, *Ad Gentes*, chap. 2, 'Mission Work Itself', http://www.vatican.va/archive/hist_councils/ii_vatican_council/documents/vat-ii_decree_19651207_ad-gentes_en.html.

16 Charles R. Marsh, *Share your Faith with a Muslim* (Chicago: Moody Press, 1975), p. 72.

17 Karen Kilby, 'Perichoresis and Projection: Problems with Social Doctrines of the Trinity', *New Blackfriars*, 81 (2000), 432–45. See also Lewis Ayres, *Nicaea and its Legacy* (Oxford: Oxford University Press, 2004); John Behr, *The Nicene Faith* (Crestwood, NY: St Vladimir's Seminary Press, 2004), esp. his introduction; Bruce Marshall, 'Trinity', in Gareth Jones (ed.), *The Blackwell Companion to Modern Theology* (Oxford: Blackwell, 2004), pp. 183–203; and Brian Daley, '"ONE THING AND ANOTHER": The Persons in God and the Person of Christ in Patristic Theology', *Pro Ecclesia*, 15/1 (2006), 17–46.

18 Augustine of Hippo, *On the Catechising of the Uninstructed*, 4.7–8, http://www.sacred-texts.com/chr//ecf/103/1030378.htm.

19 Aelred of Rievaulx, *Spiritual Friendship* (Collegeville, MN: Liturgical Press, 2010).

Bibliography

Bosch, David J., *Transforming Mission: Paradigm Shifts in Theology of Mission* (Maryknoll, NY: Orbis Books, 1991).

D'Costa, Gavin, *Theology and Religious Pluralism* (Oxford: Basil Blackwell, 1986).

Hick, John, *God has Many Names* (London: Macmillan, 1980).

Marsh, Charles R., *Share your Faith with a Muslim* (Chicago: Moody Press, 1975).

Pachuau, Lalsangkima, and Knud Jorgensen, 'Witnessing to Christ in a Pluralistic World: Christian Mission among Other Faiths' (2011), http://digitalshowcase.oru.edu/re2010series/13.

Race, Alan, *Christians and Religious Pluralism: Patterns in Christian Theology of Religions*, 2nd edn (London: SCM Press, 1983).

Riddell, P. G., 'Islamization, Civil Society, and Religious Minorities in Malaysia', in K. S. Nathan and M. H. Kamali (eds.), *Islam in Southeast Asia: Political, Social and Strategic Challenges for the Twenty-First Century* (Singapore: Institute of Southeast Asian Studies, 2005), pp. 160–90.

Riddell, P. G., 'Malaysian Christians and Islamisation', in A. O'Mahony and M. Kirwan (eds.), *World Christianity: Politics, Theology, Dialogues*, (London: Melisende, 2004), pp. 226–56.

Samartha, S. J., *One Christ—Many Religions: Toward a Revised Christology* (Bangalore: SATHRI, 2000).

Walters, A. S., *Knowing our Neighbour: A Study of Islam for Christians in Malaysia* (Petaling Jaya: Council of Churches of Malaysia, 2007).

Walters, A. S., *We Believe in One God? Reflections on the Trinity in the Malaysian Context* (Delhi: ISPCK, 2002).

5

With gentleness and respect: evangelism and witness in a multi-faith society

JONATHAN WONG (SINGAPORE)

The Pew Research Center released a report on 4 April 2014 entitled 'Global Religious Diversity: Half of the Most Religiously Diverse Countries are in Asia-Pacific Region'.[1] It ranked 232 nations in terms of religious diversity in their populations according to a ten-point 'Religious Diversity Index' (RDI), which measured how the population of each country was distributed among eight major religious groups as at 2010. The approach is quite straightforward: the more equally the eight major religious groups are distributed, in terms of percentage of a population, the higher will be the score. This report was a follow-up to the landmark study 'The Global Religious Landscape: A Report on the Size and Distribution of the World's Major Religious Groups as at 2010', in which 2,500 national censuses, large-scale surveys, and official population registers were analysed and interpreted as part of the Pew-Templeton Global Religious Futures project.

The country with the highest score on this RDI was Singapore, the island nation at the southernmost tip of Peninsular Malaysia, which has a total population of almost six million people. According to the report, the largest group consists of the Buddhists (34 per cent), followed by the Christians (18 per cent), the religiously unaffiliated (16 per cent), and then the Muslims (14 per cent). Hindus (5 per cent), Jews (under 1 per cent), folk or traditional religionists (2 per cent), and the remainder who are categorized as 'Other Religions' (10 per cent) make up the rest of the population. This gave Singapore a score of 9.0 on the RDI scale. For comparison, France, which was categorized as 'high', scored 5.9, and the United States, which was 'moderate', scored 4.1 on the RDI.

Singapore is the country of my birth and the place in which I now live and minister, and I am intimately familiar with its context. What was not captured on the scale was the phenomenal rate of growth of Christianity in the last thirty years. In 1980, Christians made up 9.9 per cent, but by

2010 the number almost doubled to 18.3 per cent of the total resident population.[2] On the basis of the results of a recent survey conducted in the congregation which I pastor, 60 per cent of those who attend regularly are first-generation Christians. About 35 per cent of this congregation are young people (under the age of thirty-five), and the majority of them are children of the older members. It is not too difficult to conclude from these simple statistics that evangelism and witness is something that is highly valued in the Christian community in Singapore because the majority of its members are themselves converts to Christianity.

However, as a small nation that is very dependent on the world economy, Singapore has not been immune to the changing realities of the rest of the globe. After the events of 9/11 in 2001, there has been a greater sensitivity to matters related to religious harmony, especially because we are surrounded by large nations that have predominantly Muslim populations.[3] The government has taken proactive steps to bolster the social cohesion among the various faith traditions, by encouraging various interreligious activities and setting up various grass-roots organizations to foster religious harmony. With this heightened sensitivity to harmony among the religions, questions have naturally arisen as to how appropriate it is for the church in Singapore to continue to engage in evangelism.

This chapter seeks to defend the practice of evangelism in the religiously and racially diverse country of Singapore by addressing some common objections, exploring the assumptions behind these concerns, and providing a theological and biblical case for the work of evangelism to continue to flourish in the context of the multi-faith society of Singapore. Many other parts of the Anglican Communion have also experienced the growing diversity of religious adherents in their own contexts because of globalization and the concomitant rise of immigration, and as a result may share similar concerns about the evangelism and witness of the church in such pluralistic contexts. It is hoped that some of my reflections on the situation in Singapore may be of help to others facing similar questions as they encounter different faiths and religious traditions in their own contexts.

Objections to evangelism

There are two main arguments that have been raised about the ongoing practice of evangelism in multi-faith Singapore. Firstly, there is the worry expressed by some who are proponents for a more secular society which seeks to harmonize differences, that the practice of evangelism—which inevitably accentuates the exclusive truth claims of Christianity—is an act of arrogance which is unacceptable in a multi-faith context. To say that 'there is no other name' (Acts 4.12) is perceived as a fundamental negation of other religious truth claims. One example of this objection is raised by Tom Driver, who says:

> the immoral factor in the 'scandal of particularity' today is its insistence upon a once-and-for-all Christ in a relativistic world. That is indeed a scandal—erroneous, imperial, and dangerous to humanity. It precludes Christianity's ability to affirm that all people have a right to their place in the sun.[4]

The underlying concern is the question of 'how to be a Christian without being paternalistic to those who are not'.[5] The belief is that 'if the incarnation of God in finite humanity can occur but once, the religious value of all other human history is nil'.[6] Such thinking finds its roots in the Western Enlightenment project which compares particular truths, which can be defended only on the basis of arbitrary religious authority, against the absolutes that are established by universal human reason. It is assumed that if everyone submitted to the universal truths that are plainly evident and available to all, then no one would have the corner on truth, and everyone could then speak a common language and come to the realization that the differences among the different faith traditions are only cosmetic. So, therefore, one should not impose their views on another, appealing to their own sources and authorities, to the denigration of others.

On the surface, this is a valid and noble concern. The desire to impose one's views on others, to the exclusion of other opposing views, can be problematic and has at times in the course of history led to conflict and violence. However, this attempt to relativize truth is in danger of being yet another form of cultural colonization. The universal rationality of the Enlightenment itself assumes an authority which has particular appeal mainly (or perhaps only) to those who espouse it. It purports to look behind particular truth claims of the faith traditions and practices, so as to distil 'the universal object of the transcendent' for all times and in all places.[7] The hope they have is that such an approach may open up the space for dialogue and common concerns. The intent is that no one should have a privileged position of authority, as this is inevitably intolerant of other views from other traditions.

However, this seemingly tolerant approach has its own problem. It ultimately relativizes every other truth claim and subjects all other claims to its own privileged authority. In demanding an abandonment of their particularity, its proponents strip each religion of their vital essence and what makes each of them unique. Lamin Sanneh criticizes this approach.

> Can we know ourselves as religious persons without the religious sources of our identity and without the capacity to discriminate and to evaluate? Must interreligious encounter involve making a hostage of each of our particular traditions before we can undertake it? The objection of critics of religious uniqueness that if we privilege one particular perception of religious truth as the only correct one, we make true dialogue impossible and open ourselves to the charge of intolerance sounds like an implicit attack on what makes the religious traditions of others also distinctive.[8]

When this uncritical relativism (which is itself a form of imperialism!) is mixed with the collective Western guilt that arises from their colonial past, it 'forms a lethal brew that has sapped the vitality of many Christians in the West'.[9] The result is a loss of confidence in the work of evangelism and witness of the Western church. And these same objections have made their way among those of us who operate in non-Western contexts which may have sometimes uncritically adopted such thinking.

The second objection that has been raised is that the practice of evangelism and witness among people of other faiths will aggravate the tensions inherent in a multi-faith society. They fear that such actions would upset our neighbours and cause friction in our multicultural and multi-faith context. Once again there are real dangers here, and as Christians, we cannot ignore the reality of how the insensitive actions of a small minority have created and can create unnecessary stress on the delicate peace we enjoy in Singapore.[10]

Yet we must also recognize that religious freedom, which is one of the fundamental tenets of Singapore's constitution, allows Christians to evangelize and witness despite the fact that we live in a multi-faith context. And this basic freedom should be maintained and defended. The report *Christian Witness in a Multi-Religious World*, which came out of a joint five-year study by the Pontifical Council for Interreligious Dialogue, the World Council of Churches, and the World Evangelical Alliance, stated: 'Religious freedom including the right to publicly profess, practice, propagate and change one's religion flows from the very dignity of the human person which is grounded in the creation of all human beings in the image and likeness of God.'[11]

Even so, we must still be cognizant of the need to be circumspect in how it is done. The Cape Town Commitment, which emerged from the Third Lausanne Congress on World Evangelization, is helpful in this regard.

> We are called to share good news in evangelism, but not to engage in unworthy proselytizing. *Evangelism*, which includes persuasive rational argument following the example of the Apostle Paul, is 'to make an honest and open statement of the gospel which leaves the hearers entirely free to make up their own minds about it. We wish to be sensitive to those of other faiths, and we reject any approach that seeks to force conversion on them.' *Proselytizing*, by contrast, is the attempt to compel others to become 'one of us', to 'accept our religion', or indeed to 'join our denomination'.[12]

This makes the helpful distinction between *evangelism* and *proselytizing*. The former is an attempt to respectfully persuade, whereas the other is coercive and aggressive. Scripture does not condone such proselytizing. It tells us that we are to witness to others 'with gentleness and respect' (1 Pet 3.16, NIV). In essence, the difference lies in what our attitude is towards those we witness to. If we see our witness as an exercise of power to compel and convert others, we fall into the trap of proselytizing. But if we see that our role is 'to proclaim and assert Christ's claims of Kingship over all realms of life, but to do this, just as its Lord, as a servant, even ready to be a suffering servant, and not a power dependent on rights and privileges', the way we witness will be an entirely different proposition.[13] It does also boil down to the question as to whose work it is to convert a person. I am of the opinion that those who fall into the trap of proselytizing mostly see conversion as something we do as human agents. Whereas the broad witness of Scripture is that conversion is the gracious work of God in the world (Acts 11.18; Rom 2.4; 2 Cor 7.10; 2 Tim 2.25; 2 Pet 3.9). The recognition of divine agency in conversion thus frees the Christian to be a servant to their neighbour, trusting in the power of the Holy Spirit to change their heart.

Evangelism done as 'suffering servants' does not seek to assert our rights and freedoms, or to elevate our position at the expense of others. Instead it is done by loving our neighbour, for their good. There is no place for aggressive proselytizing for those who follow the one who 'emptied himself, taking the form of a slave' (Phil 2.7). We should also do it with full recognition of the dignity of others.

> Our fellow human being is first, foremost and essentially one in the image of God, and only secondarily a Hindu, Muslim or secular pagan. So, inasmuch as his religion is part of his humanity, whenever we meet one whom we call 'an adherent of another religion', we meet someone who, in his religion as in all else, has some relationship to the Creator God, a relationship within which he is addressable and accountable.[14]

Evangelism is an imperative for the Church

This understanding that all human beings have some relationship to God and is therefore 'addressable and accountable' is the very reason why the church is called to engage the world in evangelism and witness. The incarnation of Jesus Christ, in all its particularity, is of universal significance. The revelation of God breaking into history and creation in Christ 'ennobles our humanity and enables us to have not merely a "place in the sun" but a "home in God"'.[15] As Ramachandra points out, 'the universal is always mediated through the particular, in the biblical scheme of things'.[16] And the unique message that came through the person of Jesus Christ has always, because of its universal significance and importance, compelled the church to cross geographical, linguistic, and cultural boundaries to communicate this to the world. This is not only true for the first disciples but continues to be the case even now in our day. At its heart, 'Evangelism is joining in the work of God to bring redemption to this world. It's proclaiming the revolution of love that has rescued God's world from darkness to light.'[17] If we believe in what the Bible has revealed as the purpose for the incarnation, then this message is so important, with such far-reaching implications, that the church cannot help but engage the world in evangelism and witness.

Furthermore, there is an inevitability to the practice of evangelism in the church's interaction with the world and especially in its contact with those of other faith traditions. Hendrik Kraemer points out that communication is a fundamental human fact, and that it is 'the essence of our humanity'.[18] As a result, we have in every contact with our neighbours to communicate with them. If that communication is to go beyond the superficial, we as Christians must at some point have to bear witness to the Gospel, the good news that Jesus Christ came, died, and rose again to reconcile us to God. This is because the Gospel is what brought the church into being. It is what God did when he redeemed his people and gathered them as his body. In fact, I believe that evangelism and witness are the *raison d'être* for the church.

> [The Christian message] is not a message about which the bearers have the right to decide whether it should be communicated or not, whether one should keep it as a precious private possession for oneself or not. It *must* be communicated because it issues from the prophetic consciousness that is the Word of the Lord of the universe...It has called a community into being, the *Church*, which exists for the sake of the world, and not for its own sake.[19]

The resurrected Lord made this clear when he said, 'As the Father has sent me, so I send you' (Jn 20.21). The church is therefore sent into the world to continue and reflect that which was revealed in and through the life and death of Jesus Christ. As Jesus came to serve and to reveal God's love to the world, those who are called by his name are to do likewise. To be witnesses of this love of God in Christ then becomes an imperative for us. 'The communication of the gospel is not a...cause for glorification, but...a divine must, laid upon the Church.'[20] Furthermore, this message 'conveys the revelation of God, not an idea of God which enters into competition with other conceptions of the divine. Revelation means that God wants to be known.'[21] And the way he has appointed to be known to the world at large is through his people, the church.

Some additional thoughts

This impetus and mandate for the church were articulated in the Lausanne Covenant. 'Our Christian presence in the world is indispensable to evangelism', which is obvious. But the covenant goes on to point out that what is also absolutely necessary 'is that kind of dialogue whose purpose is to listen sensitively in order to understand'.[22] On the surface, it would seem incongruous to speak about evangelism and dialogue in the same breath. The assumption is that evangelism immediately shuts down any path to dialogue, since it is an act of persuasion, and thus seems antithetical to the practice of dialogue, which requires complete openness. Or at least, that is what the rules of the dialogue game insist. 'Authentic listening requires a total openness to the possible truth of what the other person is presenting. In fact, it requires each partner to presume the truth of the others' positions . . .'[23] This presupposition, however, has been challenged. It presumes the questionable 'view from nowhere', and has the similar Enlightenment roots of relativism and progressivism which were discussed earlier in this chapter.[24]

> It is...a discursive practice with strictly imperialistic tendencies: it wants and intends that its rules and modes of procedure should be dominant (even the only) ones in play when the game has to do with intercourse among different religious communities. Such dialogue is also a practice that ought to cease: it has no discernible benefits, many negative effects, and is based upon a radical misapprehension of the nature and significance of religious commitments.[25]

It is little wonder that so many such efforts at interreligious dialogue have been confined to religious elites and esoteric philosophical debates, with little significant traction in religious communities at large. 'Thou shalt be nice to everyone' is the first commandment of such dialogue, and so similarities are celebrated while differences are downplayed or ignored. However, 'such conversations may be socially pleasant but they are not religiously productive'.[26] Paul Griffiths instead suggests that what would be more productive is interreligious apology. This is not 'apology' as in 'apologies for offending you' or 'sorry, I'm wrong'. Rather it is apologetics as in a 'reasoned argument in defense of what one takes to be true against views that one takes to be false—against, that is, potential or actual challengers to one's own beliefs'.[27] This is the apology of 'be ready to make your defence to anyone who demands from you an account of the hope that is in you' (1 Pet 3.15). Christians 'are under both ethical and epistemic obligations to argue for the truth of what they take themselves to believe when they are faced with religious others who appear to believe something different and to act differently based upon such difference in belief'.[28] This makes evangelism not just nice to have, but necessary to have as part of our interaction with people of other faiths.

If we believe sincerely in the saving truth that comes through the Gospel, and that it has the power to transform and change the lives of all who receive it, how can we withhold it from them and still claim to be morally upright and honest? If I saw a truck coming at speed down the road and a person standing directly in its path, and yet stood by in silence because I was afraid to offend or was too polite to raise my voice, how could I be considered a good or loving neighbour to that person?

Conclusion

This dialogue with people of other faiths is not merely an academic or theological exercise for us in Singapore. It is an everyday reality. I myself often meet up with a group of old friends from my secondary school days, and among them are those who are Buddhists, Christians, Muslims, Hindus, and even some religious 'nones', representing many of the religious groups identified by the Pew Research Center study cited at the start of this chapter. For me, interreligious encounters are not just some ivory-tower practice but a concrete reality. They take place not just among the upper echelon and the elites of the religious hierarchy, but especially among those who make up our multi-faith society.

I have found that genuine dialogue under such circumstances need not dilute the message, nor is there a need to suppress our convictions in the name of peace. Nevertheless, we cannot see this as some kind of debate or contest in which we become belligerent. 'If in this dialogue religious persons press their cases resolutely, they also do so religiously; that means, with compassion, sensitivity, and, yes, politeness.'[29] In other words, it should be done with gentleness and respect!

Response

CHRISTOPHER WELLS (UNITED STATES)

Catholic apologetics: for a renewed classicism and conservation

A friend is writing his dissertation on lying in Thomas Aquinas—Thomas's rich account of what it means to tell the truth, tied to an Aristotelian understanding of character, habit, and virtue, incorporating grace and much else. He chose his topic years ago as substantively worthy and understudied. Then, as rarely happens in academia, his subject suddenly became practically urgent, in our dawning 'post-truth' era. In our country, we have been inundated for two years with private email servers, probably-possibly 'rigged elections', fake news, and a concomitant erosion of confidence in all mainstream media on grounds of bias.

For traditionally minded persons, a root problem is the widespread disdain for and dismissal of our own history and culture, which has not been taught and so is forgotten in the name of progress, diversity, alleged justice; also in the name of self-interest, national security, and whatever else we install in place of careful analysis, argument, the right of law, protection of minorities, virtue, order, genuine pluralism, and created difference. As Camille Paglia and Jordan Peterson recently agreed in a fascinating conversation,[30] at some point, perhaps soon, our pseudo-progressive, would-be utopian Western culture will be unmasked as the coercive, anti-liberal fraud it always was—'the artificial, mechanized or brutalized control which is a desperate remedy for its chaos', in T. S. Eliot's pungent formulation (*The Idea of a Christian Society*, p. 12).[31]

We need goads to retrieval of the old ideals, and here, Eliot observes, a critical liberalism might come in just as handy as a preservationist conservatism in so far as both habits are placed in service of a classicism of the good, the true, and the beautiful (p. 13). Just here—in the space of freedom *from* tyranny, *for* the common good—*all*, including the heterodox, by both old and new measures, may live and thrive, in a commonly shared gentleness and respect, as Wong insists, beyond the paltry homogeneity of 'spaces' mostly made safe for social media and shopping. Here, as well, Christians and others may cultivate the conditions of coherent community life centred on actual justice, fairness, order, and reason, and speak of their divine basis as created. We may, in other words, find ourselves engaged in the old-fashioned labour of apologetics, that is, defence and propagation of the faith.

Thomas Aquinas: discursive pedagogue

Here, as Paul Griffiths demonstrates, the *heart of Catholic reason* appears. For our purposes, allow me to sketch several brief lines of thought from the aforementioned Thomas Aquinas: a scholastic theologian, Dominican monk, and saint of the thirteenth century who I take to be the best, 'classic' exemplar of reason in the Catholic tradition.[32]

Theology as argument about revealed things

First and foremost, theology, says Aquinas, operates just as other sciences do *in that* it takes certain things for granted as givens, and then goes on to 'prove' other things—and answer objections of one and another sort. Aquinas takes the analogy of music: 'The musician accepts on authority the principles taught him by the mathematician', one science building on another (1.1.1).[33]

The 'principles' of Christian theology are, explains Aquinas, the articles of faith, revealed by God (1.1.1, 1.1.8). Taking these principles in hand, the core task of Christian theology is to articulate the sense of the faith, in the same way that St Paul argues from Christ's resurrection to the general resurrection in 1 Corinthians 15 (1.1.8). This is first-order Christian argument, within the bounds of the orthodox faith: pushing and pulling it in pursuit of understanding.

A second kind of discussion is between different Christians who disagree about fundamental matters. Here the very basis of the argument is our common acceptance of 'at least *some* of the truths obtained through divine revelation. Thus we can argue with heretics from texts in sacred Scripture, and against those who deny one article of faith, we can argue from another' (1.1.8).

Thirdly, we will find ourselves engaging those who believe nothing of divine revelation. In this case, says Aquinas, 'there is no longer any means of proving the articles of faith by reasoning, but only of answering their objections—if they have any—against faith'. But of course, Aquinas adds: 'Since faith rests upon infallible truth, and since the contrary of a truth can never be demonstrated, it is clear that the arguments brought against faith cannot be demonstrations, but are difficulties that can be answered' (1.1.8).

Thomas is not bluffing with reference to reason. He has confidence in its proper role. What is that role? Not 'natural' apologetics. *Pace* Anselm, there are no 'necessary reasons' to be given for basic Christian truths that will have persuasive purchase for the non-believer *sans* acceptance of the means by which they are borne to us, namely, revealed sources, inspired by God. That being said, the place of reason in theology is robust and relentless—not in order 'to prove faith (for thereby the merit of faith would come to an end), but to make clear other things that are put forward in this doctrine'.[34]

Aquinas is famously interested in how revealed truths about God may be *known* and so characterized as science: because, as he says, theology takes up 'all things' *from God's perspective*. This is because God is the subject and object of the discipline—already eternally, as the Son is begotten as the word of the Father. Augustine's picture in *De trinitate* is basic for Aquinas, and he follows Augustine all the way in his theology of the Word of God, who is a *fountain* of language in which we share through our own creation and in the revealed discourse of Scripture, thence by the association of other words with God in Christ, sacramentally and imitatively.

Fundamentally, theology may and must be called a science because it begins with God's own knowledge of himself and all things as creator: *God's* science or knowledge. Aquinas says, in effect: we will now discuss God and all things as related to him, following his lead. We will do so for our salvation; and we will do so ordered to the end that God has planned for us, namely, 'eternal bliss'. As we proceed, we will continually circle around God's own imparted knowledge of himself in Scripture, which can and will contend with all the other sciences and demonstrate itself, on its own divinely-appointed grounds, to be wholly reliable and of supreme certitude, value, and nobility.[35] The mood, as the hoped-for end, can only be doxological: 'You show me the path of life. In your presence there is fullness of joy; in your right hand are pleasures for evermore' (Ps 16.11).

Catholic and conservative

Turning to the cultural work of evangelization and apologetics, let me briefly suggest three applications.

Taxonomy of evangelization

A major gain in thinking with Aquinas on these questions is that we start to get a feel for the different sorts of conversations that we rightly engage in, as we move in various circles to varying ends. Rudimentary socialization delivers a similar lesson: I am now on the farm; I am now in the palace. I am preaching to the humble faithful; I am speaking to the uninitiated, or the rebellious. Thus St Paul in Acts—respectfully: 'I think myself happy, king Agrippa, because I shall answer for myself this day before thee touching all the things whereof I am accused of the Jews: Especially because I know thee to be expert in all customs and questions which are among the Jews: wherefore I beseech thee to hear me patiently' (Acts 26.2–3, KJV). And, by contrast, to the Corinthians: 'I, brethren, could not speak to you as to spiritual *people* but as to carnal, as to babes in Christ. I fed you with milk and not with solid food; for until now you were not able *to receive it*, and even now you are still not able' (1 Cor 3.1–2, NKJV). Context, therefore, and wise discernment in service of the Gospel yield a taxonomy of evangelization under the heading 'by any means necessary'; that is:

> though I am free from all *men*, I have made myself a servant to all, that I might win the more; and to the Jews I became as a Jew, that I might win Jews; to those *who are* under the law, as under the law, that I might win those *who are* under the law; to those *who are* without law, as without law (not being without law toward God, but under law toward Christ), that I might win those *who are* without law; to the weak I became as weak, that I might win the weak. I have become all things to all *men*, that I might by all means save some. (1 Cor 9.19–22, NKJV)

Corpus mixtum

The point naturally leads to ecclesial applications in the mixed body of the church: so says our Lord in the parable of the wheat and the tares (Mt 13.24–30), and the Augustinian tradition synthesizes a rich account of sacrament and structure, visibility and invisibility, operative and cooperative grace, and election in order to handle the necessary pastoral and ascetical challenges, subject to divine freedom. Though this was not a focus of Wong's chapter, a good—and necessary—question concerns the responsibility of Christian teachers to engage in *evangelism and witness in a multi-faith church*: a church divided and riven in countless ways.

I have already noted Aquinas's assumption that debate will be necessary at times between divided Christians who estimate their differences to be a matter of heresy. In these cases of *intra-ecclesial apologetic*—and/or *inter*-ecclesial, perhaps, in cases where the point of division is schism—we proceed, says Thomas, precisely with reference to Scripture (and presumably other authorities) in the hope of establishing common bases of agreement from which better to pinpoint, thence eradicate, neuralgic difference. Certainly, in the absence of such exchange, division cannot be overcome, and this is Paul's own tactic vis-à-vis Corinthian and other disorder, incorporating discipline and ordered boundary when necessary.

Several associated considerations therefore come quickly into play—making sure that a verdict of heresy is accurate and in accord with charity; and care taken to ensure that discipline by the church does not risk schism, bearing in mind the principle of the wheat and tares. Moreover, 'excommunication is medicinal' (3.82.8, undertaken with a view to correcting the brother or sister in the hope of their changing their mind and publicly renouncing the false doctrine, so that 'his spirit may be saved on the day of the Lord', as Paul says (1 Cor 5.5).

Short of formal censure by the church, the brother or sister with whom we disagree may be thought of as *erring*, that is, as potentially teaching heresy, which should inspire vigorous engagement with him or her in the mode of 'challenge or dialogue' within the bounds of the visible body. The purpose of such engagement is primarily to offer and teach the truth and to convince the person or group of the inadequacy of their propositions.

Cultural conservation

T. S. Eliot, in his discussion of the sociology of sect and cult, wants Christians to invest in rich cultures and sub-cultures of literature, art, and devotion that are not flattened or homogenized. Yes, he says, we must avoid a simple *identification* of religion and culture; at our most imperious moment 'we make many errors and commit many crimes' (*Notes towards the Definition of Culture*, p. 74).[36] Imagining, however, the reunion of all Christians, as we must, we ought not seek thereby *uniformity* of culture. Rather, a reunified church would include a variety of local cultures, which 'would and should vary very widely indeed' (p. 76). Why? Because we are bound to note the fruitfulness of multiple forms, for which the doctrine of providence provides a ready theological alibi. In England, for instance, Methodism, 'in the period of its greatest fervour, revive[d] the spiritual life of the English, and prepare[d] the way for the Evangelical Movement [within the Church of England] and even for the Oxford Movement' (p. 80).

Accordingly, Eliot concludes, 'it would seem that a constant struggle between the centripetal and the centrifugal forces is desirable. For without the struggle, no balance can be maintained.' He goes on:

> Christendom should be one: the form of organization and the locus of powers in that unity are questions upon which we cannot pronounce. But within that unity there should be *an endless conflict between ideas*—for it is only by the struggle against constantly appearing false ideas that the truth is enlarged and clarified, and in the conflict with heresy that orthodoxy is developed to meet the needs of the times; *an endless effort also on the part of each region*

> *to shape its Christianity to suit itself, an effort which should neither be wholly suppressed nor left wholly unchecked.* (p. 83, italics mine)

This *is* the work of enculturating the Gospel wherever it may be found, among every land, nation, and people across time and space, in service of a what Eliot calls an ecumenism of 'common faith': a communion formed in and through the furnace of necessary debate, not least in the defence *and* propagation of the one faith. As the church and our institutions turn to this work, we will reclaim the old task of Christian apology, and make some progress in mending our divisions as well.

Notes

1 Pew Research Center, 'Global Religious Diversity: Half of the Most Religiously Diverse Countries are in Asia-Pacific Region' (Apr. 2014), http://www.pewforum.org/2014/04/04/global-religious-diversity/.

2 Saw Swee-Hock, *The Population of Singapore* (Singapore: Institute of Southeast Asian Studies, 2012), p. 42.

3 Malaysia to the north has a population of 31 million, of which 61.3 per cent are Muslim. Indonesia, which surrounds Singapore to the south, has a population of 261 million, of which 87 per cent are Muslims, making it the largest Muslim country in the world.

4 Tom F. Driver, *Christ in a Changing World: Toward an Ethical Christology* (New York: Crossroad, 1981), p. 58. While such proponents of pluralism have mostly recognized the inadequacy of this view and have since adopted a more nuanced position, these concepts continue to exert their influence on secularists and other exponents of religious pluralism.

5 Ibid.

6 Ibid, p. 60.

7 George R. Sumner, *The First and the Last: The Claim of Jesus Christ and the Claims of Other Religious Traditions* (Grand Rapids, MI: Eerdmans, 2004), p. 2.

8 Lamin O. Sanneh, 'Response I', in Gerald R. McDermott and Harold A. Netland (eds.), *A Trinitarian Theology of Religions: An Evangelical Proposal* (New York: Oxford University Press, 2014), pp. 295–300 at 296.

9 Vinoth Ramachandra, *Faiths in Conflict? Christian Integrity in a Multicultural World* (Downers Grove, IL: InterVarsity Press, 1999), p. 128.

10 I remember being in a government-organized forum in Singapore where a senior Buddhist monk complained about how he was accosted by an over-zealous Christian young person insisting on sharing his faith to him as he walked in a shopping mall, despite the fact that he was wearing his bright saffron robes!

11 World Council of Churches, *Christian Witness in a Multi-Religious World*, 'Principles', sect. 7, https://www.oikoumene.org/en/resources/documents/wcc-

programmes/interreligious-dialogue-and-cooperation/christian-identity-in-pluralistic-societies/christian-witness-in-a-multi-religious-world.

12 *The Cape Town Commitment* (25 Jan. 2011), sect. IIc, 1, https://www.lausanne.org/content/ctc/ctcommitment#p2-3.

13 Hendrik Kraemer, *The Communication of the Christian Faith* (Philadelphia: Westminster Press, 1956), p. 87.

14 Christopher J. H. Wright, 'The Christian and Other Religions: The Biblical Evidence', *Themelios*, 9/2 (1984), 5.

15 Ramachandra, *Faiths in Conflict?*, p. 129.

16 Ibid.

17 Justin Welby, 'Sharing Jesus: The Revolution of God's Love', https://www.archbishopofcanterbury.org/priorities/evangelism-and-witness.

18 Kraemer, *The Communication of the Christian Faith*, p. 11.

19 Ibid., p. 22.

20 Ibid., p. 23.

21 Ibid.

22 The Lausanne Covenant (1 Aug. 1974), https://www.lausanne.org/content/covenant/lausanne-covenant.

23 Paul F. Knitter, *No Other Name? A Critical Survey of Christian Attitudes toward the World Religions* (Maryknoll, NY: Orbis Books, 1985), p. 208.

24 One obvious result of this is the secularists' insistence on relegating religion truths to the private sphere, while accepting only truths that conform to 'universal reason' in the public square, which is at the heart of the insistence on the sacred–secular divide in civil society.

25 Paul J. Griffiths, 'Why we Need Interreligious Polemics', *First Things*, 44 (1994), 32.

26 Paul F. Knitter, *Introducing Theologies of Religions* (Maryknoll, NY: Orbis Books, 2002), pp. 186–7.

27 Griffiths, 'Why we Need Interreligious Polemics', p. 35.

28 Ibid.

29 Knitter, *Introducing Theologies of Religions*, p. 187.

30 At the University of the Arts in Philadelphia, published online on 2 Oct. 2017; see https://www.youtube.com/watch?v=v-hIVnmUdXM.

31 T. S. Eliot, *The Idea of a Christian Society* (London: Faber and Faber, 1939).

32 See John Paul II, *Fides et ratio* (1999), http://w2.vatican.va/content/john-paul-ii/en/encyclicals/documents/hf_jp-ii_enc_14091998_fides-et-ratio.html.

33 Aquinas, *Summa theologiae*, 2nd and rev. edn (1920), trans. Fathers of the English Dominican Province, http://www.newadvent.org/summa/1001.htm.

34 'Since grace does not destroy nature but perfects it, natural reason should minister to faith...Hence the Apostle says: "Bringing into captivity every understanding unto the obedience of Christ" (2 Corinthians 10:5). Hence sacred doctrine makes use also of the authority of philosophers in those questions in which they were able to know the truth by natural reason (as Paul quotes a saying of Aratus: "As some also of your own poets said: . . ." (Acts 17:28). [2]

Nevertheless, sacred doctrine makes use of these authorities *as extrinsic and probable arguments*; but properly uses the authority of the canonical Scriptures as an incontrovertible proof (*ex necessitate argumentando*), [3] and the authority of the doctors of the Church as one that may properly be used, yet merely as probable. [4] For our faith rests upon the revelation made to the apostles and prophets who wrote the canonical books, and not on the revelations (if any such there are) made to other doctors. Hence Augustine says (Epis. ad Hieron. xix, 1): "Only those books of Scripture which are called canonical have I learned to hold in such honor as to believe their authors have not erred in any way in writing them. But other authors I so read as not to deem everything in their works to be true, merely on account of their having so thought and written, whatever may have been their holiness and learning"' (1.1.8). Cf. 1.1.5.

35 1.1.5: 'this science surpasses other speculative sciences; in point of greater certitude, because other sciences derive their certitude from the natural light of human reason, which can err; whereas this derives its certitude from the light of divine knowledge, which cannot be misled: in point of the higher worth of its subject-matter because this science treats chiefly of those things which by their sublimity transcend human reason; while other sciences consider only those things which are within reason's grasp. Of the practical sciences, that one is nobler which is ordained to a further purpose, as political science is nobler than military science; for the good of the army is directed to the good of the State. But the purpose of this science, in so far as it is practical, is eternal bliss; to which as to an ultimate end the purposes of every practical science are directed. Hence it is clear that from every standpoint, it is nobler than other sciences.'

36 T. S. Eliot, *Notes towards the Definition of Culture* (New York: Harcourt, Brace and Company, 1949).

Bibliography

The Cape Town Commitment (25 Jan. 2011), section IIc, 1. https://www.lausanne.org/content/ctc/ctcommitment#p2–3.

Driver, Tom F., *Christ in a Changing World: Toward an Ethical Christology* (New York: Crossroad, 1981).

Griffiths, Paul J., 'Why we Need Interreligious Polemics'. *First Things*, 44 (1994), 31–7.

Knitter, Paul F., *Introducing Theologies of Religions* (Maryknoll, NY: Orbis Books, 2002).

Knitter, Paul F., *No Other Name? A Critical Survey of Christian Attitudes toward the World Religions* (Maryknoll, NY: Orbis Books, 1985).

Kraemer, Hendrik, *The Communication of the Christian Faith* (Philadelphia: Westminster Press, 1956).

The Lausanne Covenant (1 Aug. 1974), https://www.lausanne.org/content/covenant/lausanne-covenant.

Pew Research Center, 'Global Religious Diversity: Half of the Most Religiously Diverse Countries are in Asia-Pacific Region' (Apr. 2014), http://www.pewforum.org/2014/04/04/global-religious-diversity/.

Ramachandra, Vinoth, *Faiths in Conflict? Christian Integrity in a Multicultural World* (Downers Grove, IL: InterVarsity Press, 1999).

Sanneh, Lamin O., 'Response I', in Gerald R. McDermott and Harold A. Netland (eds.), *A Trinitarian Theology of Religions: An Evangelical Proposal* (New York: Oxford University Press, 2014), pp. 295–300.

Saw, Swee-Hock, *The Population of Singapore* (Singapore: Institute of Southeast Asian Studies, 2012).

Sumner, George R., *The First and the Last: The Claim of Jesus Christ and the Claims of Other Religious Traditions* (Grand Rapids, MI: Eerdmans, 2004).

Welby, Justin, 'Sharing Jesus: The Revolution of God's Love', https://www.archbishopofcanterbury.org/priorities/evangelism-and-witness.

World Council of Churches, *Christian Witness in a Multi-Religious World*, 'Principles', sect. 7, https://www.oikoumene.org/en/resources/documents/wcc-programmes/interreligious-dialogue-and-cooperation/christian-identity-in-pluralistic-societies/christian-witness-in-a-multi-religious-world.

Wright, Christopher J. H., 'The Christian and Other Religions: The Biblical Evidence', *Themelios*, 9/2 (1984), 4–15.

6

The disciples' misconceptions of mission and Jesus' correctives: insights for evangelism and witness today

MUTHURAJ SWAMY (INDIA)

> To be in mission means to change continually as the gospel encounters new and diverse contexts.[1]

The general understanding about Christian mission, as I have observed through my conversations, interactions, and readings, is that it is something we, Christians, have received from God, or have been commanded and commissioned to do, and that it is done primarily towards others, that is, non-Christians. The understanding goes something like this: God has given us a mission through Jesus (or Jesus has commanded), and this is found in the Bible, and we need to do it towards other people so that they know Christ and become Christians. Even though this understanding seems to be simple and straightforward, there are limitations with it. First, we are living in a context which is constantly changing and which requires changes in our understanding and practice of God's mission in the world too without diluting the constants of the Gospel. In fact, historically, the context of Christian mission has always been changing during the last two thousand years. Secondly, biblical accounts of mission show us that even the understanding of mission among the disciples of Jesus was not without errors, and that they constantly needed correctives from Jesus in spite of being with him and witnessing to his life and work for years. The conversation between Jesus and his disciples about mission and witness in Acts 1.6–8 can help us to understand the need for a continuous engagement with Jesus for progressing in our conception and practice of mission. This reflection comes from some of my observations about how mission is understood and practised in India, and some issues may be similar in other contexts too.

The context and text

Christian mission and changing contexts

It is now an unquestionable fact that the changing global context is very important for talking about, understanding, and practising Christian mission. The evolution of Christian mission and its practice in changing contexts are not new developments—the entire history of Christianity has witnessed them—but awareness of and reflection on these developments have become crucial and necessary in the contemporary context.[2]

The most important change that has been talked about during the last few decades is the changing landscape of Christianity.[3] The general argument is that while Western Christianity is in decline because of various factors such as secularization, atheism and rationalism, scientific and technological developments, and other similar issues, Christianity in the non-Western world (the Global South or majority world) is growing. The decline of Christianity is a contested issue,[4] but in the context of Christian mission, what is important is the awareness and initiatives taken for mission in the non-Western world. There are now a number of indigenous mission organizations and bodies which send missionaries to different parts of their own countries and to the wider world, including North America and Europe, places which in previous centuries sent missionaries to the non-Western world. In fact in India, visions for indigenous mission organizations began as early as the nineteenth century, and in the early twentieth century the first Indian bishop in the Anglican Church in India (now the Church of South India), V. S. Azariah, took a number of initiatives to found and set up indigenous mission organizations in India.[5] In the last century there have been similar indigenous efforts towards mission in Africa, Asia, and other parts of the world as well.

A related factor that has to be taken into account when talking about the missionary initiatives in non-Western contexts today is the resurgence of other religions and the missionary thrust and message that come with that resurgence. In the Indian context, the missionary nature of Hinduism has become quite strong since the early nineteenth century (though, of course, it has always been there),[6] primarily as a reaction to Christian mission and the Christian message.[7] Islam is another religion that promotes a strong missionary message. The missionary nature of other religions is not a new issue, but what is significant is that it is often ignored or undermined in the context of Christian mission except for the purpose of polemics aimed at these religions.

Second, the world is also changing to a large extent, both culturally and demographically. Globalization has come to define the way people live today. People from different walks of life, cultures, traditions, and religions find themselves living close to one another. This in itself is not a new development, at least in some contexts, but what is important is the awareness of it, and the importance attributed to such awareness. During the last five centuries, European colonial expansion into the non-Western world led Christians to encounter people from different religions and traditions, but today global migration does most of that work. In fact, migration has become multi-directional as people move from anywhere to anywhere, particularly from the non-Western world to the Western world, and this has intensified the need for multiple cultures to exist close to each other. This results in a situation where religious and cultural plurality, and a growing awareness of such a plurality, are increasing. Such an awareness also has implications for our faith in God, salvation, and religious practices. In such a context, Christian mission cannot continue to be the same by simply and strictly following its traditional approaches. It has to continue to find new ways of communicating the Gospel, growing churches, and building communities.

Third are the continuing challenges posed by the socio-economic realities of our societies. In spite of scientific and technological advances and factors that help people to come together and exist together, social and economic injustice, inequality, and discrimination have not decreased; rather they are increasing. One does not always need evidence and statistics to prove this, as it has become an everyday reality. Further, in addition to the discrimination and justice issues among human beings, human destruction of and irresponsibility towards the environment have also become a serious issue that needs immediate attention from anyone who cares about human beings and about all of God's creation. Christian mission and witnessing cannot ignore these realities. Poverty, social and economic inequality, violence, the human onslaught on the environment, challenges in health care: these concerns are crucial in the context of thinking about and practising Christian mission today.

I want to reiterate that in no way are these changing contexts or the reflections on these changes new. They have been there for quite some time now. However, it is fair to say that Christian mission does not always address these issues adequately. True, a number of churches and Christian institutions are working to address the issues and making efforts practically to change the conditions, but in my understanding, there is still a long way to go in terms of how these concerns inform and shape Christian mission, evangelism, and witness in our times.

Acts 1.6–8 as a foundational text for Christian mission

> So when they had come together, they asked him, 'Lord, is this the time when you will restore the kingdom to Israel?' He replied, 'It is not for you to know the times or periods that the Father has set by his own authority. But you will receive power when the Holy Spirit has come upon you; and you will be my witnesses in Jerusalem, in all Judea and Samaria, and to the ends of the earth.' (Acts 1.6–8)

From a mission perspective, I am sure biblical scholars and mission practitioners would agree that this is one of the important mission texts in the New Testament, and definitely the most important one in the book of Acts. What fascinates me about this text, in comparison to other texts like the Great Commission, to which most Christians return quite often for thinking about mission, is that the conversation about mission, evangelism, and witness here is in a dialogic form—a conversation between Jesus and his disciples. More importantly, the text unambiguously records the false assumptions the disciples had about mission, which stood to be corrected by Jesus. In other words, the disciples' understanding of mission evolves in conversation with Jesus, where they express their misconceptions and misperceptions of God's mission and Jesus offers correctives. For me this shows that mission has an interactive nature, and it suggests that the shortcomings in our understanding of mission today are similar to those of the disciples. Jesus' correctives to the misconceptions offer important insights for our shortcomings too.

The disciples' misconceptions of God's mission

Interestingly, the disciples' misconceptions and misperceptions persist in spite of the fact that Jesus continues to teach about the kingdom of God after his resurrection (Acts 1.3). Yet the question that they ask here shows they have totally misunderstood his teaching. John Stott in his commentary on the book of Acts succinctly summarizes the disciples' errors thus:

> Their question must have filled Jesus with dismay. Were they still lacking in perception? As Calvin commented, 'there are as many errors in this question as words.' The verb, noun and the adverb all betray doctrinal confusion about the kingdom. For the verb 'restore' shows that they were expecting a political and territorial kingdom; the noun 'Israel' that they were expecting

> a national kingdom; and the adverbial clause 'at this time' that they were expecting its immediate establishment. In his reply...Jesus corrected their mistaken notions of the kingdom's nature, extent and arrival.[8]

For me, there are three important issues that can be identified in the disciples' question that need serious attention in relation to the contemporary context of mission and which may also be related to some misconceptions and misperceptions: (a) the question about the time, (b) the question about power and the kingdom, and (c) the question about the location and movement of mission.

The question about the time

The disciples' question 'is this the time?' suggests a sense of urgency. The disciples, in spite of witnessing to the resurrection of Jesus Christ, are not aware that their idea of time is limited and that they do not have control over time that is set by God. Their concept of time is only empire-based: Israel has been a ruling nation in the past, but is now subjected to or put to serve other empires, and the disciples want this to change and Israel to be restored. The question clearly shows some uneasiness about the delay in restoring the kingdom to Israel and implies that the disciples want it to be established immediately.

Further, the disciples' question also indicates a feeling of accomplishment. The disciples think that the mission of God has already been accomplished by Jesus Christ, and that they are already at the end of the mission. The realization that Christian mission is a continuing act is lacking here. Also, the disciples do not see themselves at the centre of doing something, but rather are thinking of something being done for them. They think that the work has been completed on their behalf, and they want Jesus to do the remaining work quickly. They fail to realize that God has inaugurated the mission in Jesus but that it is they, the disciples, who should continue it, and that in terms of time there is still a long way to go!

The question about power

Second, the disciples are here concerned with power, and the power they are interested in is political power. They talk about Jesus restoring the kingdom for them. Here, no doubt, by talking about the kingdom, the disciples are still thinking of Christ's mission merely in political dimensions. This is in spite of the fact that they are actually in a conversation that involves Jesus talking about the kingdom of God (Acts 1.3). The disciples' apprehension is understandable given the context of Roman oppression of the Israelites and others for centuries, but the question completely betrays their experience of being with Jesus and their witnessing to all that he did.

Without undermining the need for Christians to engage with the wider society and political structures, I must say that Christianity and Christian mission have collaborated with political power at various periods in Christian history—for good and bad reasons. During the time of persecution in early Christianity the followers drew power from God through the Holy Spirit and withstood the political powers and persecution. But after the arrival of Constantine, Christianity easily succumbed to his offer of political power.[9] There is certainly a difference in how mission was carried out before and after Constantine. Christianity's privileged status as a state religion certainly led to a situation where witnessing to Christ was not always seen as a primary task.

I do not wish to argue here for any essentialized binary, such as political versus religious/spiritual, but I would like to highlight that there has been often a preference for political and human power in the context of Christian mission. This in fact began with the disciples themselves, and Jesus corrected them immediately, but unfortunately it would show up again and again in Christian life and mission. The love–hate relationship between imperialism and Christian mission in the past five centuries is another example.[10]

The question about Israel

Third, the disciples' narrow understanding of God's mission comes out in their limiting of God's plan and action to Israel, in spite of seeing Jesus moving with the Gentiles very freely and extending the good news, miracles, and healing to them. Their talk about Israel indicates that there is a monopolization of Jesus Christ and his work within the nation of Israel. The disciples do not yet realize that God's kingdom has a place for all, and that there are many others, for instance the Gentiles, in God's mission and kingdom. In talking about restoring the kingdom to Israel, the disciples assume a disconnection between God's mission and the rest of humanity, although they had all along watched Jesus' mission, which was just the opposite: to connect people with each other and reconcile divided communities and warring groups.

Some misconceptions in Christian Mission today

What is found in the disciples' question in Acts 1.6 is not simply a historical problem that happened some two thousand years ago. The disciples' misconceptions and questions resemble the many issues we have today in mission in our own context, though the misconceptions may not necessarily be precisely the same. But in my understanding we can relate a number of contemporary perceptions of missions with the misconceptions that the disciples had.

First, the time factor and urgency are one of the most important issues in contemporary mission. Often there is a sense of urgency or rush in the way the Christian mission is designed and the missionary message is propagated. While developing serious mission plans and strategies and raising awareness about the importance of mission are important, sometimes (or often) Christian mission does have the number of converts or saved souls in a short time frame as its primary focus or the only focus. In India I have often seen missionary organizations keep this at the centre of their mission discourse and practice, and it often leads to suspicion, opposition, and attacks from various quarters. Among other things, it also plays into the hands of the extremist Hindutva forces, who accuse Christianity of disturbing the social and cultural fabric of Indian society.

Also in the Indian context, I have often come across situations where there is a prevailing sense of accomplishment when missionaries are sent to other places, especially from South India (where I come from) to North India.[11] While sending missionaries is indeed an accomplishment, what is problematic about it is that for many Christians the mission ends there. They have done their work by handing the mission over to the missionaries, and it is now the latters' responsibility to do the work and the responsibility of the 'unreached' to repent and convert to Christianity. Beyond that, they often have no awareness of how Christian mission continues to have significance in their own back yard (apart from sending missionaries) and in their own lives.

Second, the disciples' expectation of the restoration of the power of the kingdom resonates with contemporary Christian mission's lack of will to identify with and address the concerns of the powerless and marginalized. In some ways, Christian mission still struggles when it comes to engaging with these concerns. We may recollect the ongoing struggles between mission as conversion and mission as social action. In spite of many efforts by churches and Christian institutions, my observation and experience are that many Christians in India (like those in many other parts of the world) still see Christian mission as separate from social justice. We seldom think that being silent about the powerless is wrong, and Christian mission cannot neglect this.

In India one often comes across situations where if there is any talk at all about the powerless in the Christian mission discourse, it concerns Indian Christians themselves, who are a religious minority (along with other religious minorities such as Muslims and Sikhs). Just as the disciples *felt* powerless (and hence asked Jesus to restore the kingdom to Israel), Christians in India often see themselves as powerless while doing mission work. This results in often showing 'persecution of Christians' as the only framework in which they express their relations with non-Christians.[12] In fact there are a number of problems with such an approach in India, although this is not to say that there are no attacks and violence against Christians.[13] However, the narrative that other religions are opposed to Christian mission and the projection of other religions and secularism as powerful enemies to be competed with have serious limitations.

Third, in spite of the changing contexts, conceptions of the location and movement of the Christian mission still remain narrow. In some ways, 'reaching the unreached' is one such misunderstanding, since it puts the focus of the mission on the 'unreached'. My biggest difficulty here is that while the disciples limited God's mission narrowly to Israel, Christians today narrowly (though it may appear more broadly) limit God's mission to the unreached or 'those who do not know Jesus Christ' (this is the terminology I quite often come across in the mission context). Also, as the disciples limited God to Israel, Christians often limit God to Christians and their understanding of mission. The change required in the non-Christian 'recipients' of the mission is always at the centre of the message, and hence the mission has become too much oriented towards the recipients of the Gospel. In other words, the primary goal of the mission is believed to be to effect change in those receiving it. Because of this, the self-interrogative nature of Christian mission is usually lost.

Jesus' correctives

Jesus' response in Acts 1.7–8 comes as a corrective and challenge to the disciples' misconceptions about God's mission. I stated above that I am fascinated by this text because it is a conversation between Jesus and his disciples. In the entire New Testament, the dialogues between Jesus and his disciples and the people around him are always interesting because when Jesus is asked questions, he always corrects the questioners' mindset rather than answering their questions. He does it again for one last time before his ascension.

First, regarding the question of the time, Jesus very clearly and firmly tells the disciples not to worry. He says that 'it is not for you to know the times or periods that the Father has set by his own authority'. This unambiguously shows that time does not need to be the primary concern in the context of mission. However, the history of Christian mission is filled with ideas like 'converting the world for Christ in this generation'. Jesus' corrective of the disciples' misapprehension clearly shows that he has inaugurated God's mission and that Christians should continue to participate in without worrying about the time available. Also, against any feeling of accomplishment and seeing the responsibility for and in mission only among others, Jesus' corrective points out to the continuous responsibility of those who are his disciples.

In this corrective, Jesus also points out human limitations and puts God's transcendence over human expectations in the context of Christian mission. Although this should not be the case, the link between God's transcendence and Christian mission is often lost or undermined in our thinking about and practising mission. But in Jesus' correctives, the fact that Christian mission is linked with God's transcendence, and not with our limited imagination and perception, comes clear. This is important because God's way of extending his kingdom is beyond our narrow understanding and is not controlled or conditioned by our work in mission. The Bible is full of stories about the fact that there are others in God's mission (e.g. Lk 4.25–27) and that God has his own ways of reaching out to others which are not known to the disciples and are not affected by their understanding of 'reaching out' (e.g. the story of Peter and Cornelius in Acts 10).

Second, Jesus responds to the disciples' question with a powerful 'you will be my witnesses'. In fact it is a direct challenge to his disciples' understanding of power and the kingdom, which they thought Jesus would restore by establishing a kingdom for Israel while taking it away from the hands of the Romans. The question about the restoration of power is answered with an invitation to be the witnesses of Jesus: 'you will be my witnesses'. Interestingly, 'my witnesses' conveys that Christian mission exists primarily in the relationship between Jesus Christ and those who participate in his mission. It is important that 'the unreached' recipient of the mission does not figure at all in Jesus' reply. The act of witnessing is centred on the missionary, and Christian mission ceases to exist without this. This has very powerful implications for those participating in mission context, having implications for those participating in God's mission. It is a simple truth, but often neglected under the illusion that mission is only to do with those who are there to receive it. God's mission is carried out by the person who participates in it as a witness to Christ, rather than simply passing on the mission to the 'unreached'.

Third, Jesus challenges the disciples' narrow attitude of limiting God's mission only to Israel. His corrective is 'in Jerusalem, in all Judea and Samaria, and to the ends of the earth'. These words offer many insights for the location, method, and movement of Christian mission. It is important that Jerusalem is not excluded in witnessing. It is not true to say that mission is only for 'others'. Mission is needed in Jerusalem as well. For me 'Jerusalem' implies that mission is both internal and external at the same time. It is not simply mission from Jerusalem to the others. Jerusalem cannot be ignored as a privileged place of already having Jesus. It is also important that Judea and Samaria are connected in Jesus' response. In fact this is the only mission text which has Judea and Samaria together in the context of witnessing. Given the background and history of the relations between Judea and Samaria, I cannot read this simply as Jesus talking about places in sequence. Rather, while the disciples are concerned with disconnecting the rest of the humanity from Israel, based on their understanding of power and the kingdom, Jesus points out the importance of connecting Judea and Samaria and connecting the entire world by the disciples being his witnesses.

This also should be read as the gradual movement of Christian mission, rather than its rapid movement outward or *from* one region *to* the other. Somehow in the history of Christian mission the words 'to the ends of the earth' have often been identified with the need to move quickly from Jerusalem to the ends of the earth (or later from the West to the rest of the world). Jesus challenges this. Moreover, the words 'Jerusalem in all Judea and Samaria, and to the ends of the earth' refer to the fact that mission is multi-directional rather than moving strictly from one place to the other. The importance of Christian mission as connecting and relating the different parts of the world in the name of the Gospel comes out clearly in the corrective Jesus offers to his disciples.

What holds Jesus' various correctives together is his promise of the Holy Spirit, who is not bound by human understanding of time, power, and space. When the disciples are concerned with the power that comes from an earthly kingdom, Jesus promises the power of the Holy Spirit, who crosses not only the boundaries of time and space, but also community boundaries and other boundaries based on identity and hostility for those who are Christ's witnesses, wherever they are.[14]

The implications for evangelism and witness today

The correctives that Jesus offers to his disciples about not worrying about the time have significant insights for Christian mission today. As mentioned earlier, time-bound attitudes and obsession with the numbers of saved souls or converts in Christian mission have not worked well for Christian impact in society, nor can they be helpful in the rapidly changing context today. The urgency of reaching out to the entire world often compromises the values of the Gospel. Just as the disciples erred, contemporary Christianity too is mistaken in connecting Christian mission with the establishment of a 'Christian kingdom'. Of course, it must be said that both in the past and in the present not all missionaries have been concerned with rushing to add numbers. Bernard Lucas, a British missionary to India in the early twentieth century, famously asked the whether Christian missionaries should be involved in proselytizing Hindus or evangelizing India. For him, while the former was to do with numbers without minding the impact of the Gospel's values, the latter was about Christianity making a long-lasting impact on Indian society. There are also examples of European missionaries in India who made people wait for several years before they could be baptized in order to ascertain their commitment to Christ. What St Teresa of Avila said in a personal contemplative life can be true for Christian mission too: 'God is willing to wait for us for many a day, and even many a year.'[15]

Jesus' correctives also offer insights in contexts where Christian mission is carried out as a power struggle. Acts 1.6–8 clearly says that the disciples were indeed concerned with the power of the kingdom. Jesus corrects them and replaces the restoration of the kingdom with the power of the Holy Spirt and the need for them to witness to Christ. Today, unlike the disciples, we may not always be talking about the political power achieved through Christian mission. Nevertheless the concern about power continues, albeit of course in different ways, and occupies a central place in the way mission is carried out. The image of Christian mission as a battleground has not disappeared entirely, in spite of the increasingly realized multi-religious and multicultural context in which we exist today.

In contexts like India, other religions are often seen as enemies to be won by Christian mission. One might think that considering other religions as 'heathen', 'pagan', 'devilish', and so on is a thing of the past, but in fact this is not the case. In one way or another way, the notion that the other religions are problematic and premodern, have nothing to offer, and should be replaced by Christianity still dominates the missionary discourse in India. A triumphalist approach, in addition to playing in the hands of the Hindutva extremist forces, antagonizes ordinary Hindus and Muslims and people of other faiths and no faith who otherwise live in relatively good relationships with the Christians in India. Another perceived enemy of Christian mission both in the West and in the Global South is secularism or secularization. In fact, blaming secularization in the context of Christian mission has become a fashion which has serious limitations.[16]

I am of the view that the old idea of Christian mission as a battleground in a war between good and evil and the language of 'winning' in such a war is no longer helpful and indeed never has been.[17] In the multi-religious and multicultural contexts we need to unearth and utilize the images of hospitality in Christian mission.[18] Christian mission should involve 'giving place to, and embracing, those who are alien, and even hostile to our culture. This is not merely a corollary of the Gospel but is of its essence....'[19] In our treatment of other religions, the following statement by a missiologist in the context of training missionaries is important:

> We may prepare and take our own bread with us, or we may, in the spirit of Jesus, take no bread for the journey (Mark 6:8)...Unless we believe that those to whom we go have some bread for themselves, and unless we trust that they will share their bread with us our journey will be travesty of the Christian mission.[20]

In other words, participation in Christian mission means not only to teach, but also to learn. In fact there is extensive evidence of Christian mission having been successful when the missionaries were willing to learn from other cultures, traditions, and religions, though this has not always been the case. This has had a huge influence on the way the Gospel values have impacted societies all over the world. The approach is not to change gears or invent new methods because we think that we are losing relevance. Rather, the existing methods and approaches remain fundamental to the sharing of the good news and have been used by some, though neglected by many. It is time for Christian mission to take them seriously.

Jesus' correctives also bring out the importance of God's transcendence in mission. Because of our narrow understanding of time, space, and God's ways of doing mission, we often end up betraying God's transcendence and authority in Christian mission. Often, 'the medium becomes the message' in the negative sense in the context of mission. Jesus' correctives not only affirm the authority of God in the context of mission (which other mission texts in the New Testament do too), but more importantly declare that God's authority is beyond what we do and expect in Christian mission.

Jesus' correctives challenge the idea that Christian mission is something which has already been completed, and is handed over to us to forward to others. Rather, Jesus has inaugurated God's mission, and we are called to participate in it by first appropriating it for ourselves. In South India I have often come across an attitude among Christian families and local churches who support missions and send missionaries to North India which is something like: 'fund mission, send missionaries, and stop there!'

Jesus' words 'you will be my witnesses' have missional implications for mission-doers before mission-receivers. The change expected is first in those who witness, before the change among those to whom they will witness can be expected. The peculiarity of the mission text under study, in comparison to other texts like the Great Commission in Matthew 28.19–20, is that it puts the whole emphasis on the participants in mission witnessing to Christ rather than on those whom the mission is aimed at.[21] There is a prevailing belief that because we have received a mission and we are passing on it to others, everything is fine with us, as if we no longer need to appropriate the message ourselves. But Christian mission is not simply concerned with what should be done *to* or *by* the 'unreached'. It 'is no longer from "us" to "them", whoever "we" and "they" might be...[On the contrary] the missionary is as much a recipient of the *Missio Dei* as Peter was at the time of his "conversion" when confronted by the work of God in the Gentile Cornelius.'[22] In other words, witnessing does not mean change only in non-Christians. It is first, and most importantly, a change in those witnessing. It is easy to talk about the conversion of non-Christians but not about the conversion of the missionary, which is essential for witnessing. Mission is equally important for the conversion of the one who hears the Gospel and for the conversion of the missionary.

The reference to Jerusalem in Jesus' corrective has some important insights for contemporary mission. This verse is often interpreted as meaning that mission should flow from Jerusalem to the ends of the earth—from the privileged to the margins, from those who have the Gospel to those who do not have the Gospel. In the last few centuries it has been from the West to the rest. The jump is immediately towards the global, international, and one-directional. But the reality is that Christian mission is also local as well as multi-directional, both internal and external (to Jerusalem and the ends of the earth). A mission document from the World Council of Churches states:

> Mission has been understood as a movement taking place from the centre to the periphery, and from the privileged to the marginalized of society. Now people at the margins are claiming their key role as agents of mission and affirming mission as transformation. This reversal of roles in the envisioning of mission has strong biblical foundations because God chose the poor, the foolish, and the powerless (1 Cor. 1:18–31) to further God's mission of justice and peace so that life may flourish. If there is a shift of the mission concept from 'mission *to* the margins' to 'mission *from* the margins,' what then is the distinctive contribution of the people from the margins?[23]

'Mission from the margins' means that today we no longer can speak only about mission from Jerusalem to the rest of the world, but also mission to Jerusalem as well. Christian mission to Europe and North America from the Global South has indeed become a reality.[24]

Witness also has wider implications in today's changing social and economic contexts. For me it points to a holistic understanding of Christian life and mission built on the life and work of Jesus Christ rather than a compartmentalized notion of mission as conversion versus mission as liberation and so on. Hence the idea that concerns like poverty, social justice, violence, environmental degradation, and so on exist outside and separate from Christian mission has serious limitations today. In fact in the context of power struggles everywhere, the primary task of Christian mission is to be with those who are powerless.

Finally, the expansion of mission is not simply adding one place to another or moving from one place to another. The idea here is not 'foreign missions' but rather mission that crosses borders and boundaries: connecting communities rather than taking the Gospel to the unreached places. The disciples tried to *disconnect* Israel from the rest and ask for a kingdom to be restored for Israel. But Jesus *connected* Jerusalem with the rest of the world.[25] The reference to Judea and Samaria together clearly suggests that Christian mission is more than moving from one place to another. As Jesus Christ's mission involved connecting and reconciling hostile communities, he invited his disciples to continue to do the same.

Conclusion

In Acts 1.6–8 Jesus helps the disciples to re-imagine themselves in Christian mission. The changing contexts facing us challenge us to continue this re-imagining. Jesus offers correctives to the disciples' question that expects him to restore power and the kingdom to Israel quickly, and he changes their mind-set. Thus we have been offered a direction whenever we too are caught up in Christian mission with those misconceptions. Jesus' correctives to his disciples' misconceptions offer us a model of Christian mission in which we continue to appropriate its content for ourselves, both personally and geographically, and through our witnessing to Christ we share it with others. Jesus's correctives also invite us as his disciples to affirm and practise the gradual and multi-directional growth of the kingdom of God in terms of connecting and reconciling people, groups, nations, and communities based on Gospel values.

Response

ROBERT S. HEANEY (IRELAND)

Power, time, and scope in Christian witness

Swamy's chapter suggests that contemporary missionaries, particularly in an Indian context, misunderstand the mission of God in ways not dissimilar to ways the first disciples of Jesus misunderstood the mission of God. In the face of such a missiological muddle Jesus provides dialogic and remedial work in Acts 1.7–8. Swamy argues that the misunderstandings of the disciples—relating to time, power, and scope—and the correctives that Jesus offers can renew evangelism and witness today.

In this short response I would like to attempt two things. First, without entirely agreeing with Swamy's reading of Acts 1.7–8, I will identify some questions for missiological reflection. Second, in light of those questions and the work of Swamy, I will begin to suggest how we might imagine further developments in Christian witness in continuity with a reading of Christ's ascension.

Possible questions

In identifying questions for reflection, I will re-order the main themes from the chapter as this will aid inter-contextual or inter-cultural reflection by beginning in the particular and moving towards a broader view. The first theme to be addressed is power, as this theme immediately situates the witness of Jesus in the originating imperial context. The theme of time or temporality is addressed next because how one understands the breaking in of God's mission to human history and human activity informs how one thinks of the church and the call of the church. Finally, the scope of God's witness in Jesus is addressed as the subversive and religio-political lordship of Christ is considered.

Power and witness

In reading the verses from Acts 1.6–8 Swamy hears the disciples make a series of mistakes about the purpose of divine power in the mission of Jesus. Central to their misunderstanding about Jesus' purposes is their expectation that he is a political actor who will bring about political renewal. In the words of Swamy, they see Jesus' mission 'merely in political dimensions'. He rightly wants to avoid any 'essentialized binary' defining the political over against the spiritual. I wonder, however, if there is not precisely this tendency at work in Swamy's chapter. In reading the passage from Acts, a contrast between the disciples' over-politicized understanding with Jesus' message of the kingdom of God is identified, before the later Constantinian over-politicization of Christian witness in relationship with empire is identified.

The New Testament again and again expresses the mission of God in political terms familiar and in wide use in Palestine and the Roman Empire. Further, at least one section of the religious community in Jerusalem was assimilated into the imperial status quo to the extent that preaching the good news of God's kingdom was, understood as a direct threat (Mt 21).[26] The mission of God is a direct challenge to Caesar and an inbreaking of a renewal of Israel that is always both theological and political. The mission of God is religio-political. In the end, it is such politicking that gets Jesus killed.

I am not convinced that the missiological misunderstandings of the disciples can be ascribed to their dullness of mind or, for that matter, the pedagogical inadequacy of Jesus. Might the mistake instead be ours? That is to say, both the disciples and Jesus were correct. Jesus' witness is religio-political. It is just that the disciples did not understand when and how that religio-political mission was to be fulfilled. In the text, Jesus does not rebuke them for their question but rather for their insistence that they be told when the kingdom is to be realized.[27] The first question that emerges, therefore, is twofold. How might we understand the mission of Jesus in thoroughgoing religio-political terms? What would that do to our hermeneutics and our understanding witness and evangelism today?

Time and witness

Swamy states that the 'urgency of reaching out to the entire world often compromises the values of the Gospel'. This is a rather provocative claim. Swamy sees the disciples' impatience with God being infected by an 'empire-based' understanding of time. As well as criticizing the disciples, he rightly criticizes any contemporary approach to Christian witness that emphasizes an evangelistic urgency at the expense of deeper and dialogic witness. In India, such proclamatory urgency today only plays into the hands of extremists and non-Christian authorities. One wonders to what extent we might have chided the Apostles for a similar kind of urgency that, according to Acts, meant they ran foul of the expectations of other religions, economic systems, and a variety of governing authorities (Acts 4; 5.17–42; 6.8—8.3; 9.19–22; 12.1–19; 16.16—17.9; 18.12–17; 21.27—26.30).

I detect a tension at work here between human agency and divine agency and between a 'progressivist' understanding of mission and what Swamy calls an 'already accomplished' understanding of mission. The stress in Swamy's chapter is towards a progressivist understanding of mission. Swamy urges the church towards 'a continuous engagement with Jesus for progressing in our conception and practice of mission'. Given this, he is critical of the disciples:

> The disciples think that by now the mission of God has been already accomplished...and that they are already at the end of mission. The realization that Christian mission is a continuing act is lacking...They fail to realize that God has inaugurated the mission in Jesus but that it is they, the disciples, who should continue it, and that in terms of time there is still a long way to go!

This quotation captures well the issue I would like to reflect on. How do we understand what God's mission in Christ accomplished? How does that divine mission, wrought through divine agency and God's own proclamation of God's self, inform how we understand the agency and work of the church today?

Scope and witness

Swamy sees the resurrected Jesus correct the disciples understanding of the scope of God's mission. He hears the disciples limit 'God's plan and action to Israel, in spite of seeing Jesus moving with the Gentiles very freely and extending the good news, miracles, and healing to them'. Does this overstate the Lukan mission of Jesus? In Luke's Gospel, Jesus may transgress boundaries of acceptability to restore the marginalized into his renewal movement to Israel but his ministry to Gentiles is much more circumscribed. For Joel Green, the inclusion of the Gentiles is 'not highlighted much in the ministry of Jesus...Generally...the inclusion of the Gentiles is a matter of future significance . . .'[28] While Luke may understand the purposes of God as bringing salvation to all people, 'Jesus himself prepares the way for this universal mission, not by engaging much with non-Jews, but by repeatedly calling into question those barriers that divide ethnic groups, men and women, adults and children, rich and poor, righteous and sinner'.[29] The disciples' focus on the restoration of Israel is, therefore, not in contrast to Jesus' mission but in continuity with it.

I do not hear Jesus criticizing the disciples in Acts 1 for too narrow a missional scope. Rather, by calling them to be his witnesses and by promising the gift of the Spirit he points them towards a fuller realization of his mission to restore Israel. He is calling them into an Israel that will be refined and re-defined by the inclusion of Gentiles as a result of the gifted Spirit of Pentecost (Acts 2; see Rom 9—11) that will, in turn, move this Jesus-movement towards the Council of Jerusalem (Acts 15). But this move of the Spirit is predicated upon the religio-political ascension of Jesus of Nazareth (Acts 1.9–11). In ascension, this Jewish Messiah now stands above all claims to ultimate authority and thus, once more and decisively, challenges the power of Caesar.

> The ascension is...the vindication of Jesus as Israel's representative, and the divine giving of judgment...in his favour and against the pagan nations who have oppressed Israel and the current rulers who have corrupted her . . . This is how the kingdom is being restored to Israel: by its representative Messiah being enthroned as the world's true lord.[30]

The mission of God, in and through this vindicated saviour and ascended Lord, directly challenges and displaces Caesar. The ascended Jesus is Lord. Caesar is not Lord. Further, the lordship of this colonized and marginalized Jew subverts the empire's understanding of lordship and divinity.[31]

Possible developments

Given this reading and re-reading of Acts 1.6–8 and as a first step towards resourcing the questions raised in the previous section, I would like to point towards some theological themes that take into account the issues Swamy raises in relation to power, history, and scope.

Christian witness as religio-political

Swamy rightly points to the complicated relationship between imperialism and colonialism in the history of Western Christian mission. At the heart of our Anglican tradition is an established church, and, in many cases, the Communion we are part of has its genesis in white settler colonialism. The temptation towards syncretism and the instabilities of enculturation or contextualization must not be presented as issues particular to theologies and practices beyond the so-called West. Colonial histories and the way they impact theological education and ecclesiology are increasingly being interrogated by theologians and historians.[32]

Swamy complicates and enriches an understanding of power relations by setting his reflections on Christian witness in the context of indigenous mission movements, globalization, migration, and socio-economic and ecological injustice. He also identifies the missionary expansionism of other religions and the militant, militaristic, triumphalist language used by all sides in India as creating a 'battlefield' in which co-religionists see each other as enemies. Given these issues, how does a religio-political understanding of the mission of God address the complicity at the heart of Anglicanism and the ongoing political and interreligious power relations at work in the world?

The mistake in Anglican history is not that mission was politicized but that mission politics often justified and supported the domineering power of empire against movements for contextualizing theology and movements for self-determination. The mistake was not that the mission was political. The mistake was that the politics were Caesarian. Given the subversive lordship of Christ, a different exercise and understanding of power are at the heart of the Gospel and, thus, at the heart of a Christian theology of witness. For Swamy this means an immediate decommissioning of militant and militaristic language in place of a mission theology that centres on hospitality. Indeed, non-believers and those of other faiths are to be treated always as neighbours and teachers. He makes the profound and often overlooked observation that the mission of God is not simply external: it is also internal. Thus, categories like 'evangelist' and 'evangelized' are problematized. The extension of such thought means that Christian witness and evangelism involved commitment to deeper interreligious exploration and cooperation. Further, Christian actors will be allies of secular movements that seek to challenge militancy and nationalisms that depend on a demonizing of others. In short, Christian witness is always a resistant movement against the powers that dehumanize. The inreach that Swamy identifies should not simply be understood as activism or even public missiology (that is, discourse and action in the public square understood as mission). It also resources a particular understanding of intentional discipleship or mission formation.[33] Such formation requires taking heed of God's religio-political mission hermeneutically and historically.

Christian witness as inter-contextualization

Given the imperial and colonial context, the witness to Jesus as Lord that emerges from the significance of the Gospel was, and remains, religio-political. To fail to read the New Testament in such contextual terms will inevitably forestall an inter-contextual practice of Christian witness today.

I have already argued that rather than correct the disciples' political framing of the restoration of Israel Jesus answers their question directly. 'Jesus', they ask, 'is this the time when you will restore the kingdom to Israel?' Luke understands Jesus' answer to be in the affirmative.[34] The rest of Acts, beginning with the ascension, is a demonstration of this affirmative response as Israel is restored in the Jesus-movement in Jerusalem, Judea, Samaria (Acts 8), and the world (Acts 10, 13—28). Swamy's insight is important when he argues that the mission of Christ's followers is not a movement centred on or confined to Jerusalem or Israel but is a migration and counter-migration (Acts 2.5) of cross-cultural and inter-cultural witnesses that meet the Spirit in Jerusalem. Given Jesus' affirmative response to the disciples' question, the ascension, and the day of Pentecost, there is a very important sense that the disciples are indeed recipients of the completed and fulfilled work of God in Christ. Restoration took place in the person and work of Jesus. If, at the beginning of a theology of witness, there stands a strong sense of God's completed work in Christ (2 Cor 5; Eph 2), then this has implications for how we understand the historical and contextualizing witness of the church. Contextualization will not be understood as theological innovation or progress or evolution. Contextualization is, rather, a return and a rediscovery of the spirit of Christ. It is a turn back to the day of Pentecost, to Easter, to the nativity of God incarnate. When it is understood in such terms, we are saved from a progressive temporality that was absent in the first witnesses of Christ.[35] Unfortunately, a progressivism was often at work in the modern missionary movement. This led to the elevation of cultures purportedly 'enlightened' by their discontinuity from the past. In contrast, contextualization, as the life of the Gospel, is the articulation and demonstration of the continuity of the message of Jesus Christ in a given culture. Of course, these selfsame cultural resources can veil the Gospel. However, all cultures and all branches of the church are called back to the reconciliation wrought by God in Christ for all cultures. Thus, the Anglican Communion is not less than a network of contextualizations held together by a commitment to inter-contextual discernment and fellowship. It is an exercise and a pilgrimage in catholicity-from-below. In Swamy's terms, such witness is a travelling outward from Jerusalem but is also always a journeying or pilgrimage back to Jerusalem. All contextualizations turn back to the incarnation and to the marginalized Christ of Palestine.

Christian witness as the declaration of Christ's (subverting) lordship

The Christian Gospel is a direct challenge to the reigning powers. The good news is that there is another Lord and that Lord lays aside his glory that we might know the reconciling healing of divine love. The God of love is the missionary God always reaching out to creation. Despite our sin, the God who is love comes to us and in doing so lays aside the glory that is his right in a series of profound boundary crossings. The missionary God, come in Christ, continues to transgress, question, and step over boundaries until he is faced with the ultimate boundary that all humans will face. Christ is cast aside by the empire in execution. Yet, in the very act of being thrown to the margins, Christ subverts Caesarian power.

When we centre ourselves on the Lord's table we are fed by the body and blood of the Lord crucified by empire. In centring ourselves on the table we are, simultaneously, turned to the margins. Given this christological heart of Christian witness, Swamy poignantly defines mission as crossing boundaries. He sums up the practical implications of such boundary-crossing as Christian presence with the powerless: 'the primary task of Christian mission is to be with those who are powerless'. Given God's own witness in Christ, it seems that Swamy is saying that presence with the powerless is the very definition of proclaiming the (subversive) Lordship of Jesus. Yet, despite a conversional and liturgical centring on the Lord of the margins and despite Christ's ascension displacing the power of Caesar, Swamy observes a hesitancy in the church to 'identify with and address the concerns of the powerless and the marginalized'. The challenge of such an observation is that despite the intellectual ascent to holistic witness he sees an absence of this commitment in actual mission practice. To what extent is this the case in my context and your context? For if such commitment is absent, then, in practice, we disagree with Swamy's assertion that the primary task is to be present with the powerless. At the very least, he wants his readers to consider that the corollary of declaring the lordship of Christ is this kind of call to self-interrogation. For those of us from dominant cultures such a picture of Christ and call to witness must surely make us pause to consider our predilection to make Christ in the image of Caesar.[36]

Conclusion

I do not see Jesus correcting the religio-political expectations of the disciples in Acts 1. There is continuity between the witness of Jesus and the hopes of the disciples. Jesus came to renew Israel and to interrupt Caesarian understandings and practices of power. The disciples understood the former but, prior to Pentecost, struggled with the latter. However, the rest of the Acts of the Apostles bears testimony to the willingness of the followers of Jesus to give up their lives and embody a different practice of power. The restoration of Israel, which included the incorporation of Gentiles, did indeed take place with the coming of the power of God's Spirit that continued to challenge and subvert the power of Caesar.

Summary of questions for reflection

1 How might we understand the mission of Jesus in thoroughgoing religio-political terms? What would that do to our hermeneutics and our understanding of holistic mission today?
2 What did God's mission in Christ accomplish? How does that divine mission, wrought through divine agency and God's own proclamation of God's self, inform how we understand the agency and work of the church today?
3 What does it mean for a theology of mission to say that Jesus is Lord of all and that Jesus' exercise of lordship subverts domineering (imperialist) understandings and exercises of power?
4 Despite the intellectual ascent to holistic mission there seems to be an absence of commitment to it in practical ministry. To what extent is this the case in different contexts?
5

Notes

1 Stephen Bevans and Roger Schroeder, *Constants in Context: A Theology of Mission for Today* (Maryknoll, NY: Orbis Books, 2004), p. 72.
2 There is a quite a lot of literature on this. For instance, see Todd M. Johnson and Kenneth R. Ross (eds.), *Atlas of Global Christianity* (Edinburgh: Edinburgh University Press, 2009); Bryant Myers, *The Changing Shape of World Mission* (Monrovia, CA: MARC, 1993); Michael Pocock, Gailyn Van Rheenen, and Douglas McConnell, *The Changing Face of World Missions: Engaging Contemporary Issues and Trends* (Grand Rapids, MI: Baker Academic, 2005); Todd M. Johnson and others (eds.), *2010Boston: The Changing Contours of World Mission and Christianity* (Eugene, OR: Pickwick Publications, 2012); and Ogbu Kalu, Peter Vethanayagamony, and Edmund Chia (eds.), *Mission after Christendom: Emergent Themes in Contemporary Mission* (Louisville, KY: Westminster John Knox Press, 2010).
3 See Philip Jenkins, *The Next Christendom: The Coming of Global Christianity* (New York: Oxford University Press, 2002); Jonathan Y. Tan and Anh Q. Tran (eds.), *World Christianity: Perspectives and Insights* (Maryknoll, NY: Orbis Books, 2016); Ogbu E. Kalu and Alaine Low (eds.), *Interpreting Contemporary Christianity: Global Processes and Local Identities* (Grand Rapids, MI: Eerdmans, 2008); Charles E. Farhadian, *Introducing World Christianity* (Chichester: Wiley-Blackwell, 2012); Lamin Sanneh and Joel A. Carpenter (eds.), *The Changing Face of Christianity: Africa, the West, and the World* (Oxford: Oxford University Press, 2005).

4 Elizabeth Koepping, 'Exploring the Past for a Stronger Future: A Reflection on Meaning and Hope', in Paul Silas Peterson (ed.), *The Decline of Established Christianity in the Western World: Interpretations and Responses* (London and New York: Routledge, 2017), pp. 267–82.

5 See Carol Graham, 'The Legacy of V. S. Azariah', *International Bulletin of Missionary Research* (Jan. 1985), 16–19. See also A. R. Chelliah, *Bishop Vedanayagam Samuel Azariah: A Life in Indigenisation* (Delhi: ISPCK, 2016).

6 See Arvind Sharma, *Hinduism as a Missionary Religion* (New York: SUNY Press, 2011).

7 Paul D. Devanandan, *Resurgent Hinduism: Review of Modern Movements* (Bangalore: Christian Institute for the Study of Religion and Society, 1959). Devanandan's was one of the earliest Indian Christian voices in post-colonial India to take the resurgent Hinduism seriously and engage with it in the context of Christianity rather than ignoring or undermining it.

8 John Stott, *The Message of Acts: To the Ends of the Earth* (Downers Grove, IL: Inter-Varsity Press, 1991), pp. 40–1.

9 For a discussion of Christian embrace of political power offered by Constantine, see Alistair Kee, *Constantine versus Christ: The Triumph of Ideology* (London: SCM Press, 1982).

10 For a discussion of the relationship between colonialism and Christian mission see Andrew Porter, *Religion versus Empire? British Protestant Missionaries and Overseas Expansion*, 1700–1914 (Manchester and New York: Manchester University Press, 2004).

11 In India, South India has a good presence of Christians in comparison to North India, and this is primarily due to the work of foreign mission societies during approximately the last five centuries. Sending missionaries to North India is one of the main ways in which both the mainstream and independent churches, as well as independent mission organizations, are involved in the mission enterprise.

12 While there have been many attacks and incidents of violence against Christians in India during the last few decades, especially since the Hindutva forces started to acquire political power, narrating such events as Hindu–Christian violence or Hindu attacks on Christianity betrays the complexities of factors and identities involved. It also completely undermines the nature of Hindu–Christian relations in ordinary life situations, and ignores how religious communities with the same identities which are (or are said to be) in conflict with each other often actually help each other during times of persecution, attacks, and violence.

13 I am working on the problems with such narratives in my current ethnographic research project on Indian Christianity: *Reactions to Christianity in Contemporary India: Perceptions, Interpretations and Responses* (Philadelphia: Fortress Press, forthcoming).

14 Theological and missional reflection on Holy Spirit in the context of Christian mission is relatively a new area of study, and several works have been published. For instance, see Kirsteen Kim, *Joining in with the Spirit: Connecting World*

Church and Local Mission (London: SCM Press, 2010); Gary Tyra, *The Holy Spirit in Mission: Prophetic Speech and Action in Christian Witness* (Downers Grove, IL: InterVarsity Press, 2011); Amos Yong, *The Missiological Spirit: Christian Mission theology in the Third Millennium Global Context* (Eugene, OR: Cascade Books, 2014); and John V. Taylor, *The Go-Between God: The Holy Spirit and the Christian Mission* (Eugene, OR: Wipf and Stock, 2015). In this chapter, I have not attempted to do a detailed study of this.

15 Teresa of Avila, *The Interior Castle: or, The Mansions*, trans. Benedictines of Stanbrook (New York: Benziger Brothers, 1912), p. 29.

16 I have difficulty with Christianity antagonizing what it terms as secularism or secularization. First of all, whether a strict secular–religious binary exists at all in practice is my fundamental question. Second, I cannot think of the evolution of the idea of secularization outside the development of Christianity. Third, though it appears that Christianity is opposed to secularism, in fact, if secularism is to mean enlightenment, rationality, and scientific and technological advances, Christianity has heavily made use of these in its approach to other religions, particularly in looking down upon them.

17 Joerg Rieger in his recent book states that today the main struggle in the context of Christian life and witness has to be between the values that the Gospel promotes and the values that the Gospel resists. See his book *Jesus vs. Caesar: For People Tired of Serving the Wrong God* (Nashville: Abingdon Press, 2018).

18 See Frances S. Adeney, *Graceful Evangelism: Christian Witness in a Complex World* (Grand Rapids, MI: Baker Academic, 2010). See also Terry C. Muck and Frances S. Adeney, *Christianity Encountering World Religions: The Practice of Mission in the Twenty-First Century* (Grand Rapids, MI: Baker Academic, 2009). My own model of Christian mission is an invitation to share the joy of the good news. Invitation is a recurring theme in the entire Bible, and for me the good news can never be shared in a hostile way. See Muthuraj Swamy, 'Doing Mission in Context: Christian Mission as Invitation in Contemporary India' (2016), http://www.missiontheologyanglican.org/article-mt/doing-mission-in-context-christian-mission-as-invitation-in-contemporary-india-/.

19 Roger Bowen, 'Biblical Principles for Calling and Training for Mission', in Francis Bridger and James T. Butler (eds.), *Conversations at the Edges of Things: Reflections for the Church in Honor of John Goldingay* (Eugene, OR: Pickwick Publications, 2012), pp. 105–15 at 108.

20 Sherron Kay George, 'The Quest for Changes of Missionaries', *Missiology*, 30 (2002), 51–63 at 57.

21 Joseph Pathrapankal offers an excellent study comparing the Great Commission text in Matthew 28 and the text in Acts 1.8. 'Making Disciples (Matt 28:16–20) and Being Witnesses of Christ (Acts 1:8): Theology of Mission and A Study in Contrast', https://www.vanderbilt.edu/AnS/religious_studies/SNTS/pathra04.htm.

22 Bowen, 'Biblical Principles for Calling and Training for Mission', p. 107.

23 World Council of Churches, *Together towards Life, Together towards Life: Mission and Evangelism in Changing Landscapes. With a Practical Guide* (2012), https://www.oikoumene.org/en/resources/publications/TogethertowardsLife_SAMPLE.pdf.

24 Of course, mission to the West is not a new idea. See Eugene L. Stockwell, 'Conciliar Missions', in James M. Phillips and Robert T. Coote (eds.), *Toward the Twenty-First Century in Christian Mission: Essays in Honour of Gerald H. Anderson* (Grand Rapids, MI: Eerdmans, 1993) pp. 21–9 at 25–6.

25 For a discussion of the connected nature of Christianity in a context of Christian mission see Graham Kings, *Christianity Connected: Hindus, Muslims and the World in the Letters of Max Warren and Roger Hooker*, Indian edn (Delhi: ISPCK, 2017).

26 Central to imperial order was the Jerusalem 'temple-state' operating, quite literally, under the Roman imperial eagle. See Richard A. Horsley, *Jesus and Empire: The Kingdom of God and the New World Disorder* (Minneapolis: Fortress Press, 2003), pp. 15–43; Leo G. Perdue, Warren Carter, and Coleman A. Baker, *Israel and Empire: A Postcolonial History of Israel and Early Judaism* (London: Bloomsbury, 2015), pp. 217–91.

27 See N. T Wright, *The Resurrection of the Son of God* (London: SPCK, 2003), pp. 653–4.

28 Joel B. Green, *The Theology of the Gospel of Luke* (Cambridge: Cambridge University Press, 1995), p. 90.

29 Ibid., pp. 47–8.

30 Wright, *The Resurrection of the Son of God*, p. 655.

31 Ibid., p. 656.

32 Seen particularly in the ongoing emergence of post-colonial theology. See Ian T. Douglas and Kwok Pui-Lan (eds.), *Beyond Colonial Anglicanism: The Anglican Communion in the Twenty-First Century* (New York: Church Publishing, 2001); Kay Higuera Smith, Jayachitra Lalitha, and L. Daniel Hawk (eds.), *Evangelical Postcolonial Conversations: Global Awakenings in Theology and Praxis* (Downers Grove: IVP, 2014); R. S. Wafula, Esther Mombo, and Joseph Wandera (eds.), *The Postcolonial Church: Bible, Theology, and Mission* (Alameda: Borderless Press, 2016); Robert S. Heaney, *Finding God and Each Other amidst the Hate: The Intent and Practice of Post-Colonial Theology* (Eugene, OR: Cascade, forthcoming).

33 See John Kafwanka and Mark Oxbrow (eds.), *Intentional Discipleship and Disciple-Making: An Anglican Guide for Christian Life and Formation* (London: Anglican Consultative Council, 2016).

34 Wright, *The Resurrection of the Son of God*, pp. 649–61.

35 See John S. Mbiti, *New Testament Eschatology in an African Background* (London: Oxford University Press, 1971); and Bruce J. Malina, *The Social World of Jesus and the Gospels* (London and New York: Routledge, 1996), pp. 179–214; Robert S. Heaney, *From Historical to Critical Post-Colonial Theology* (Eugene, OR: Pickwick, 2015), pp. 62–93.

36 For the pathology possible in dominant cultures and the potential and dangerous effects of the colonization of the mind see, for example, Ashis Nandy, *The Intimate Enemy: Loss and Recovery of Self under Colonialism* (Delhi: Oxford University Press, 1983).

Section 3

MIDDLE EASTERN PERSPECTIVES

7

Models of 'evangelism' and 'witness' in the Anglican/Episcopal Church in Egypt

SAMY FAZY SHEHATA (EGYPT)

There is a controversy related to the difference between mission and evangelism. The word 'evangelism' is used more narrowly than 'mission'. Roman Catholics and ecumenical Protestants use the word 'mission' for ecclesial activities. Therefore, evangelicals have avoided using the word and used only 'evangelism'. Some evangelicals claim that historically the mission of the church was evangelism.[1] There is also a tendency to understand 'mission' and 'evangelism' as synonyms. In ecumenical literature, mission, evangelism, and witness are interchangeable concepts. I cannot deny the degree of confusion that arises when some evangelicals use 'evangelism' in relation to proclamation, dialogue, service, and presence.

How to refer to the activities of the church in contemporary Egypt? Is it mission, evangelism, or witness? Theologians prefer the word 'witness' when they refer to the ministry of the church in the Middle East. Catholicos Aram I states that 'because of the historical connotations attached to term "mission" particularly in this region the Middle East Council of Churches prefers to use "witness"'.[2]

Evangelism should be viewed as an essential element in the total activity of the church. It is witnessing to what God has done, is doing, and will do. Evangelism aims for a response; conversion involves turning from a life of separation from God and turning to a new life of obedience and fellowship with God. The evangelist is a witness. 'I am witness to him who is both utterly holy and utterly gracious. His holiness and his grace are as far above my comprehension as they are above that of my hearer.'[3] In the witnessing act of the Anglican Church in Egypt, evangelism remains an essential aspect and cannot be replaced. Mission is not merely evangelism but denotes all activities of love, service, preaching, and healing.

Evangelism and mission in the Anglican Church in Egypt can be seen in three models. The work with the Coptic Orthodox Church offers us a model of unity. The mission to Muslims offers us a model of witness. The social, educational, and medical mission offers us a model of service. Here I need to add that I am not creating a new policy or vision for the Anglican Church in Egypt, but mainly observing the ministry of the church and relating the different aspects of the work of the church to models for contemporary ministry. For each of these models I will survey the historical background and examine its application to and relevance in contemporary Egyptian society.

Unity

The policy of the early mission of the Church Mission Society (CMS) was one of cooperation with Eastern churches in their revival and the ultimate winning of the 'heathen'. There was to be no formation of Anglican congregations in this early period (1815–40). In 1825 five men from Basel were sent to Egypt, where they sold and distributed Bibles and tracts. A boys' boarding school was established in Cairo, which in 1842 was changed into a theological seminary for the training of the Coptic Orthodox clergy. The Rev. John Lieder revised the Coptic and Arabic New Testaments and translated into Arabic some of the works of St Macarius, whose authority is greatly respected in the Coptic Orthodox Church. However, Anglican work in Egypt ground to halt with the death of Lieder in Cairo in 1865, the last member of the Mediterranean mission.

CMS's mission in Egypt deliberately avoided building up an Anglican church at the expense of the Coptic Orthodox Church. As late as 1908 the leaders at the society's headquarters in London expressed their desire to keep the door open for a possible amalgamation with the Coptic Orthodox Church, 'if reformed', of any congregation built up in connection with its work in Egypt.[4] The early mission's aim was to support and revive the church in Egypt.

We need to evaluate this early mission and ask a few questions. What alternatives were planned if the mission did not succeed in reviving the traditional church? What exactly do we mean by reviving the church? In 1921 it became obvious that the failure to develop the Arabic branch of the Anglican Church was a major weakness in the mission's work. The problem which forced the discussion of this matter was the shortage of ordained members in the mission's staff who were qualified to provide pastoral services for the Arabic-speaking congregation. The solution proposed by Rev. W. Temple Gairdner, a missionary scholar to Islam, was the ordination of native pastors.[5]

The principal objective was to develop a vigorous, evangelistic church, admitting into membership those who were prepared to endorse its evangelistic principles. Gairdner wrote in 1924: 'we are agreed that when Jesus Christ found His Church He purposed to spread His message of Salvation everywhere by means of that Church'.[6]

> The Episcopal Church in Egypt does not desire to increase its membership by accessions from other organizations, whether Coptic Orthodox, Presbyterian or otherwise...it is inevitable also to recognize the practical fact that circumstances have caused certain individuals, and will continue to cause others, to come into such close contact with this community that they end by seeking membership of the same.[7]

The document expressed the church's intention of cooperating with other Christian communities, to live in spiritual unity with them, and to press forward to the day when this fellowship would become 'full cooperate union'.

One of the reasons for not developing the Arabic Anglican Church was the early policy. A decision to create an indigenous church has to be followed by practical steps to full indigenization, but this did not take place until after the departure of the missionaries due to the Suez crisis in 1956. At this point the bishop left without handing the church to the indigenous clergy, the funding stopped, and the church was left simply to die. However, the Church of Christ always managed to carry on in its work in spite of loss of vision or funds. After 1956 the map of the church changed dramatically, resulting in the loss of some of our churches and social institutions. It took the Anglican Communion twenty years to form the Province of Jerusalem and the Middle East and accept an Egyptian bishop, something which should have happened after the retirement of Bishop Gwynne 1945, after the revolution of 1952 and the resignation of Bishop Allen, or before the deportation of Bishop Johnston in 1956.

Unity does not mean ceasing to exist for the sake of the other but cooperating with other churches. The concept of the church as communion combines the several Bible images of the church (the body of Christ and the People of God); these images popularize the notion of the church as supernatural organism vivified by the Holy Spirit, a fellowship sustained by the outpouring of divine grace. This type of ecclesiology has a basis in the biblical notion of communion (*koinonia*) in the book of Acts and in the Pauline description of the church as the body of Christ. This approach is ecumenically very fruitful, and is far more acceptable to most Protestants, Catholics, and Orthodox than the institutional model of the church. This type of ecclesiology explains the personal relationship between the faithful—individually and collectively—with the Holy Spirit, and helps to revivify the life of spirituality and the life of prayer.

The Church of Christ upon earth is essentially, intentionally, and constitutionally one, consisting of all those in every place who profess faith in Christ and obedience to him in all things according to the Scriptures. Unity as *koinonia* is more than cordiality towards those who differ from us, more than a warm feeling of belonging to one family, to the one flock of Christ. Fellowship is more than an idea. If it is to become effective it must assume form and structure. Unity includes real, tangible relationships and structures that constitute our life together. Unity means that we share in the experience of faith and mission in such dramatic ways that both we and the world can see and know that Christians are one.[8]

Furthermore, to understand the church in the terms of communion confronts us with the scandal of our divisions. Christian disunity obscures God's invitation to communion for all humankind and makes the Gospel we proclaim harder to hear. But the consideration of communion also enables Christians to recognize that certain, yet imperfect, communion that they already share. Christians from many traditions are coming to acknowledge the central place of communion in their understanding of the nature of the church and its unity and mission. This is the unity we need to examine in the context of Egypt.[9]

There are sixteen Protestant denominations in Egypt. The work of unity is carried out on three different levels. On a global level, there is a dialogue between the Anglican and Oriental Orthodox Churches, which has produced signed documents on the nature of Christ and the procession of the Holy Spirit.[10] The fellowship of the Middle East Council of Churches is aiming towards unity between the churches in the Middle East. Moreover, the Egyptian Council of Churches unites the main denominations: Coptic and Greek Orthodox, Catholics, Protestants, and Anglicans. Our mission as a bridge church is evident in the friendship with Coptic, Catholic, and Protestant Churches. The Anglican Church hosts a monthly ecumenical meeting for clergy from all denominations, and our theological education is recognized and accepted by all denominations.

The church's mission in Egypt is to participate in God's mission, which is the establishment of the kingdom of God. Unity has to be understood in the perspective of the kingdom. It is related to the very essence of *koinonia* as fellowship in the triune God. In Egypt, the churches are striving for visible unity and a common mission in the midst of conflict and turmoil. The question of unity is important to the churches in any part of the world, but it is of paramount importance in Egypt. It is God himself in Jesus Christ who is present in and acts in the church's continuous struggle for unity and mission.[11] We are in open dialogue, and the churches in Egypt are cooperating with each other, yet we are still working towards the day when we will reach full unity. It is our duty to share in the hopes and burdens of the churches within the social, religious, and economic issues in contemporary Egypt. The search for unity takes us again to the cross of Christ. Through the cross we can discern and accept the shape of Christian unity.

Witness

The year 1882 was significant for the resumption by CMS of its work in Egypt. The earlier mission, which had sought to revive the Christian faith of the Coptic Orthodox Church, had ended with the death of John Lieder in 1865. In 1882, the mission resumed with an entirely different policy. In the same year the British army defeated the Egyptian army at Tel-el Kabir, which also influenced this process. Now the mission started to focus on reaching the Muslims who formed the majority of the Egyptian population.

With the arrival of Gairdner and Douglas Thornton in 1898–99, CMS launched a specialized method of working among Muslims. Gairdner and Thornton explored a variety of methods and approaches, using as a starting point the failure of the previous missionaries of 1882–1900 to learn about Islam. It also seems that Gairdner had only a limited, superficial, understanding of Islam, as Michael Shelly concludes in his thesis about the early years of Gairdner's mission, before 1910.[12]

The development of the mission's work with Muslims depended mainly on Gairdner, whose new approach to mission in Egypt started in 1921. The work shifted away from contending with Islam and trying to win converts and towards the creation of the Anglican Church as a true indigenous church. Gairdner used dialogue, literature, and drama as ways of meeting Muslims, discussing theological issues with them and communicating Christianity by presenting Christ and not controversy.

The missionaries' use of dialogue with Muslims was different from the way we understand it today. They understood it mainly as a method for converting Muslims. One needs to remember that their efforts in reaching Muslims and listening to their beliefs and thoughts were a great step forward over the polemics of their day. Gairdner hated controversy because it did not achieve any fruit; he abandoned this method a few years after the departure of Thornton in 1907 and began to use literature as a method for reaching all Muslims without controversy. Gairdner had gone to Cairo committed to creating Christian literature for educated Muslims. He achieved his goal to a remarkable degree by preparing over a score of Arabic works before his death.

Gairdner's experiments in the medium of drama reveal how he adapted poetic and musical talent for the purpose of apologetic work. In Egypt, people have a natural affinity for drama. The first play was presented in a church with the approval of Bishop Gwynne. Five presentations drew nearly two thousand Muslims and Christians, and Gairdner gained a new hope that Egypt might receive the Gospel. But the use of this medium was too advanced for CMS's supporters at home. The CMS committee, fearful that gifts might be withheld, confined the use of drama to hospitals and schools, thus stopping Gairdner's creative venture.

The model of witness calls us not only to work for the renewal of the local community of faith, but also to work for the renewal of the entire human community. The mission of the church is not a doctrinal consensus, but fundamentally the renewal of the broken fellowship with Christ. It is essentially the transformation of human beings, community, and the whole creation. The model of witness is understood in the Muslim context as the church as the light of the world and the salt of the earth. In the Muslim context, we must never say: 'God so loved the Christians . . .'[13]

It is through the presence of committed Christians that a sense of their faith will always be available for the world. The role of the Anglican Church is to encourage Christians to be humble and honest in the midst of the majority population, articulate when opportunities occur and questions emerge, but always embodying the evidence as disciples of Jesus. Christians and Muslims in Egypt should not live in two exclusive communities. The vision for work with Muslims should be transformed: the church is part of the society and should be a living witness to Muslims through the life of her members. The cultural centres in Cairo and Alexandria offer open doors for the community, especially young artists, thinkers, and the church's members, to cross the boundaries and share life together.

The church needs to understand its context. The People of God need to know the world in which they are living in some depth. The church must engage in dialogue, but dialogue as controversy is not beneficial and widens the gap between Muslims and Christians. More beneficial is an informal dialogue of life that takes place between friends who live together and share together in work or study, each testifying to their own beliefs and spiritual values. It is in this kind of dialogue that the church should also offer correct teaching for its members. Christians should understand Islam correctly and respect other beliefs, yet at the same time be able to witness of the work of Christ in their lives.

Formal dialogue is important in removing misunderstanding. This kind of dialogue takes place between Islamic and Christian leaders. When terrorists attack Christians or the government, formal dialogue offers a unique opportunity to correct misperceptions of religion and to assure the world at large that Muslims and Christians want to live in peace and build the community. Two new projects, 'Together for Egypt'[14] and 'Together We Develop Egypt',[15] are initiatives of the Anglican Church of Egypt. 'Together for Egypt' has brought together priests and imams to work side by side in humanitarian and social work, while 'Together We Develop Egypt' educates Muslim and Christian youth from villages experiencing conflict to be able to live together in peace.

The church has established many initiatives to engage in formal dialogue and life dialogue in Egypt. The Al Azhar formal dialogue with the Anglican Communion is one of the most important and influential forums. This daily encounter with Islam has greatly affected our theological outlook, our values and traditions, and our understanding of ourselves. In other words, the church's entire existence is shaped by Christians living among Muslims. Christian mission in Egypt is not aimed at the conversion of Islam. We are living with people who are different in many respects and who intend to remain different. But the church cannot abandon her mission of spiritual transformation. Christians in Egypt must engage in a dynamic process of spiritual renewal. Islam can become an encouraging factor in the church's search for their true identity in Christ. We need a coherent and relevant theology to make us more reliable partners of our neighbours in our common mission for community building. We need a new theology that is strong enough to be open to 'mutual witness' yet at the same time resistant to any temptation to possible compromise. Padwick in her biography of Gairdner wrote:

> It is sometimes said that little mission churches will be as islands in the sea of Islam—but let us not be enslaved by dreary metaphors. Let us rather say that such churches will be centres of life and heat and light, serving and saving the Islamic peoples round them.[16]

Service

The history and development of social, educational, and medical mission are very important to our understanding today of the mission of the Anglican Church in Egypt. Social mission existed from the very early stages, and the new policy of creating an indigenous church provided the opportunity for those who were involved in its social work, if they wished, to be full members of the Anglican Church. The work offered an opportunity to serve the society on a very small scale in comparison with the population or size of the Egyptian community.

CMS made a substantial commitment to various kinds of education. Female education was a pioneering venture in societies that traditionally did not give girls formal training; Henry Venn stated, 'female education as a means of training Christian mothers and female native teachers presents at the present time one of the most important fields of missionary labours'.[17] The medical missions were still in their infancy in 1850, and the medical profession had not yet won public confidence. It was another generation before medical missions were accepted among missionary societies. CMS considered preachers, rather than doctors, to be its responsibility.

Independent work was carried out by Mary Whately, daughter of the Anglican Archbishop of Dublin, who came to Egypt for her health in 1856 and was grieved to find no schools for Muslim girls. Miss Whately wrote:

> The schools opened doors which might never have been opened for the gospel without it, for Egyptians are shy of receiving total strangers without some reason, and having their girls under our care was of course the best reason...[18]

1885, CMS appointed Dr F. J. Harpur, a Dublin graduate in the arts and medicine, to start a medical mission in Aden. This work was taken over by the Church of Scotland in 1888 and Harpur was transferred to Egypt, where he founded in Old Cairo the famous hospital which came to be known as 'Harmul' (the Egyptian pronunciation of Harpur). The hospital was to become the most effective witness to the power of the Christian Gospel as presented to the people of Egypt by the Anglican Church for the next seventy years.

In 1889 Harpur travelled by boat along the canals of the Nile delta, founding dispensaries at Ashmoun and Hannoul, and in 1915 a new hospital was opened at Menouf. Among the future leaders of the church who served their 'apprenticeship' at Old Cairo Hospital were Girgis Bishai, the first Egyptian to be ordained into the Anglican Church, and Ishaq Musaad, the first Egyptian bishop, who gained valuable experience as a hospital administrator after the Suez crisis of 1956. The work of Harpur, together with that of Gairdner, was to become the main source of membership and leadership in what was to become the Anglican Church in Egypt.

In the history of the church, one cannot fail to notice the importance of the service offered by missionaries to the community. It was service that opened closed doors that would have remained shut. Similarly in Egypt, the motivation of the missionaries from the beginning was to offer service without discrimination between Muslims and Christians, even though at times winning converts has also been an aim in such works. Their social work was administered in relationship with the church. The role of the church today is to extend its service to all in love, and to show that the Anglican Church is not promoting itself but serving the community.

The church in Egypt should follow the practical example of Christ washing his disciples' feet and engage in practical mission to the poor and needy. The Anglicans in Egypt cannot engage in mission as witness and communion fully without serving the community. The model of the church as a servant is in its essence a visible sign of the love and grace of God given to his people to serve in the community. Service is offered to all without discrimination on the basis of denomination or religion. The work of the Deaf School in Old Cairo serves Christians from all denominations. The social centres and the hospital offer service to Muslims and Christians alike. The results of such service should not be seen as a way of increasing the membership of the Anglican Church but as the visible sign of the love of God to all.

The understanding of the church as a visible sign is very appropriate to the mission of the church as a servant. Service is the practical expression of the life-transforming Gospel. Faith without works is dead. We serve others just as Christ, servant of all, served those who came to him. Bonhoeffer in his early work *The Communion of Saints* places a heavy emphasis on the nature of the church as a communion of people drawn together by Christ. He calls for a humble and a servant church:

> The Church is the church only when it exists for others. To make a start, it should give away all its property to those in need. The clergy must live solely on the free-will offerings of their congregations, or possibly engage in some secular calling. The Church must share in the secular problems of ordinary human life, not dominating but helping and serving.[19]

Conclusion

The Anglican Bishop John Robinson argues in *The New Reformation* that 'the house of God is not the Church but the World. The Church is the servant, and the first characteristic of a servant is that he lives in someone else's house, not his own.'[20] Therefore, the church should have a structure to enable her to unite with other churches, reach out in dialogue with Muslims, and serve all without discrimination.

The church's mission, in the perspective of this theology, is not primarily to gain new recruits for its own ranks, but rather to be of help to all people, wherever they are. The special competence of the church is to keep alive the hope and inspiration of all for the kingdom of God and its values. In the light of this hope the church is able to discern the signs of the times and to offer guidance and prophetic criticism. In this way it is a witness and initiates people in various ways into the kingdom of God.[21] The three models of the church—service, unity, and witness—are all essential in our understanding of a missionary church.

> We need to have an image of the church rather similar to the 'big bang' of creation in which from the centre, energy and vision go forth to govern and sustain new life. We need to regain our confidence in the Church as God's instrument; and we must restructure church life to enable each person, in their context and ministry, to serve God more effectively.[22]

Response

STEPHEN SPENCER (UNITED KINGDOM)

This fascinating chapter opens many windows onto the Anglican Church in Egypt. It describes a church with a ongoing history of interaction with a majority Muslim population and with a minority ancient church of the region, the Coptic Church. It is a story that throws into sharp relief the difficulty of promoting evangelism and so constructively challenges the theme of this conference.

Shehata begins by highlighting the different and confusing ways in which the terms 'mission' and 'evangelism' are used, a helpful place to begin. It shows that anyone working in this area needs to define carefully what they mean by such terms and then stick to those definitions. Such definitions will need to be influenced by context: the culture, language and politics of the location where these activities are taking place. It is instructive to hear that the Middle East Council of Churches uses the word 'witness' instead of 'mission', because of the latter's historical connotations. The word 'mission' easily evokes uncomfortable colonial memories. This hesitation over the word could be applied elsewhere: we use it widely and freely, but does it have negative connotations for those beyond the walls of our own churches? Does it evoke negative images of coercion by Christians? Shehata's chapter is a reminder that theologians must be contextually-sensitive in their use of language.

He provides a clear definition of evangelism: 'Evangelism should be viewed as an essential element in the total activity of the church. It is witnessing to what God has done, is doing and will do...[it] aims for a response; conversion involves turning from a life of separation from God and turning to a new life of obedience and fellowship with God'. The main sections of his chapter, however, show that this kind of evangelism has not had a place in the life of the Anglican Church of Egypt. The three approaches to mission/witness that he describes are very different. He begins in the early nineteenth century, when Swiss missionaries sent by CMS began with translation and educational work on behalf of the Coptic Church, hoping to revive the life of that church (1815–40). This work developed into efforts to achieve Christian unity between this and other churches, including the Roman Catholic Church, which continue to this day and are now based on a rich ecumenical communion ecclesiology. The second approach was that of Rev. W. Temple Gairdner (1873–1928) in the 1920s, using respectful dialogue with Muslims and producing apologetic literature and drama. Here the point was to mix and mingle with the Muslim population so that the church could be salt and light without confrontation. Today this kind of witness continues with both formal dialogue at an official level and informal dialogue in community centres with young artists, thinkers, and church members. At this point Shehata clearly tells us that Christian mission in Egypt is not aimed at conversion of Muslims. Then there is the third approach, which is service expressed through social, medical, and educational initiatives. This came to prominence in the late nineteenth century through the impressive Harmul hospital and other medical institutions. These became the main source of membership of the church, service 'which opened the closed doors that would have remained shut'. But, again, this work was not done to convert people and increase the membership of the church but done for its own sake.

It is immensely helpful to be told this story. But, as mentioned, it highlights the difficulty of promoting evangelism, or intentional evangelism (to use the current phraseology), across the board. It shows that there are contexts where this type of mission is not appropriate. The mission of God is advanced through other means, such as working for Christian unity, engaging in respectful dialogue, and serving the humanitarian needs of all people. But this conference is all about promoting evangelism, and so the question can be pressed as to whether evangelism might not be possible in certain situations in the Egyptian context. Are there sometimes ways in which Muslims may be clearly and deliberately told about the Gospel of Christ in a way that 'aims for a response'? It is obvious that there cannot be the noisy stadium-filling kind of mass evangelistic campaign found in other parts of the world. But that may not be the only way. Other forms are possible, such as one found in the Mara region of Tanzania, within their Anglican dioceses, which has resulted in a *tenfold* growth of church membership over recent years. Might there be scope for this approach in the Egyptian context or, indeed, in other contexts?

The Mara type of evangelism begins with a deliberate decision to engage in a limited period of intentional evangelism with a specific community of people.[23] It occurs through a team which includes experienced evangelists from elsewhere and some local Christians. It includes some events in public spaces that allow contact with a cross-section of people. In Mara these tend to involve singing by the church choir and some preaching. But these events are not the evangelism itself, and so their form and content can be adapted to make them appropriate to the respective context.

The evangelism takes place when passers-by, who see the choir or hear the preaching, indicate that they are interested in finding out more. A couple of members of the team arrange to come and meet them in their own home at their own convenience. Crucially, the evangelism takes place through open-ended conversation in that home. The team members are guests and therefore in a position of vulnerability in the host's home. They can offer only what will be received, and they can bear witness to their faith only if the conversation allows this to happen. Questions and answers are central to the whole process, showing that the way the faith is presented is intimately related to what the enquirers are willing and able to hear. It is therefore deeply and intimately contextual. It also shows that the power dynamics are the opposite of those in a classroom or church setting where the teacher or minister is in charge of the setting.

It is important to add, though, that in Mara the evangelists will challenge certain aspects of the culture of that context, such as female genital mutilation (FGM), which is still found in some districts. The prophetic edge of the Gospel will not be blunted. Also, connections will be made with the wider mission work of the church, especially its educational, medical, and developmental work in the villages and towns of the diocese. It will be made clear that the offer of faith and forgiveness in Christ is part and parcel of the wider holistic or integral mission of God served by the wider life of the church.

Finally, prayers will be said by the evangelists asking God to bless the home and lead the enquirer forward in their spiritual journey. This demonstrates that the conversation is not a simple dialogue between two parties, the host and the evangelists, but a trialogue, as it were, in which God through his Holy Spirit is active and present within the conversation and within the lives of them all. The invitation to conversion is shown to be about much more than joining a local church: it is about the whole of life and the Spirit's presence within that. The evangelists then offer to come back if the enquirer wants to know more or take things further, showing the free and voluntary nature of what is being offered. If the hosts and others in their community then come to faith, they will be entrusted with forming and running their own new church (with support from a neighbouring priest and the diocese).

This conversational and non-coercive type of evangelism, in which a team deliberately invest their time and resources in a specific act of invitation (which itself shows how much they value the offer they are making) to a chosen community of people, who are being honoured and respected through that offer, is an approach that with planning and commitment could be translated across to other contexts. Is it possible, then, that this type of approach could find a place in the unfolding story of the Anglican Church in Egypt? Might there be scope for using it in the future in that increasingly plural and challenging context?

Notes

1 Donald McGavran, 'What is Mission?', in A. F. Glasser and D. A. McGavran (eds.), *Contemporary Theologies of Mission* (Grand Rapids, MI: Baker, 1983), p. 17.
2 Aram I Keshishian, *For a Church beyond its Walls* (Antelias, Lebanon: Armenian Catholicosate of Cilicia, 2011), p. 19.
3 Lesslie Newbigin, 'Cross-Currents in Ecumenical and Evangelical Understandings of Mission', *International Bulletin of Missionary Research*, 6 (1982), 151.
4 CMS Archives, Birmingham, Special Collection, G3 E P2, 1908.
5 CMS Archives, Special Collection, G3 E O, newspaper extracts, 22 Nov. 1920.
6 W. H. T. Gairdner, 'The Christian Churches as a Home for Christ's Converts from Islam', *The Moslem World* (July 1924), 235–6.
7 CMS Archives, Special Collection, G3 E O, Cash to Manley, 21 July 1922.
8 Paul A. Crow, *Christian Mission: Matrix for Unity* (New York: Friendship Press, 1982), pp. 95–7.
9 ARCIC II, *The Church as Communion: An Agreed Statement by the Second Anglican–Roman Catholic International Commission* (London: Anglican Consultative Council, 1991), pp. 9–10.
10 Anglican–Oriental Orthodox International Commission, Agreed Statement on Christology (2002), http://www.anglicancommunion.org/media/103487/AOOIC-Agreed-Statement-of-Christology.pdf, and *The Procession and Work of the Holy Spirit*, http://www.anglicancommunion.org/media/312561/the-procession-and-work-of-the-holy-spirit-dublin-agreed-statement.pdf.
11 Keshishian, 'Unity and Mission from a Middle Eastern Perspective', pp. 445–52.
12 Michael T. Shelly, 'The Life and Thoughts of W. H. T. Gairdner, 1873–1928: A Critical Evaluation of a Scholar-Missionary to Islam', doctoral thesis, University of Birmingham, 1988, p. 53.
13 Kenneth Cragg, *Cathedral on the Nile: A History of All Saints Cathedral, Cairo,* Perspective and Prospect (Oxford: Amate Press, 1984), chap. 10, p. 88.
14 'Imams and Priests Celebrate the Together for Egypt Project' (10 Dec. 2015), Anglican Communion News Service, http://www.anglicannews.org/news/2015/12/imams-and-priests-celebrate-the-together-for-egypt-project.aspx.
15 'Together We Develop Egypt Celebrates the Graduation of Menya Youth' (18 Mar. 2018), Diocese of Egypt with North Africa and the Horn of Africa,

http://dioceseofegypt.org/2018/03/together-develop-egypt-celebrates-graduation-menya-youth/.

16 Constance Padwick, *Temple Gairdner of Cairo* (London: SPCK, 1929), p. 176.

17 Quoted in Wilbert R. Shenk, *Henry Venn: Missionary Statesman* (New York: Orbis Books, 1983), pp. 39–40.

18 Quoted in Lyle L. Vander Werff, *Christian Missions to Muslims: The Record* (Pasadena, CA: William Carey Library, 1977), p. 168.

19 Dietrich Bonhoeffer, *The Communion of Saints* (New York: Harper & Row, 1963), p. 350.

20 J. A. T. Robinson, *The New Reformation?* (Canterbury: SCM, 1965), p. 92.

21 Avery Dulles, *Models of the Church: A Critical Assessment of the Church in All its Aspects* (Dublin: Gill and Macmillan, 1976), pp. 83–96.

22 George Carey, in Cyril Okorocha (ed.), *The Cutting Edge of Mission: A Report of the Mid-Point Review of the Decade of Evangelism* (London: Anglican Communion Publications, 1996), p. 32.

23 The following paragraphs are based on my book *Growing and Flourishing: The Ecology of Church Growth*, published by SCM Press (2019), which is an extended analysis and discussion of 'the Mara approach' to church growth.

Bibliography

Published materials

ARCIC II, *The Church as Communion: An Agreed Statement by the Second Anglican–Roman Catholic International Commission* (London: Anglican Consultative Council, 1991), pp. 8–15.

Bonhoeffer, Dietrich, *The Communion of Saints* (New York: Harper & Row, 1963).

Bradshaw, Tim, *The Olive Branch: An Evangelical Anglican Doctrine of the Church* (Carlisle: Paternoster, 1992).

Cragg, Kenneth, *Cathedral on the Nile: A History of All Saints Cathedral, Cairo,* Perspective and Prospect (Oxford: Amate Press, 1984), chap. 10, pp. 86–100.

Crow, Paul A., *Christian Mission: Matrix for Unity* (New York: Friendship Press, 1982), pp. 95–104.

Dulles, Avery, *Models of the Church: A Critical Assessment of the Church in All its Aspects* (Dublin: Gill and Macmillan, 1976).

Gairdner, W. H. T., 'The Christian Churches as a Home for Christ's Converts from Islam', *The Moslem World* (July 1924), 235–6.

'Imams and Priests Celebrate the Together for Egypt Project' (10 Dec. 2015), Anglican Communion News Service, http://www.anglicannews.org/news/2015/12/imams-and-priests-celebrate-the-together-for-egypt-project.aspx.

Keshishian, Aram I, *For a Church Beyond its Walls* (Antelias, Lebanon: Armenian Catholicosate of Cilicia, 2011).

Keshishian, Aram I, 'Unity and Mission from a Middle Eastern Perspective', *International Review of Mission*, 79/316 (1990), 445–52.

McGavran, Donald, 'What is Mission?', in A. F. Glasser and D. A. McGavran (eds.), *Contemporary Theologies of Mission* (Grand Rapids, MI: Baker, 1983), pp. 15–29.

Newbigin, Lesslie, 'Cross-Currents in Ecumenical and Evangelical Understandings of Mission', *International Bulletin of Missionary Research*, 6 (1982), 146–51.

Okorocha, Cyril (ed.), *The Cutting Edge of Mission: A Report of the Mid-Point Review of the Decade of Evangelism* (London: Anglican Communion Publications, 1996).

Padwick, Constance, *Temple Gairdner of Cairo* (London: SPCK, 1929).

Robinson, J. A. T., *The New Reformation?* (Canterbury: SCM, 1965).

Shelly, Michael T., 'The Life and Thoughts of W. H. T. Gairdner, 1873–1928: A Critical Evaluation of a Scholar-Missionary to Islam', doctoral thesis, University of Birmingham, 1988.

Shenk, Wilbert R., *Henry Venn: Missionary Statesman* (New York: Orbis Books, 1983).

'Together We Develop Egypt Celebrates the Graduation of Menya Youth' (18 Mar. 2018), Diocese of Egypt with North Africa and the Horn of Africa, http://dioceseofegypt.org/2018/03/together-develop-egypt-celebrates-graduation-menya-youth/.

Werff, Lyle L. Vander, *Christian Missions to Muslims: The Record* (Pasadena, CA: William Carey Library, 1977).

Unpublished materials

All in CMS Archives, Birmingham, Special Collection

G3 E P1–5: books containing a summary of each letter or document received from the Egypt mission.

G3 E O: the original letters received by the CMS headquarters from the Egypt mission. Every file is assigned to a year, and the items are arranged in numerical order.

G3 E P2, 1908–98.

G3 E O, 1920–77, newspaper extracts, 22 Nov. 1920.

G3 E O, 1922–56, Cash to Manley, 21 July 1922.

Agreed Statements on Christology and the Procession of the Holy Spirit

Anglican–Oriental Orthodox International Commission, Agreed Statement on Christology (2002), http://www.anglicancommunion.org/media/103487/AOOIC-Agreed-Statement-of-Christology.pdf.

Anglican–Oriental Orthodox International Commission, *The Procession and Work of the Holy Spirit* (2017), http://www.anglicancommunion.org/media/312561/the-procession-and-work-of-the-holy-spirit-dublin-agreed-statement.pdf.

8

Christian witness of the Turkish church: challenges and opportunities

ENGIN YILDIRIM (TURKEY)

The Christian message is all about the good news of Jesus Christ, and Jesus' identity and his work are inherent parts of this message. The Synoptic Gospels set the scene by proclaiming this new era, whereby the kingdom of God has come near and God is about to do something new. The Gospel of Luke begins with the announcement of an angel proclaiming this good news to Mary at the birth narrative of Jesus. He says, 'I have been sent to speak to you and to bring you this good news' (Lk 1.19). The Gospel of Mark calls his message 'the beginning of the good news of Jesus Christ, the Son of God', and Jesus later says, 'The time is fulfilled, and the kingdom of God has come near; repent, and believe in the good news' (Mk 1.15). The Greek word for 'good news', *euangelion* (ευαγγελιον), is used in various religious and non-religious contexts as well. In the biblical usage of the word, Jesus himself says that he is to bring good news to the poor at his 'inauguration' message at the beginning of his ministry (Lk 4.18-19), that this news comes with signs and wonders (Mt 4.23; 9.35; 11.5), and that it must be preached to all nations (Mk 13.10; 16.15). The word 'evangelism', therefore, is derived from this word, and while it has different connotations in various circles today, it literally means sharing the good news and often implies preaching or proclaiming it in words.

Another Greek word is *martus* (μαρτυς), meaning a witness: eye or ear witness. Initially used in the legal context, the word *martus* is frequently used in the Bible as well. When Jesus promises his disciples that they will be filled by the Holy Spirit he says, 'But you will receive power when the Holy Spirit has come upon you; and you will be my *witnesses* in Jerusalem, in all Judea and Samaria, and to the ends of the earth' (Acts 1.8, emphasis added). This word is used many times in the book of Acts, in the context of bearing witness to Jesus; a greater emphasis is given to his resurrection. In return, this bears more fruit of conversion by the hearers. Even though the meanings are different, 'evangelism' and 'witnessing' are often used as synonyms.

I would suggest that witnessing to the risen Christ, that very experience of encountering him, is very much in the heart of the apostolic testimony. Through this encounter they were able to reinterpret the life, the death, and the resurrection of Christ in retrospect. While the terms 'evangelism' and 'witnessing' are often used synonymously in modern Christianity, their meanings are not the same. It seems that bearing witness conveys a broader meaning, a rather more holistic approach, while evangelism is a subset. In other words, bearing witness is a task of making Christ visible and tangible in the world. As Christians, part of our vocation is to bear witness to Christ and his redeeming work. This vocation is unfolded in the life and experience of the Christian community as Christians follow this unique call of God. By so doing, we make Christ known through the life and testimony of this community—church—and show the world the ultimate hope and reign of God. This definition describes witnessing as a lifelong vocation expressed and unfolded in a variety of ways. Evangelism on the other hand would be telling the story of Jesus (good news) and extending an invitation to the hearers to respond to it.

So, then, what does witnessing entail? What are some cultural and contextual issues that one should keep in mind with regard to bearing witness today? Evidently, modern-day Christians are not living in the apostolic age, and their experience with Christ is not the same as that of those who have seen the risen Christ. So how is it relevant to bear witness to Christ today? In this chapter, I would like to share some of my reflections on these questions based on my ministry experience, observations, and theological formation. The scope of this study therefore will be largely based on the experiences of the emerging Turkish church. As I tackle these questions below, I aim to draw out some principles, which may be applicable in other contexts as well.

Key characteristics of witnessing to Christ

In the apostolic tradition, the climax of Christian witnessing focuses on the personal experience with the risen Christ. The book of Acts provides ample examples whereby apostolic proclamation is shaped in the light of the resurrection (Acts 2.14-39; 3.12-26; 4.8-12; 5.30–32; 10.34-43). The experiences with the risen Christ have given the Apostles a new understanding as well as courage, wisdom, and favour to proclaim the good news. This experience becomes an essential part of early Christian witnessing, so much so that when they feel they need to appoint another member for Judas's place, for example, their primary criterion is that the new Apostle will be someone who has been with Jesus during his earthly ministry and witnessed his resurrection (Acts 1.21-22). Later, we see the same pattern of witnessing in St Paul's words. He draws deliberate attention to the apostolic testimony to Christ's resurrection in his first letter to the Corinthians. He provides the readers (listeners) with a list of people who witnessed to Jesus' resurrection, which starts with Cephas (St Peter) and continues with the twelve, five hundred brethren, St James, and St Paul himself (1 Cor 15.5-8).

Like Christians, the Holy Spirit also bears witness to Christ. John the Baptist says: 'I saw the Spirit descending from heaven like a dove, and it remained on him. I myself did not know him, but the one who sent me to baptize with water said to me, "He on whom you see the Spirit descend and remain is the one who baptizes with the Holy Spirit"' (Jn 1.32-33). Later, when Jesus assures his disciples about his departure, he promises the Holy Spirit, who will testify to him. He says, 'When the Advocate comes, whom I will send to you from the Father, the Spirit of truth who comes from the Father, he will testify on my behalf' (Jn 15.26). St Paul, in his letter to the Romans, says, 'For you did not receive a spirit of slavery to fall back into fear, but you have received a spirit of adoption. When we cry, "Abba! Father!" it is that very Spirit bearing witness with our spirit that we are children of God' (Rom 8.15-16). Finally, the book of Revelation ends with an open invitation to those who hear the good news. Jesus himself says this: 'The Spirit and the bride say, "Come." And let everyone who hears say, "Come." And let everyone who is thirsty come. Let anyone who wishes take the water of life as a gift' (Rev 22.17).

This testimony always invites the hearers to respond in repentance and faith in Jesus Christ. When Peter preached on the day of Pentecost, the hearers responded saying, 'Brothers, what should we do?' Peter invited them to repentance (Acts 2.37-38). Therefore faith in Christ and his redeeming work is vital for repentance. Those who believe in the good news are to be baptized and join the community. As has been said, before Jesus ascended into heaven, he left this community of people who witnessed his resurrection. I would like to propose at least seven characteristics of a Christian community, which I believe are intrinsic to the church's vocation, identity, and witnessing in the world. In other words, these are some of the key signs of the church's witnessing to the risen Christ today: it has a claim to truth, it is incarnational, it is led by the Holy Spirit, it goes on a transformational journey, it proclaims the good news, it embraces the poor, and it faces suffering.

Firstly, the good news of Jesus Christ has been a truth claim which is inherently offensive to the hearers. Jesus said to Thomas, 'I am the way, and the truth, and the life. No one comes to the Father except through me' (Jn 14.6). The Apostles preached that 'there is salvation in no one else, for there is no other name under heaven given among mortals by which we must be saved' (Acts 4.12). Christians perceived Jesus as the saviour and Lord who brings salvation and reconciliation between God and people. Therefore an appropriate response to this message always involves faith in Jesus Christ. St Paul says, 'For by grace you have been saved through faith, and this is not your own doing; it is the gift of God—not the result of works, so that no one may boast' (Eph 2.8-9). It is important to note that this truth claim has always been perceived as offensive: then and now. We live in an age of relativity where many people tend to refuse any truth claims. This, naturally, makes the Gospel's claims even more offensive in the Western world. What is more, the Christian message clashes with Islam in places like Turkey, where there is historical competition between the two religions.

Secondly, similar to the life of Jesus Christ, the church is called to live incarnationally. This is formed and unfolded in two ways. On the one hand, the Gospel is transmitted through cultural and geographical contexts by finding a way that is relevant (contextual) while it maintains its substance. On the other hand, this means that the church often lives in a constantly fragile state. In fact, the history of the church demonstrates that the church is most effective in her witnessing to Christ when she is under pressure and persecution. This has been the case in the early times of Christian witnessing as well as today.

Thirdly, the church is faithful to her vocation only if she is following the lead of the Holy Spirit. As mentioned above, both the church and the Spirit are witnessing to Christ. It is important to understand the true nature of the relationship between the two. It is often said that It is not the church of God that has a mission in the world, but the God of mission that has a church in the world. Certainly, the mode of witnessing depicted in the book of Acts indicates that the Holy Spirit drives this relationship. There are ample examples of how God the Holy Spirit leads the Apostles and other Christians according to his purposes (Acts 9.1-18; 10.1-33; 16.6-10). The lesson to be learned is that the church has to be in constant discernment of what the Spirit is saying today in order to be faithful to her vocation and witnessing. Prayer of course is one important means of communication in this process of discernment.

Fourthly, faith in Jesus Christ and the Christian journey involve a journey of transformation where both individuals and communities are transformed into the likeness of Christ. One can trace this from the beginning of Jesus' call of his disciples: those who have left their nets and boats are transformed in and throughout their journey of following Christ. There are many others who encounter Jesus during his earthly ministry, and their lives are changed. St Paul uses various analogies, such as the 'renewal of the mind' and the act of 'clothing oneself with a new self'. He prays for those for whom he has laboured, saying that 'I am again in the pain of childbirth until Christ is formed in you' (Gal 4.19). The book of Acts provides us with a glimpse of the communal depiction of this transformation in the life of the early church. They were 'of one heart and soul, and no one claimed private ownership of any possessions, but everything they owned was held in common...There was not a needy person among them . . .' (Acts 4.32-34).

Fifthly, the proclamation of the good news always remained at the heart of the Christian witnessing. Jesus commissioned his disciples before his ascension saying, 'Go into all the world and *proclaim* the good news to the whole creation' (Mk 16.15, emphasis added; see also Mt 28.19). The Greek word for 'to proclaim' is *kerusso* (κηρυσσω), which means to preach, to proclaim, to be a herald, and to officiate as a herald. When they were threatened and forced not to speak about the good news of Jesus, they responded saying, 'Whether it is right in God's sight to listen to you rather than to God, you must judge; for we cannot keep from speaking about what we have seen and heard' (Acts 4.19-20). Later, St Paul exhorts his young friend Timothy to 'proclaim the message; be persistent whether the time is favourable or unfavourable . . .' (2 Tim 4.2).

Sixthly, bearing witness to Christ often involves embracing the poor, the marginalized, and the disadvantaged groups of people in a society. Thus, the good news is declared not only by words but also by deeds. This pattern is evident in the life and ministry of our Lord. He intentionally reached out to the marginalized, the poor, and the disadvantaged individuals. It is also apparent in the life and ministry of the early church. The Apostles acknowledge this need in the very early stages of their ministry when they appoint people to do the work of distribution of food to the widows (Acts 6). Later St Paul also reminds us of this call in his ministry when he says, 'They [the Apostles] asked only one thing, that we remember the poor, which was actually what I was eager to do (Gal 2.10).

It is important to mention that this testimony of the early Christians was often met with mixed reactions. There are many occasions where we see a 'confirmation' of the Holy Spirit as he provides signs and wonders and miracles, which in turns bear the fruit of conversion and repentance. There are also many occasions where obstacles, challenges, suffering, and persecution are faced. This brings us to the last point I would like to mention here: suffering. Suffering is an integral part of Christian witnessing. Christians who come from the Jewish background experienced this at the very early stage of Christianity. When Christianity spread out to the Gentile and Roman world, there were waves of persecution and suffering over some fundamental issues such as whether Caesar or Jesus was the king. Nearly all of the Apostles and many more Christians throughout the centuries have given their lives for the sake of the Gospel. In fact, the Greek word for 'witness' mentioned above (*martus*) and the word for 'martyr' come from the same root. In other words, to be a witness is to be a martyr. Martin Luther rightly observed 'suffering' as a mark of the church.

The Turkish experience: characteristics and challenges

The small church in Turkey continues to survive and bear witness to Christ amid numerous demographic, legal, and social challenges. Turkey, with its 99 per cent Muslim population, is a country that is often depicted as having a religiously homogeneous society. Non-Muslims make up only 1 per cent of the population. The number of Christians amounts to 150,000—approximately only 5,000 of whom are from an ethnically Turkish background—in a country of 80 million. Legal challenges create constant limitations and ambiguities that add to the continual vulnerability of the church. While Turkey has a secular constitution, which theoretically forces the separation of state and religion, the state is heavily involved in shaping and teaching Islamic religious dogma and teaching as well as providing Sunni Islamic religious services. In contrast to many Middle Eastern countries, conversion from Islam to other religions is not prohibited; however, social challenges for converts remain. As far as Turkish Christians are concerned, the lack of legal status for churches as places of worship, the inability to establish theological schools that can provides formal degrees, and accusations of missionary activities—a term carrying immense historical baggage—are only some of the challenges. These contextual circumstances, naturally, make the Christian witness much harder at times.

The systematic disinformation about Christianity and its fundamental doctrines constitutes an important obstacle for the Gospel. The Islamic tradition and its public teaching in state schools and via other means have been extremely successful in instilling the idea that the Bible has been changed, that Jesus has not died and risen, and that he is not the Son of God. This teaching has been so deeply rooted in Turkish society that without any significant enquiry, average persons would consider the current teaching and practices of Christians to be false. These notions are engrained into the individuals over time through school education, accounts from family members, teachings of religious organizations, and even the narratives in the media. Contemplating the huge task of the church, to reach 80 million with the good news with its small size and limited resources, and engaging in a constant struggle against the effective systematic disinformation, it seems overwhelming.

On the basis of my personal experience as well as my observation of the experiences of my fellow Christian brothers and sisters in Turkey, the most difficult challenge faced by new Turkish Christians is that of identity. I came to faith in Christ at the age of twenty from a Sunni Islamic background. Although I was not a very devout Muslim, there were still some considerations and concerns about losing some of the 'privileges' of my immediate society. Christianity has always been perceived as the religion of the infidel in Turkey. Historically speaking, most 'Christian nations' have been viewed as hostile by Turkish people. For these reasons becoming a Christian was certainly not the most popular decision at that time, nor is it today. An 'ideal' Turkish citizen always needs to be a Sunni Muslim. When a Turkish person becomes a Christian, it means that they will lose their most immediate group of support. That is the family and friends, from which one's identity comes. Since, to date, a semi-tribal culture permeates most part of Turkey, one's communal identity always precedes one's 'individual' identity. Therefore the decision to become a Christian leads the person to a very fragile place in society. The new Christian loses their immediate sphere of support and orientation. This certainly has been my experience as a young Christian, and also the experience of many other Turkish Christians at that time and even today. The experience is even harder for women and for people who live in small villages or cities.

It is also important to note here that the kind of Christianity I was introduced to was a very individualistic version of Western Christianity where there was very little emphasis on the church as Christian community. This may be explained by the lack of an immediate model of ecclesiology known and embraced by Turkish Christians in the early years. This 'dim' understanding of the church has left many early Turkish Christians in a place of disorientation in their journey of faith. They have not had the opportunity to experience the church as a place to reorient their new identity as Christians. I argue that there were at least two reasons behind this. Firstly, the early Turkish church was never equipped to undertake this task of being a new home for reorienting one's identity in any form. While Christianity was not new in Turkish soil, it was very new for ethnically Turkish people who came to faith from Islam. In fact, we cannot really speak of a Turkish church until the late 1980s, when early fellowships, consisting only of a handful of new believers, sprang up in large cities like Istanbul, Ankara, and Izmir. Also, as mentioned above, these churches have come into being via evangelical and Western missionary work, and there has been very little interaction, if any, with the existing ethnic churches such as the Armenian Apostolic, Greek Orthodox, or Roman Catholic Church. So in many ways, early Turkish Christians have found themselves in a place of isolation where they had to discover what it means to be a church by experience. I would also suggest that since the primary influences in the early stage were diverse Western mission agencies, all of which are essentially para-churches, they, too, were inadequate in providing a proper and sustainable ecclesiology for the emerging Turkish church. In addition, since the primary emphases have been on personal salvation and having a personal relationship with Jesus, there was less emphasis on communal life of the church in the early years. All of these factors cumulatively contributed to the difficulties of finding, nurturing, and being grounded in a new Christian identity when one had cut off fundamental ties with the identity and identity-linked groups as a result of becoming a Christian.

Along with the identity and ecclesiological challenges, it is important to take into account the historical challenges and the clash with Islam. The land of Turkey, while once a very important centre for Christianity, has been occupied by mainly Muslim Turkish people for over a millennium. This land has always been a place of tension between these two religions, both of which seek more adherents. Since the purpose of this chapter is not to depict the historical challenges that were faced by Christians who lived in this land in the past, I am not going to go into more detail on this subject. Nevertheless, I would like to note that there is always historical baggage, including the negative experiences and attitudes linked to the Crusades, in many people's minds when it comes to Christianity.

Now, in light of this brief depiction of the context, let us turn to an evaluation of the nature of the experiences of the Turkish church in relation to the key characteristics of witnessing. The vulnerability of the Christian community in Turkey, attributable to its small size, the negative perceptions of the general population about Christians, and the legal limitations, as well as the immense disinformation machinery at work against the teachings of Christianity, has led the Turkish church to rely on the Holy Spirit and individual Christians to depend on the important functions of 'being a church' as a place where one finds support and where one's new identity is formed. Suffering has also been a mark of the Turkish church. Research indicates that Christians are not tolerated, that they are often targeted with abuse in the media, and that their places of worship are subject to attacks. A relatively recent incident, the brutal killings of three Christians in the city of Malatya, in south-eastern Turkey, has had the effect of impressing on the small group of Turkish Christians that being killed because of one's faith is a real possibility in this day and age. Since becoming a Christian is very costly, the suffering element also plays a selection role; only those who truly seek and feel they have found the truth continue on the journey of being a Christian.

Christianity's claim to the truth, that Jesus is the way, truth, and life, meets disinformation about Christianity head on. While younger generations in Turkey tend to be drawn by deism, the majority of the population is dogmatic. One could argue that the unbending general culture about claims to truth makes it easier for the Turkish church also to proclaim that the Gospel is the truth. The broad culture aids in creating an environment of a competition of claims of truth as opposed to many different truths being equally valid. Hence, in contrast to the contemporary Western culture dominated by a disdain of any absolute truth claim, the Turkish context may be more conducive to a competition of claims of truth, in spite of the unequal conditions.

That the life of faith is a journey and one progressively matures in this journey is also reflected in the young life of the Turkish church. This progressive maturity is perhaps most evident in the unity of the churches, their leadership development, and the outreach to those in need. One of the greatest tests of reaching out to the poor and marginalized, which is also one of the signs of effective witnessing, was the massive earthquake of 1999, which killed thousands of people. The Turkish churches acted in coordination and swiftly mobilized their people to assist the survivors of the earthquake in their camps. This has become the pattern of outreach and cooperation, and it has been repeated during other times of crises and more recently during the influx of Syrian refugees as a result of the civil war in Syria.

Despite efforts to counter disinformation about Christianity through online material, literature, and other media resources that provide the possibility of reaching out to millions, the most effective means of witnessing that has led to conversions has been incarnational witnessing. The latter, often and popularly referred to as friendship evangelism, has brought many to church and has resulted in many remaining in the church.

Conclusion

In conclusion, the growth of the Turkish church from a handful Christians in the early 1980s to approximately 5,000 in 2018 is attributable to numerous and diverse factors, without a doubt. When all these characteristics are in place, an environment that is conducive for effective witnessing is created. Witnessing is truly a process, and one element of effective witnessing is not sufficient in isolation. The Holy Spirit is the sovereign and works with and amid our challenges to fulfil his purposes. The Turkish church continues in its journey of faith, and one can only hope for better days for this beloved land and people.

Response

VICTOR LEE AUSTIN (UNITED STATES)

Yildirim's chapter is important for Christians throughout the world because it arises from a distinctive context with a long and complicated history: an ancient land that was a centre of world Christianity, where today Christians number but a fraction of a fraction of 1 per cent—and most of those Christians, he tells us, are not ethnically Turkish. To witness and evangelize faithfully in Turkey today presents an almost unique problem. This chapter raises a rich variety of questions—and therein is its importance; to address all the questions it raises would require a book-length history of Turkish Christianity (and more)! I will confine myself to three questions, one for each part of the chapter.

Firstly, doubtless the largely hostile Turkish context drives Yildirim's distinction between evangelism and witness. He does not say so explicitly, but many heirs of liberal strands of Western theology are, I think it is fair to say, a bit too comfortable with witness that shuns the articulation of the good news. I have had people quote to me, with self-satisfaction, the line that goes something like 'Witness to God and, if necessary, use words.' One fears that they are not accustomed to using words ever. This dead-end Yildirim's first part will not allow us to take. He will distinguish between witness and evangelism, but he will not let them be divorced—which can lead, of course, to existential difficulties (to say the least) when one speaks of the good news in a place like Turkey.

But should we speak of the evangel and witness without speaking also, in fundamental biblical terms, of mission? Mission, etymologically, concerns the propulsion of being sent. So while in Christian consciousness we begin with the announcement of Jesus, quickly we find it necessary to reflect on how the incarnate Son sent into the world for our salvation opens up into the eternal mission of the Son from the Father. This is not to de-centre Jesus or Christology but to ask whether our understanding of mission is incomplete in so far as it is not explicitly Trinitarian. Built into any Trinitarian affirmation is that mission is of the essence of God's *being*; it is not only something God has done but did not have to do.

Secondly, Yildirim shows that, biblically speaking, the point of witness is a personal encounter with Jesus Christ, which is necessarily an individual encounter; and yet the witness that leads to that encounter is ecclesial, that is, communal. His seven or so characteristics of witness provide a balanced missional ecclesiology (although, as noted above, I would root all talk of mission in the self-sending being of the triune God).

Particularly of importance to comfortable Christians in, for example, the United States is the note of suffering. Here I wonder: do we need a more political understanding of the good news? That is to say: should we articulate more robustly the authority that Christ has and how that authority in fact relates to and rules over earthly political authority? For the evangel includes the message that Christ the king has come and is drawing his people to himself. 'Everyone who belongs to the truth listens to my voice', Jesus says to Pilate: an invitation to acknowledge the kingship that Jesus has (Jn 18.37). In this context Oliver O'Donovan's account of Christian political theology is illuminating. As Yildirim says, sometimes the evangel is received with joy, and at other times it is resisted and opposed. This can be put in political terms: sometimes people accept Jesus as their Lord and become citizens of his kingdom; at other times they rise up in revolt and oppose him. There is no middle ground. And thus, O'Donovan says (drawing out the implications for the church), she, the church, will be a suffering community, and the sign of that is the Eucharist.[1]

Thirdly, the para-church, individualistic, missionary Christianity that first reached Yildirim, as he rightly shows, is not sufficient for the maintenance of Christian identity: one needs community, strong community, in order to withstand the myriad ways of a hostile culture. I particularly commend the need for clear Christian thinking, intelligently presented, as a piece of a witnessing strategy. One avenue of introduction to Christ is to show how what is widely assumed to be true about him (in this hostile culture) is not what Christians actually believe. (Let the comfortable Western reader understand!) But such truths must be lived out as well, as Yildirim instances following an earthquake, and importantly in the formation of friendships. The first 'moment' of the church for O'Donovan (it comes before suffering) is that she is a gathering community.

In the twentieth century, Turkey went through a secular period, but under its current leader, the country has de facto (if not *de jure*) become Muslim, as Yildirim helps us see. Yet whether it is Islamic or secular, we are speaking here of a land that once was profoundly shaped by Christianity, a principal jewel of the Christian world, home indeed to some of the greatest scholars of the early church. The eclipse of those past glories puts one in mind of the biblical history in the books of Kings, as it raises questions of divine providence.[2] I also get the impression from Yildirim that the non-ethnically Turkish Christians who remain—a remnant of but two-tenths of 1 per cent of the whole population, which is yet some thirty times larger than the ethnically Turkish Christians—are impotent. I was glad to learn in our discussions of increasing Christian solidarity between these groups. I was also left wondering: could Christianity in the United States, or even more so in Texas, become so eclipsed that most people were left ignorant of Gospel claims, and Christianity all but vanished?

Such questions are far beyond the scope of Yildirim's chapter, yet it is part of its virtue that it raises them for our reflection.

Notes

1 See Oliver O'Donovan, *The Desire of the Nations: Rediscovering the Roots of Political Theology* (Cambridge, UK: Cambridge University Press, 1996), particularly chapters 4 and 5. Indeed, the ecclesiology of chapter 5 could be mined for much insight by theologians under oppressive regimes.

2 In this regard one thinks of the work of Ephraim Radner.

Section 4

LATIN AMERICAN AND CARIBBEAN PERSPECTIVES

9

Church witness and evangelism and the politics of identity: entitlement and exclusion

JOANILDO BURITY (BRAZIL)

Since the late 1960s, Latin American theology has offered a contribution to contemporary understandings of mission which stresses the inseparable connection between the content of the Gospel message and the socio-historical conditions in which it is heard and responded to. Not always indigenous,[1] this reflection, however, has left an indelible mark on the way Latin American Christians have reassessed God's mission in the region. Its political proclivities were, over time, reinterpreted and extended to other areas of human interaction, leading to a more acute awareness among church leaders and Christian activists of the 'social dimension' of the Gospel, the 'integral' or holistic nature of the church's mission, and the preferential option for the poor and the vulnerable when missiological decisions need to be made in concrete contexts of violence, poverty, and oppression.

Despite fierce opposition from conservative Catholics and Protestants, the reception—under various guises—of these mission theologies took root in most Christian churches, including the major group among Protestants in the whole region, Pentecostals. No serious articulation of mission strategies and thinking has, since the mid-1980s, been able to ignore or sidetrack a summons to integrate 'preaching' and 'serving' to produce a public impact on social life, in addition to calls for personal commitment or response to the Christian message (see Freston 2015; Álvarez 2016, 2017; Salinas 2017).

But this whole process, not accidentally, interwove mission thinking, mission strategies, and social trends. How could it be otherwise? If the Gospel must always be heard and practised in a concrete setting, respond to concrete questions, and produce concrete transformations, there is no possibility of its articulation (in preaching, ecclesial life, and witness to the world) remaining untouched by the challenges faced by both Christians and non-Christians in their concrete situations. This means that the 'solutions' found to the issues and questions churches have had to tackle or respond to will not remain the same over time, because the latter change as a result of social dynamics in which resistance to accept them as legitimate, struggles for their recognition in society at large, and theological attempts to describe and address them alter the very circumstances in which those issues are identified and acted upon.[2]

One of the more recent trends that has had a huge socio-political and theological impact has to do with the *increasing recognition of diversity, plurality or difference*, through which societies and churches are challenged to acknowledge: (a) the *multiple constituencies* which make them up; (b) the *asymmetrical relations* involving these varied constituencies; and (c) the *historical processes of invisibilization, victimization, and exclusion* that have rendered some of these constituencies illegitimate, ignored, or targets of active prejudice or discrimination over long periods of time. As a result of processes starting in the struggles of the 1960s for civil rights, women's rights, black and indigenous peoples' rights, and sexual and reproductive rights, a whole range of demands have been raised to the state and organized civil society, particularly in the West (North and South), and such movements entered the agenda of the churches. *Culture* and *identity* became badges for a wide array of movements and demands that have shaken the ground of traditional views held by national societies and states, by bringing to the fore questions of *justice*, *entitlement*, and *exclusion*. Theologies focusing on such underplayed dimensions have emerged and raised highly contentious issues for Christian churches, too (see Vuola 2002; Cleary and Steigenga 2004; Tamez 2006; Bohache 2008; Memoria Indígena Declaration 2015; Ngong 2017; González Nieves 2017; Roussel 2018).[3]

The last few years have seen, as the debate has evolved and a number of achievements have taken place and empowered *minority groups* globally and locally, signs of a counter-tendency. A reaction against the extension of social, cultural, and political rights to ethnic, gender, sexual, religious, and cultural minorities has spread, leaving a strong impression of a backlash, mobilizing conservative groups in defence of traditional values, exclusive claims to representing national identity, and outright fascist claims to purge the social body of the hyper-diversity that has ensued over the past five decades of struggles for justice worldwide. This trend has also found its Christian counterparts, setting off a mounting wave of disputes over truth, and pastoral and humanitarian responses to the justice claims involved.

This chapter seeks to explore a few missional implications of and challenges for Latin American Anglican churches in relation to the developments and intimations of the process briefly introduced above, with emphasis on Brazil. Starting with some sociological traits of the recent context, I will then explore how the growing awareness of culture and identity has impacted church life and debates about the church's mission. Finally, I will ponder a few aspects of the current challenges that the conservative reactions against identity politics have brought to the fore and what may be lying ahead for Latin American Anglican thinking and practice on evangelism and witness in such regards. Throughout, I have tried to keep company with Latin American theologians, missiologists, and social scientists, as I am also convinced that there is a urgent decolonial task to carry out in this area and that it is time to hear voices that have been largely ignored in North Atlantic debates. I do not think it is a question of better, deeper, and broader thinking, but one of justice, so listening to these voices is less a search for originality or erudition than an exercise in listening to the other from their own perspective in a dialogue that desperately needs a levelling ground—and also in mission thinking and practice. Dialogue can be rough and disconcerting, and I think that this is what is happening at the moment, for good reasons. If we persist in dialogue, a common mind and a mutual acceptance of what cannot be held in common will both emerge as we take seriously the Pauline call to bear one another's burdens and the Johannine call to love one another (beyond our differences) as a direct expression of Jesus' own love.

I am deeply aware of the limits of my argument if it is seen as a theological one. It is admittedly only indirectly theological, in far as it is about theology and draws from a number of theological sources. However, my voice is, here, basically placed between social theory, socio-political analysis, theology, and personal commitment. I hope this will spark a helpful conversation at the frontier, rather than put people off. As I stated above, dialogue can be disconcerting. But it can be rewarding for those willing to cross boundaries, even if only for a while.

Evangelism in the age of identity politics

Globalization has ushered in the intensification of awareness of the other—both their existence and their demands. It has also led to a growing sense of threat posed by others near and far. If the process favours flows of people and representations of otherness across virtually every national context in the world, its amplification has also brought in uncertainties and losses to local groups or less powerful nations that spurred real and imagined senses of trespassing, subordination, and vulnerability among such groups.[4] Awareness of the other has required both acknowledgement of differences within and willingness to make arrangements that expressed hospitality and (mutual) respect. This has problematized conventional views of what are the proper, legitimate, and non-negotiable elements of national or local identity, pluralizing it and raising political implications, such as, for instance, how to grant representation and voice to the newly acknowledged differences.

In Latin America these trends have prompted a much needed recognition of the colonial and slave-owning past—and the enormous debt towards indigenous people and African descendants—as well as vicious forms of subordination of and violence against women. Social and cultural policies of recognition and legal changes enforcing them have spread regionally to an unprecedented level, deeply impacting constitutional arrangements in Bolivia and Ecuador, and policy-making in Brazil, Chile, Colombia, Peru, and Argentina, to name a few examples.[5] Assumptions about cultural homogeneity or naturalized views on gender and sexual identities have come under attack from vocal social activists.

In the context of faith identities, Latin American societies were historically marked by the weight of Catholicism and the Catholic Church's privileged status vis-à-vis religious and social minorities. Long-standing forms of assimilationism and syncretism defined prevailing politics of culture and faith, leaving space for condescending or hierarchical forms of inclusion, though it also allowed for resistance and religious belonging from below (see Parker 2002, 2016; Sanchis, 2001; Brandão 2006; Peterson and Vásquez 2008; Leavitt-Alcántara 2008; Steil and Toniol 2013). This particularly impacted African American and Amerindian religious forms, which came under the protection and control of the church, while Protestant churches by and large demonized the former and refused the Catholic syncretic model. Since the mid-1980s, intensified global flows have allowed for local initiatives to break the Catholic quasi-monopoly in the religious landscape of the region, but also to spread faith expressions influenced by neoliberal ideology (so-called neo-Pentecostalism being a prime example, with its blend of entrepreneurial spirituality and increasing adoption of neoliberal views on social and economic issues). In several countries, the past few decades have also witnessed a self-driven process of transnationalization of Pentecostal and charismatic missions and a complex renegotiation of ecumenical relations among Latin

American and North Atlantic partners (see Burity 2016a, 2016b; Medina and Alfaro 2015; Oro and Alves 2015; Freston 2007, 2008).

The recent rise of identity politics has shown a two-way trend cutting across faith dynamics: (a) the achievement of legal and policy recognition, as well as increased cultural acceptance of claims to justice and respect, by ethnic, gender, sexual, and regional or local cultural identities; and (b) the growing pluralization of religious alternatives, including a steady loss of members by the Catholic Church in contrast with the growth of hugely influential Pentecostalism and with de-syncretized African American religions. The cross-currents of these trends have created momentum for (a) the emergence of an identity-centred agenda and related social movements and Christian-based social activism engaging those from within, and (b) the emergence of new religious minority actors among Christian and non-Christian religious groups, arousing heated debates, as religious pluralization has actually empowered conservative Christianity—both Pentecostal and evangelical—rather than traditional historically Protestant churches.

Whereas the latter have become more porous to the calls for recognition—opening up access to church attendance, membership, and lay and ordained ministry and leadership by black and indigenous persons, women, gays, and lesbians—the most dynamic sectors of Pentecostal and evangelical churches have frontally rejected such openings, engaging in sustained initiatives to resist or even reverse legal and policy changes favouring those minorities and promoting a veritable cultural war through preaching, political representation, and (new) media propaganda. Many such initiatives have gathered support from Catholic circles, forming conservative Christian alliances. The recent return of neoliberal politics with a vengeance against left and centre-left governments across Latin America (and elsewhere, of course) has roused even further the conflicts around minority rights by covering them with right-wing ideological overtones. Some sort of belated 'new Christian right' has emerged in Latin American Christianity since the mid-2000s as a direct consequence of the new political and cultural climate of rights affirmation, distributive policies, and cultural pluralization. Although conservatism has always been predominant within Christian churches, it has now reached a qualitatively distinct level of articulation, funding, and propagation.

The period since the late 1970s has witnessed major changes among Christians at every corner. Liberation theology challenged social and political conformism in arguing that the call for conversion and faithfulness to the Gospel is inseparable from conversion to social and environmental justice. Evangelical holistic mission, though initially portraying itself as an alternative to liberation theology, moved steadily closer to it during the 1990s, creating a visible tension with the emerging Pentecostal churches (which basically opposed the proclamation of the Gospel to any other task). However, by the early 2000s, a general accommodation as to the legitimacy of social service as part of most churches' understanding of mission had been reached.

The new development, nevertheless, has been the emergence of a concerted, Pentecostal-led reaction to identity politics that ironically exhibits all the features of the movement it resists. Using all the resources also available to minority rights movements (from legislation to repertoires of action and argumentation), *conservative identity politics* has developed a media-based *cultural war* against anti-racist policies (clumsily confused with acceptance of Afro-Brazilian religions), women's rights (considered to violate traditional gender roles, although women have found remarkable opportunities for recognition, including ordained ministry, in charismatic and Pentecostal churches), social equality policies (deemed to stimulate dependence on state grants and to hamper entrepreneurship), and gay rights (equated with an assault on traditional family values). Political power has been harnessed as a means to halt or reverse such developments, leading to coalitions that have led to the delegitimization or dismantling of several achievements of excluded groups, within a clear strategy to undo those changes, accompanied by inflammatory language against minorities—including their representation in churches. An argument about the common Christian background of Brazilian society, which is a classical Roman Catholic one, has become a moot point for the convergence of conservative Christians and even secular conservatives.[6]

Alongside these trends, a powerful *aggiornamento* has impacted traditional evangelistic practices: styles of preaching, music, church buildings, Christian education, social provision coupled with explicit or implicit forms of ecumenical work, and public engagement as part of an apologetic strategy. A third strand of theological discourse has taken root, in tension with liberationist and holistic ones, spreading the prosperity gospel beyond neo-Pentecostal churches and towards most other denominations. Such influence has produced a mixed message about conversion: pulling oneself up by the bootstraps both spiritually and materially, embracing entrepreneurialism in spirituality and work behaviour, engaging in spiritual warfare, and fighting head-on public discourses and practices that are considered anti-Christian.

The Pentecostalization of Christianity increases the militant aspect of identity politics as much as the new demands for recognition of women and gay and lesbian members and clergy, anti-racism, and indigenous culture and cosmology. It also promotes limited forms of de-institutionalization and a 'new ecumenism' of conservative Christianity, lowering denominational and doctrinal barriers through increased convergence in spirituality styles and political conservatism, as well as circulation of people among different but like-minded churches. There is a lot of innovation in evangelism, public witness, and organizational management techniques, together with a general trend towards more vertical forms of authority and subordinated participation: people tend to be recruited to do things rather than having the power to make decisions in church; these are increasingly the preserve of an elite of bishops, apostles, pastors, and professional lay managers.

But the process has also set apart church sectors which have responded affirmatively to the calls for justice and acceptance from minority groups in all churches, inspired by liberation theology, integral mission, and other recent brands of minority theology. Those view Pentecostalized churches as largely indifferent to injustice (particularly through prosperity theology), individualistic, intolerant of religious diversity (there have indeed been many incidents of profanation and physical assaults against Afro-Brazilian religions and Roman Catholic worship places and followers), and politically prone to corruption. In turn, they are charged with failure to reach out to ordinary people because of spiritual infidelity or lack of appeal to the latter's mores.

On the other hand, socially engaged Christians have become very influential among Christian non-governmental organizations and groups organized around the promotion of rights, environmental concerns, or social provision to the poor. Their organizations are accepted within secular civil society as truly committed to human rights and to social and environmental justice. They increasingly develop a 'public theology' approach that seeks to carve a space for progressive Christians in the overall public arena of political debate and cultural pluralism as a form of witness to their understanding of the implications of being followers of Jesus (Sinner 2012; Jacobsen, Sinner, and Zwetsch 2012; Caldas 2016; Sinner and Panotto 2016). The relational dynamic that has pushed conservative Christianity into identity politics has also led to a deep rethinking among historic denominations— and fringes of the Pentecostal-evangelical world—of what it means to do mission under the present circumstances.

Joanildo Burity

Pluralism and the call to conversion in an age of entitlement and resentment

I argue that the challenges of pluralism (recognition of difference and diversity) and justice (addressing inequality, discrimination, and violence) are the most important issues for church mission today in Latin America, as they call for a thorough reassessment of what conversion, church membership, ethical commitment, and Christian societal influence imply. It cannot be assumed that a linear march towards increasing complexity and a voice for underprivileged people is beyond reversal. It cannot be assumed that the debates and engagement that led to politicized theological views and practices consolidated holistic mission or liberation discourses beyond questioning. It cannot be assumed that more opportunities for Christian witness necessarily result in wider social influence, locally or globally. And despite rampant individualistic trends, coming to Christ cannot be severed from the conditioning force of these questions on people.

Pluralism is a space which merely allows for difference to emerge and calls for some degree of reciprocity and forbearance from participants, within a combination of cultural and institutional frameworks. But it also intensifies the challenges of *proximity*—how to live together with such different others? What to do when the other does not simply wish to be left alone, but intends to engage, to debate, to have a say?—and the question of *identity*—how to keep one's identity unaltered and unharmed by the interaction with the other? To what extent does every advance in acceptance of one's views and practices imply deeper involvement with others, negotiations, and self-reform?

Many have taken pluralism to imply an absence of friction, of attempts to change others' identities. Liberals stick to a live-and-let-live approach that does not encourage engagement other than to affirm the other as different; engagement leads to indifference or exoticism. Conservatives stick to a notion of threatened age-old identities that has ultimately the same result: the other is affirmed as different and unacceptable; engagement becomes confrontational. To be sure, in situations, particularly in democratic societies, in which there are legal protections for different forms of life, whether communally or individually experienced, liberals and conservatives can learn to tolerate others—sometimes agreeing on tradition and cultural conformity, especially in the face of ethnic and religious difference.

However, acceptance of pluralism, when associated with notions of justice and entitlement (from both 'granting' and 'receiving' sides), does not leave things untouched. What does conversion mean when there are assumptions that different identities each have an intrinsic integrity that should protect them from 'trespasses' or 'intolerance'? What does it mean to be (or become) a Christian in a pluralistic setting? What does it mean to share a faith when identity becomes entrenched and non-negotiable but simultaneously incapable of encompassing all the loyalties and values that people adhere to?

Many features of current experiences of identity pull people apart in various directions, both individually and collectively, as much as they bring them together, and the idea of a common faith becomes fragmented along other lines. So pluralism is good and bad, and it calls for both discernment and action if we wish to retain and promote the good. Firstly, *we need to come to terms with the relational dynamics of processes of pluralization.* Affirmation of identity—including a Christian identity—impacts other identities and responds to them, appealing sometimes to the same people (who must decide whether to learn to cope with multiple identifications or to choose and withdraw from particular ones) or claiming shared spaces and allegiances as exclusive. In these contexts, pluralism involves friction, disagreement, dispute. Freedom and difference go together. And so do relentless efforts to protect certain identities through engagement with others—both forging instrumental or substantive alliances and confronting others whose different values, beliefs, and practices are deemed to be antithetical to one's own. There is a connecting line in current forms of social conflict surrounding nationalism, linguistic difference, religious competition, and attachments to place and cultural forms that renders identity politics highly ambiguous—expressing both claims to justice and, at the same time, resentful reactions to the widening of the scope and content of those forms of identity, through the activation of fear, prejudice, discrimination, and indifference.

Secondly, *pluralism produces differentiation, which creates opportunities for personal and collective religious change.* In Latin America, pluralization has accelerated de-Catholicization, with members mostly bifurcating between Pentecostal or evangelical and no-religion alternatives, although virtually all non-Catholic faiths have grown. So religious diversity and internal differentiation have resulted. The Catholic Church also experienced a difficult accommodation of a massive charismatic movement which significantly reduced the influence of liberation theology, under direct and firm action from the Vatican (throughout John Paul II's and Benedict XVI's papacies), but is now recovering some balance between social engagement and personal spirituality under Pope Francis, notwithstanding conservative resistance. The impact of a vocal Africanist black movement has led a number of highly important Afro-Brazilian Candomblé and Umbanda worship places (*terreiros*) to untie their links with Catholicism (de-syncretization) and find recognition through certain cultural policy actions (as mentioned above). In everyday life, in addition, a powerful transformation has also been unleashed, as even modest economic advancement has allowed for higher levels of consumption and openness to publicity of products, lifestyles, and consumerist values. Under the influence of neoliberal ideas, even citizen behaviour has strongly tilted towards a consumer approach based on 'service delivery' in exchange for votes and acquiescence. Cultural and moral changes, therefore, have been quite ambivalent, as millions of conversions to Pentecostal and evangelical churches and the turning-charismatic of millions of Catholics have happened simultaneously, but not at the same pace and to the same depth.

Thirdly, *pluralism confronts Christian churches with aspects of their own message that have become strained and mutually contested* as regards the connection between confession of faith and ethical behaviour. Love and justice appear to be at odds with the call to personal faith and morality, and for many Christians and preachers, piety does not translate into compassion for the suffering of others. Questions of poverty or illness are disputed by the conservative majority and regarded as a result of individual failure or demon possession, while the socially engaged minority stresses socio-historical causes. Sexuality continues to trouble many within churches, given the sinful overtones often emphasized by preachers and teachers, whereas socially engaged groups seek to support the important civil legislation changes that began to emerge with new provisions on marriage, reproductive rights, protection of women and children, and gay rights.

Although some of these changes have been uncontroversial across the board (anti-poverty, anti-racism, or child protection policies), some aspects have been met with uneasiness because of their impact on class relations (raising poor and black people out of poverty, equal access to education and decent work) or on traditional gender relations (full legal equality for women), while others, such as gay rights, have sparked deep and heated controversy because of their impact on church life – membership, participation, ministry, and leadership. Over the last few years, however, the return of neoliberal politics has further unsettled the connection between beliefs and behaviour, as its fierce opposition to the general trend that progressive governments have set off in the region (Brazil, Chile, Argentina,

Peru, Paraguay, and Colombia are cases in point, for distinct reasons) and has given voice to preachers and lay leaders who vocally oppose social and cultural policies favouring equality, in the name of fighting public overspending and making people responsible for their own fate. As a consequence, the message coming from such quarters pushes once again towards an individualistic kind of conversion that is oriented to self-gratification and indifference to the plight of the traditionally excluded or the new losers.

Anglicans in Latin America, identity politics, and mission: venturing a few propositions

South America is the site of three Anglican provinces—Brazil, South America, and the Episcopal Church—with different histories and outlooks (see Kater 2018). There are quite tenuous links between them as far as churches and their members are concerned. It is beyond my knowledge to present any consistent overall picture of their outlook regarding the issues discussed so far. A few things can be said, however. These are very small churches. With the exception of the Province of Brazil, they each span several countries. They all find it hard to even keep together and know one another because of the huge distances between parishes and dioceses. They have, however, been significant in the formation of a Reformed identity in the region and have always been relatively open to integrating proclamation and social concern, private and public witness, ecclesial identity, and ecumenical (and, to a lesser extent, interfaith) engagement. But the depth of their impact in local or national life varies hugely, according to their response to the course of pluralization both in their societies and in the Anglican Communion. They all have sought, in one way or another, to respond. And they all have been traversed by the social trends that I have described above. So in this last section I would like to venture a few propositions on the implications of this scenario for South American (and even more specifically, Brazilian) Anglicans.

The push-and-pull of identity disputes will continue, because despite its fragmenting, conflictive outcomes, *there are true unresolved questions of justice* that are part of the tensions—which means that some of the reactions against positive changes are on the side of former privileged groups having to make room for excluded ones. In this context the Gospel references to 'the little ones', 'little children', and 'the least of these', and the unambiguous affirmation of outcasts (lepers, the mentally ill, publicans, prostitutes, ethnic rivals), must once again be heard and heeded (see Mt 8.1–13; 10.42; 11.5–6, 25–27 18.2, 6, 10, 14; 21.31–32; 25.40, 45). They remind us, in our time, of the still huge portions of the population who are ignored, despised, or treated with fear and violence because of their poverty or certain identity traits that do not conform with the majority order. These people cannot find liberation in Christ if their response to the message of redemption will keep them separate, untouched, suffering, and facing discrimination just as before. They also remind us of true cultural differences between social classes, urban and rural communities, and national histories. Some of 'the little ones' are persons who suffer multiple forms of exclusion, as they embody in themselves economic, ethnic, gender, sexual, age, physical, or educational or intellectual differences. In any case, there are many 'little ones' who will have no hope outside of welcoming churches offering love and service not only out of grace and compassion, but also out of respect and for affirmation of their rights.

On the other hand, *South American Anglicans are currently being torn by a disconnect between different dimensions of God's mission.* Given Anglicanism's affirmative stance on plural forms of experience of the Christian faith, not only in relation to other families of churches but also internally, the delicate balance that their bonds of affection and interdependence require has become sorely impaired. Pentecostalization has become wrapped up in demands for keeping traditional gender and family relations untouched or barely revised in the face of enhanced equality and outright rejection of sexual difference. Conservative evangelicals, even when not impacted by charismatic emphases, follow suit. Ironically, liberal and conservative attitudes[7] towards unassimilable or unwanted differences converge here in producing multiple and successive splits within communities, which become less and less compatible, and less and less open to mutual dialogue and even to sharing communion. Loyalties and attitudes on such divisive issues have become—not for the first time in church history—fundamental points of disagreement and separation.

For those who have participated in inter-Anglican commissions, task forces, networks, or meetings of the Instruments of Communion, it is striking that so much is held in common in what Anglicans do when they share the Gospel story, worship, pray, serve local communities, and raise their voices for justice locally and globally. And yet conflicting views on and practices in relation to gender and sexual identity have become so paramount as to almost paralyze mission partnership domestically and among provinces, other than along like-minded lines. Unfortunately, there are far too many expressions of this inability to live up to Jesus' example within Christian churches, beginning with the New Testament ones themselves, although many lessons on generous love, forgiveness, hospitality, mutual support, justice-making, and peacemaking abound there, too. Passages such as John 4.1–24 and 8.1–11, Acts 6.1–7 and chapters 10 and 15, 1 Corinthians 1.10–14 and 3.1–23, and James 2.1–13 speak powerfully to the inner connections in how gender, sexual, ethnic, and theological differences both bring up tensions and express justice claims that can and must be answered in view of a united and differentiated body of Christ.[8]

However one assesses the mission achievements and strengths of the increasingly consolidated Anglican divide—ineptly dubbed Global North *versus* Global South—it seems clear that churches can be more or less successful in gathering members, provinces can spread or shrink at the behest of organizational techniques and local efforts, and there are many things happening mission-wise, with more or less consistency and numerical results. The toll of pluralization on such a situation is that (a) non-Anglicans react in various ways to our debates and divisions, and this can lead to a range of group alignments, too; (b) many people resent inflicted suffering when other people are turned down, looked with contempt, or harassed in their search to believe *and* belong; and (c) faithful Anglicans will be on virtually every side of disputes, making it very likely that passing judgement on others will incur unfairness or arrogance.

In any case, pluralization is not an alibi against faithfulness, integrity, and coherence. And that is what is at stake: if we freeze up our fault-lines, decide to walk apart, and behave like enemies or strangers, what kind of diversity, interdependence, and freedom will be embodied in our message to the world? The preaching of the same message by people who cannot live together is a capitulation to dogmatism, pride, and power-seeking. It is a Gospel divided. We are still and again retracing the steps of the church, repeating one of its worst historical lessons: splintering over particular issues and resorting to bigotry against dissenting others, and then having to acknowledge mistakes only centuries later, when it is too late for those who were denigrated and proscribed.

What pluralization can still teach us in such circumstances is: identity matters, but it is not self-referential and self-sufficient; actually, it is entirely relational and transient, historical. There is no single grasp on the whole truth, no guarantee that truth is warranted by the large numbers. On the other hand, because the Gospel is not an ideology, a blueprint, or a programme, we will always need to exercise discernment as to what its implications are for concrete situations. Identity politics is about people who have historically been made invisible, unworthy, and punishable for the wrong reasons, in most cases under religious or ideological sanction: they were cast out as sinful or impure, or because their unequal position was less important than economic inequality. The way we respond to them tells us as much about our own identity as Anglicans and as human beings.

So the Gospel is, indeed, about redeeming such 'little ones'. However, 'the little ones' are highly diverse in their needs, claims, and values.

South American Anglicans have found it hard to reconcile all these different aspects in their communities and decision-making structures. Although it is true that our provinces have reached across social and cultural differences and inequalities, they also tend to be most acceptable to the middle classes. Although it is true that in each there are dioceses where particular minorities are better represented than others in the church's missional strategies or constituencies, there is no one provincial mind on the full acceptance of such people in ecclesial life, including ordained ministry. If history teaches anything, it is that the conversation is likely to remain tense and contrived and that splits and competition will occur, but also that the struggles of 'the little ones'—embraced by Christ himself—for acceptance, dignified treatment, and full participation will continue to make inroads, sensitizing people across doctrinal battle-lines, bringing them to serve through words and deeds, and challenging the moral integrity of discourses of fidelity that thrive on conflict and hate.

I believe that we can learn from every side on questions of mission, provided that we are clear on the implications of the historical realities we are living in. This is where a reflection on mission inspired by Latin American liberation theology and holistic mission in dialogue with the myriad minority theologies of our time, energized by Pentecostal passion and flexibility and responsive to the challenges of pluralization and justice, can make a real difference in the world. Not a stubborn reaffirmation of tradition, as so many times before, but a reaffirmation of the Gospel as good news to people in need, despair, subjection, oppression, abandonment, loneliness. What would a radical evangelical, postliberal, liberationist, minoritarian Anglican missiology look like, one that responds positively to the challenges of Pentecostalization, de-institutionalization of religious affiliation, social and cultural pluralism, and the demands of identity politics? We are in the middle of things. So it is hard to see clearly. Let's not use this as an excuse for declining the challenge of moving forward together.

Response

ISABELLE HAMLEY (FRANCE AND UNITED KINGDOM)

Burity's stimulating and engaging chapter sharply analyses some of the key social and political tensions and questions around evangelism and mission today. While the chapter is clearly focused on South America, the questions he raises are echoed in many other societies across the globe. The rootedness of liberation theologies within the specific context makes the historical evolution of the tension between different forms and understandings of mission sharper, but we see similar trends towards an integration of proclamation and social transformation elsewhere, with the same hostile reactions from what is loosely known as 'the Christian right'. The chapter resonates with recurring questions from contemporary philosophy on identity and otherness, and with contemporary theological reflections on the nature of the human person. Burity's analysis of the problems we face today is crisp and incisive, but there are few solutions suggested. The chapter is brilliant sociologically, but does not drill into theological understandings of identity, faith, Gospel, kingdom, and the human person. Nor does it address the role of God as the ultimate other with an active interest in human affairs. Missiologically, it leaves us with the imperative to keep proclamation and social transformation closely linked, but does not necessarily offer us tools to think through how to do so in the face of multiple challenges. Exploring all this would, of course, be well beyond the scope of a short chapter. But I would like, in this response, to suggest directions for travel that may help explore answers to the question that Burity sharply leaves us with at the end of his chapter: 'What would a radical evangelical, postliberal, liberationist, minoritarian Anglican missiology look like, one that responds positively to the challenges of Pentecostalization, de-institutionalization of religious affiliation, social and cultural pluralism, and the demands of identity politics?'

I would suggest that interaction with the following areas would enhance reflection: biblical and theological anthropology; theology of the kingdom of God; contemporary philosophies of identity and otherness; and, finally, the intrinsic relationship of Christian faith, and therefore evangelism and mission, with questions of identity. Let us very briefly look at all these in turn, bearing in mind that I will only sketch out areas for further reflection and discussion.

Biblical and theological anthropology

What does it mean to be human, and how we can work with the reality, rather than the ideal, of what it means to be human? Here, I am thinking of working with finitude, with the constant tension between immanence and transcendence, with the need to belong, with the reality of sin. Anthropology can help illuminate what is threatening about change and how to approach it. A solid theological anthropology can also help ground the nature of conversion within what it means to be human, and the relationship between faith and social identity. The tensions mentioned in the chapter are very contemporary in the way in which they appear, yet they are in many ways already in the biblical corpus, and they are dealt with creatively as culture and society evolve over the course of the story.

Theology of the kingdom

It strikes me that the core question at stake is, what is the Gospel? Different understandings of the Gospel yield different approaches to evangelism and mission, often with little awareness of how what is considered the 'Gospel' is actually anchored within cultural and social positioning. This often results in the illusion of a 'pure' Gospel that could somehow be lifted out of the pages of Scripture, or the Christ event, and somehow barely recontextualized for contemporary consumption. Of course, this is an illusion, though a powerful one. Yet an equal and opposite danger would be to argue that there is no substance to the Gospel, only form. It seems to me that a grounded theology of the kingdom of God would help resolve some of this tension. It would also mean working within an eschatological framework, since the nature of our eschatology often affects the shape we give to our mission.

A theological framework would also, potentially, help address one of the areas of absence in this chapter: the absence of God as agent, the nature of how God relates to the world, and how this therefore needs to inform the way in which mission and evangelism are carried out by those working with God for the transformation of the world around them.

Philosophies of identity and otherness

There is much written on these topics, and I think some engagement would be beneficial, particularly in being more precise in the use of terms such as 'identity' and 'otherness'. This would be especially helpful in charting out the possibilities of conceiving of relating to the other differently, as well as being grounded in some of the psychological realities of being human (such as the need to belong and the difficulties inherent in identity being subjugated to bigger and bigger groups of belonging). Contemporary philosophies of otherness help to chart out how identity is formed for self and other, and how particular shapings of identity yield certain types of relationship to the one perceived as other. To put it simply, human beings construct their sense of identity and place in the world within a complex network of relationships with other human beings, the world around them, and the philosophical and cultural systems within which they belong. When they meet an 'other' (person or idea), their weaving of the story of the world and their own place within it is disturbed, yielding an instinctive threat reaction. This often yields one of two opposite reactions, either rejection of the other (often accompanied by an attempt at mastery over them) or a collapse of their own identity to the mastery of the other. Many traditional approaches to evangelism have reflected these dynamics. A consideration of how evangelism, mission, and identity may work together may involve a reconceptualizing of meeting the other that consciously moves away from instinctive reactions and into a more constructive approach to meeting the other within an open, third space that does not collapse or appropriate one consciousness over another.

It is helpful here to note a danger which is alluded to in the chapter and present in much contemporary writing: the risk of turning the relationship with the other into a primarily ethical framework, which then dictates that I act well towards the other, but without necessarily meeting the other and opening up to how their difference may disrupt my own stories of identity. Reducing the duty towards the other to an ethical precept of caring for the vulnerable can easily veer into benevolent patriarchy, which still does not treat those who are underprivileged or oppressed as equals, and reinforces the privileged position of the 'helper' as needed and in control.

Within this optic, one may then ask how helpful it is to consider 'identity' as immutable, and how far we need to see identity as constantly evolving within relationships. Contemporary philosophers and theologians concerned with anthropology might then extend this thinking to considering what promotes the health of the human person in terms of stability and change, what is needed for the self to be secure enough to meet the other, how group identity can be constructed without becoming oppressive, and how human beings can belong meaningfully.

Gathering these threads together, I suggest that it would be helpful to reflect on how Christianity itself is concerned with the politics of identity and therefore shapes particular models of interaction when it comes to evangelism and mission. Scripture is of course not monochrome on the subject: notions of identity in general and faith identity in particular shift and evolve together with social context and historical location. Yet at the same time, there is little doubt that faith in Yahweh in the Old Testament, and in Christ in the New, shapes persons and communities to the core of their being; it does not just shape what they do, but their entire story of who they are, and what and how the world is. Neither is this shaping static or instantaneous. By all accounts, the process of faith is the process of opening oneself to the otherness of God and, within this dynamic relationship, seeing oneself changing, and participating in the change and transformation of society.

Notes

1 The sources of Latin American theology—whether in its liberationist or integral mission veins—can be traced back to developments in Europe and the United States which sought to go beyond liberal and post-millennialist as well as fundamentalist readings between the late nineteenth- and mid-twentieth centuries, in the light of the devastating impact of the two great wars, the civil rights movement, and the process of decolonization. Political theology and various forms of response given by Protestant and Catholic theologians, as of the early 1970s, helped to articulate a dialogue between continental European theological avant-gardes and newly sensitized Latin American young theologians. In the Brazilian context, the impact of the work of Richard Shaull, a Presbyterian theology teacher and adviser to the World Christian Student Movement, sparked a Protestant counterpart to Roman Catholic developments after Vatican II that must be counted as an alternative source of liberation theology. The more radical orientation of the evangelical integral-mission approach came, initially, to a large extent from the push of Latin Americans, such as René Padilla and Samuel Escobar, advisers to the Intervarsity Movement in the region and keenly involved in the Lausanne movement. But the theological language was and remained for a long time imbued with Northern vocabularies and methods (see Alves 1969; Assmann 1971; Bonino 1997; Boff 1998; Míguez, Rieger, and Sung 2009; Heaney 2008; Padilla 2010; Santiago-Vendrell 2010; Escobar 2012; Padilla 2012).

2 There is an essential interconnection between perceptions of the world by actors and observers (whether media, academic, or theological/religious ones), their engagement with concrete situations and with others, and how they alter one another, rendering ever-changing the context in which actors make sense of the world and the issues they feel compelled to respond to. This interweaving of perception, action, and context means that our relation to the world and to the Scriptures is always *meaning-ful*, that is, always contextual, relational, and traversed by conflicts of interpretation.

3 There is a clear tension, in this theological literature as well as in socio-anthropological literature, between reassertions of identity as pre-given and ahistorical or ancestrally defined on the one hand, and emphases on identity as an open, future-oriented construction (even if marked by historical legacies) on the other. However, it is also true that there are many roads in between which may be broader or narrower at different times and places, but which always witness to less clear-cut definitions and experiences of what identity is, how it is formed and transformed, and what needs to be retained or inherited at concrete junctures. My own approach will stress the relevance of inhabiting this plural, heterogeneous, and, surely, tricky 'middle ground', understanding that it is not There is a clear tension, in this theological literature as well as in socio-anthropological literature, between reassertions of identity as pre-given and ahistorical or ancestrally defined on the one hand, and emphases on identity as an open, future-oriented construction (even if marked by historical legacies) on the other. However, it is also true that there are many roads in between which may be broader or narrower at different times and places, but which always witness to less clear-cut definitions and experiences of what identity is, how it is formed and transformed, and what needs to be retained or inherited at concrete junctures. My own approach will stress the relevance of inhabiting this plural, heterogeneous, and, surely, tricky 'middle ground', understanding that it is not so much a middle way, a balance between extremes, as an affirmation of the plural and contingent character of identity—including the ones recorded and narrated in biblical accounts.

4 A wide range of secular and theological perspectives have emerged on such issues. See Connolly 1995, 2011; Huntington 1996; Derrida 2000; Sherwood and Hart 2005; Panotto 2015; Gajardo and Valderrama Cayumán 2017.

5 On such policies of recognition and the debates around them in Latin America, see Garbarino 2008; Castro-Gómez and Grosfoguel 2007; Richard 2010; Dietz 2017.

6 The advances made by black movements in Brazil, for example, in their efforts to reach back to authentic cultural roots after centuries of forced assimilation (including de facto religious syncretism), led many activists to identify Afro-Brazilian religions as an integral part of black identity. This led both to a 'culturalization' of Candomblé (the Brazilian historically adapted form of African traditional religion) through a number of actions that identified *terreiros* (Candomblé places of worship) as cultural centres in and through which anti-racist and cultural diversity policies were implemented. Since the early 1990s, neo-Pentecostal churches had been waging a war on Candomblé and the Catholic Church as the great religious evils of Brazilian society. Such churches, in increasing convergence with traditional Pentecostal ones, succeeded in electing a sizeable number of representatives to both houses of the National Congress of Brazil (the Federal Chamber and the Senate) and crafting political alliances with governments since the mid-1990s that allowed them to occupy high-rank positions in the administration. From pulpits, in Parliament, and

through various media, Pentecostal resistance was pieced together against black rights as some sort of back-door legitimation of Afro-Brazilian religions, pulling other conservative secular and religious groups into the gravitation of Pentecostal-led reaction. Similar logics developed around an alleged 'gender ideology' which would dissolve traditional gender roles and 'proselytize' the acceptance of homosexual relations as legitimate. In the context of the increasing polarization that Brazilian society has undergone since the aftermath of the presidential election of November 2014, this complex conservative reaction embraced openly neoliberal views of economic crisis as a direct consequence of the modest progress in social legislation and social policies. Such has been the journey from a largely benign evangelical empowerment between the mid-1980s and mid-2000s to a clearly 'new Christian right' takeover since then.

7 I use these terms in a broad sense. The assumption here is not that the lines are drawn between liberalism and conservatism within churches or in society at large. It is rather that polarized discourses pitting affirmative positions to identity politics and their increasingly vocal and mobilized adversaries have intensified antagonisms and mutual accusations among conflicting groups. What actual contents such 'liberal' and 'conservative' responses have is open to varied and debated descriptions, some of which I offer here.

8 The point could be easily made in relation to First Testament sources, as intimated by Israel's journey from ethnogenesis through constant migration and eventual long-term enslavement to an ancient state–temple alliance, under constant threat from world empires of the time. The emergence of the prophetic movement and its complex links to priestly theologies produced a composite tension between a sense of special election and of universal solidarity that confronts us as contemporary readers with ambivalent orientations. Ethnic versus ethical covenant, fraternalism versus bigotry, covenant entitlement versus organized and religiously-sanctioned oppression, commitment to the poor, the orphan, the widow, and the stranger or foreigner in tension with self-referential faith: these are shades of theological tension challenging current attempts to derive dogmatic or intolerant forms of ethical orientation and message, as much as summoning us to appreciate what the First Testament can tell us about living with difference.

Bibliography

Álvarez, Miguel (2017) *Integral Mission: A Paradigm for Latin American Pentecostals.* Eugene, OR: Wipf & Stock.

Álvarez, Miguel (ed.) (2016) *The Reshaping of Mission in Latin America.* Eugene, OR: Wipf & Stock.

Alves, Rubem (1969) *A Theology of Human Hope.* New York: Corpus Books.

Assmann, Hugo (1971) *Opresión-liberación: desafío a los cristianos.* Montevidéu: Tierra Nueva.

Bohache, Thomas (2008) *Christology from the Margins*. London: SCM.

Boff, Leonardo (1998) *Ecology & Liberation: A New Paradigm*. Maryknoll: Orbis Books.

Bonino, José Miguez (1997) *Faces of Latin American Protestantism*. Grand Rapids, MI: Eerdmans.

Brandão, Carlos Rodrigues (2006) 'The Face of the Other's God: Notes on the Theology of Inculturation in Latin America', *Teoria & Sociedade*, 2 (special issue), https://socialsciences.scielo.org/scielo.php?script=sci_arttext&pid=S1518-44712006000200003&lng=en&tlng=en.

Burity, Joanildo (2016a) 'Minoritisation and Global Religious Activism: Pentecostals and Ecumenicals Confronting Inequality in Politics and Culture', in Dawn Llewelyn and Sonya Sharma (eds.), *Religion, Equalities and Inequalities*, pp. 137–48. Abingdon and New York: Routledge.

Burity, Joanildo (2016b) 'Minoritization and Pluralization: What is the "People" that Pentecostal Politicization is Building?', *Latin American Perspectives*, 43/3, 116–32.

Caldas, Carlos (2016) 'Desafios da teologia pública para a reflexão teológica na América Latina', *Revista de cultura teológica*, 24/88, 328–53.

Castro-Gómez, Santiago, and Ramón Grosfoguel (2007) *El giro decolonial: reflexiones para una diversidad epistémica más allá del capitalismo global*. Bogotá: Siglo del Hombre Editores/Universidad Central/Instituto de Estudios Sociales Contemporáneos, Pontificia Universidad Javeriana/Instituto Pensar.

Cleary, Edward L., and Timothy J. Steigenga (eds.) (2004) *Resurgent Voices in Latin America: Indigenous Peoples, Political Mobilization and Religious Change*. New Brunswick: Rutgers University Press.

Connolly, William E. (1995) *The Ethos of Pluralization*. Minneapolis: University of Minnesota Press.

Connolly, William E. (2011) *A World of Becoming*. Durham, NC: Duke University Press.

Derrida, Jacques (2000) *Of Hospitality*. Stanford: Stanford University Press.

Dietz, Gunther (2017) 'Interculturalidad: una aproximación antropológica', *Perfiles educativos*, 39/156, 192–207.

Escobar, Samuel (2012) 'Doing Theology on Christ's Road', in Jeffrey P. Greenman and Gene L. Green (eds.), *Global Theology in Evangelical Perspective: Exploring the Contextual Nature*. Downers Grove, IL: InterVarsity Press, pp. 67–85.

Freston, Paul (1997) 'Charismatic Evangelicals in Latin America: Mission and Politics on the Frontiers of Protestant Growth', in Stephen Hunt, Malcolm Hamilton, and Tony Walter (eds.), *Charismatic Christianity: Sociological Perspectives*. London: Palgrave Macmillan, pp. 184–204.

Freston, Paul (2007) 'Latin America: The "Other Christendom", Pluralism and Globalization', in Peter Beyer and Lori G. Beaman (eds.), *Religion, Globalization and Culture*. Leiden and Boston: Brill, pp. 571–90.

Freston, Paul (2008) 'Researching the Heartland of Pentecostalism: Latin Americans at Home and Abroad', *Fieldwork in Religion*, 3/2, 122–44.

Freston, Paul (2015) 'Prosperity Theology: A (Largely) Sociological Assessment', *Lausanne Movement*, 2 Oct., https://www.lausanne.org/content/prosperity-theology-a-largely-sociological-assessment.

Gajardo, Antonieta Vera, and Angélica Valderrama Cayumán (2017) 'Teología feminista en Chile: actores, prácticas, discursos políticos', *Cadernos Pagu*, 50, e175012,http://dx.doi.org/10.1590/18094449201700500012.

Garbarino, Maximiliano (2008) 'Retomar la iniciativa política, recuperar la ética militante: debates y combates en torno a la obra de Ernesto Laclau', *Sociohistórica*, 23–24, 253–70.

González Nieves, Juliany (2017) '18 Latin American Female Theologians You Should Know About', *The Global Church Project*, 31 July, https://theglobalchurchproject.com/18-latin-american-female-theologians-know.

Heaney, Sharon E. (2008) *Contextual Theology for Latin America: Liberation Themes in Evangelical Perspective*. Eugene, OR: Wipf & Stock.

Huntington, Samuel P. (1996) *The Clash of Civilizations and the Remaking of World Order*. New York: Simon & Schuster.

Jacobsen, Edneida, Rudolf von Sinner, and Roberto E. Zwetsch (eds.) (2012) *Public Theology in Brazil: Social and Cultural Challenges*. Zurich and Berlin: Lit Verlag.

Kater, John L. (2018) 'Latin American Anglicanism in the Twentieth Century', in William L. Sachs (ed.), *The Oxford History of Anglicanism*, vol. V: *Global Anglicanism, c.1910–2000*. Oxford: Oxford University Press, pp. 98–123.

Leavitt-Alcántara, S. (2008) 'Latin American Theology', in William R. Dirness and Veli-Mati Kärkkäinen (eds.), *Global Dictionary of Theology*. Downers Grove: IVP Academic, pp. 470–2.

Medina, Daniel, and Alfaro, Sammy (eds.) (2015) *Pentecostals and Charismatics in Latin America and Latino Communities*. New York: Palgrave Macmillan.

The Memoria Indígena Declaration (2015) final document of the conference 'Who Writes History? Indigenous Spirituality and Mission Identity', *Journal of Latin American Theology: Christian Reflections from the Latino South*, 10/2, 111–16.

Míguez, Nestor, Joerg Rieger, and Jung Mo Sung (2009) *Beyond the Spirit of Empire: Theology and Politics in a New Key*. London: SCM.

Ngong, David (2017) 'The Ethics of Identity and World Christianity', *Missionalia*, 45/3: 250–2.

Oro, Ari Pedro, and Daniel Alves (2015) 'Encontros globais e confrontos culturais: Pentecostalismo brasileiro à conquista da Europa', *Dados: revista de ciências sociais*, 58/4, 951–80.

Padilla, C. René (2010) *Mission between the Times: Essays on the Kingdom*. 2nd rev. and updated edn. Carlisle: Langham.

Padilla DeBorst, Ruth (2012) 'Songs of Hope out of a Crying Land: An Overview of Contemporary Latin American Theology', in Jeffrey P. Greenman and Gene L. Green (eds.), *Global Theology in Evangelical Perspective: Exploring the Contextual Nature*. Downers Grove, IL: InterVarsity Press, pp. 86–101.

Panotto, Nicolás (2015) 'Heterotopías, nomadismos e identidades populares: una relectura del concepto de pueblo desde el relato del Éxodo en las teologías de la liberación', *Horizontes decoloniales*, 1/1, 164–95.

Parker Gumucio, Cristián (2002) 'Religion and the Awakening of Indigenous People in Latin America', *Social Compass*, 49/1, 67–81.

Parker Gumucio, Cristián (2016) 'Religious Pluralism and New Political Identities in Latin America', *Latin American Perspectives*, 43/3, 15–30.

Peterson, Anna L., and Vásquez, Manuel A. (eds.) (2008) *Latin American Religions: Histories and Documents in Context.* New York and London: New York University Press.

Richard, Nelly (ed.) (2010) *En torno a los estudios culturales: localidades, trayectorias y disputas.* Santiago and Buenos Aires: Arcis/Clacso.

Roussel, Jean-François (ed.) (2018) *Decoloniality and Justice: Theological Perspectives.* São Leopoldo: World Forum on Theology and Liberation/Oikos.

Salinas, J. Daniel (2017) *Taking up the Mantle: Latin American Evangelical Theology in the 20th Century.* Carlisle: Langham.

Sanchis, Pierre (2001) *Fiéis & cidadãos: percursos de sincretismo no Brasil.* Rio de Janeiro: Eduerj.

Santiago-Vendrell, Ángel D. (2010) *Contextual Theology and Revolutionary Transformation in Latin America: The Missiology of M. Richard Schaull.* Eugene, OR: Pickwick.

Sherwood, Yvonne, and Kevin Hart (eds.) (2005) *Derrida and Religion: Other Testaments.* New York and Abingdon: Routledge.

Sinner, Rudolf von (2012) *The Churches and Democracy in Brazil: Towards a Public Theology Focused on Citizenship.* Eugene, OR: Wipf & Stock.

Sinner, Rudolf von, and Nicolás Panotto (eds.) (2016) *Teología pública: un debate a partir de América Latina.* São Leopoldo: EST/Gemrip.

Steil, Carlos Alberto, and Rodrigo Toniol (2013) 'O Catolicismo e a Igreja Católica no Brasil à luz dos dados sobre religião no censo de 2010', *Debates do NER*, 14/24, 223–43.

Tamez, Elsa (ed.) (2006) *Through her Eyes: Women's Theology from Latin America.* Eugene, OR: Wipf & Stock.

Vuola, Elina (2002) *Limits of Liberation: Feminist Theology and the Ethics of Poverty and Reproduction.* London and New York: Sheffield Academic Press.

10

Pastoral care as evangelism

MARIANELA DE LA PAZ COT (CUBA)

This chapter describes some experiences of Christians in contemporary Cuba. This living experience is embedded in a complex world context, where threats to peace and the integrity of creation, together with the lack of the justice that would guarantee a dignified life for millions of human beings, constitute not only realities but also challenges that call us to discover new ways for God's mission in this world.

In this changing and globalized world, Cuba is going through multiple economic and social changes, which generate feelings of insecurity and hopelessness in lots of people. As a result of the updating of the Cuban economic model, macro-economic indicators have been prioritized while trying to avoid the social cost. Nevertheless, it has been shown that poverty-reproducing processes and inequality have coexisted with the implementation of the state's protective apparatus and have become worse in the last few years. These changes, although gradual, have had an impact on diverse population groups, giving rise to social and economic differences that did not exist before. As a background for all these changes at an international level, there has been a deterioration in the relations between Cuba and the United States, which have become tense in several respects. This affects the families in Cuba, the relations among our churches, and those wishing to visit our country freely, in addition to the unjust fifty-year-old embargo which makes the life of my people even harder.

The Cuban religious context is diverse. Apart from Christianity there are other expressions of Cuban religions of African origin, which are known as Afro-Cuban. Judaism, spiritualism, and Islam are also present, among other smaller groups. We could say that most of our people do not think of themselves as belonging to a particular Christian church, which does not mean we are not a religious people. Rather, our life is expressed in our syncretic and popular religious practice, where the Afro-Cuban matrix is predominant. Initiation in Afro-Cuban religions cannot take place without the particular candidate's initiation in the Christian church.

The Cuban Council of Churches is developing a training programme for prison chaplains, who are mainly Pentecostal Christians. As part of the team, I was asked to support their training by developing the subject of pastoral care with people of other faiths or beliefs, of whom there are many in the prisons they visited.

The chaplains also knew that I am the priest in charge of a community in the town of Limonar in Matanzas province, which is mainly made up of low-income black women who are initiated in Afro-Cuban religions. All these women grew up in families which belonged to the Episcopal Church from its very beginning in this town. They stay loyal to the Christian faith in spite of the fact that the church was damaged in a hurricane in the 1980s, and they faithfully worship God every Sunday in the small sacristy, which is the only part of the building still standing. They identify themselves as Episcopalian, and they feel that the church has always walked alongside them. The ministers who have served there have been respectful and have not opposed their basic spirituality and religious practices. On the contrary, they have offered them all that as the church of Jesus Christ we are called to give. The women identify with the liturgy of the church, and have had their children, grandchildren, and great-grandchildren baptized throughout generations. The church has accompanied them through its pastoral rites, by tending the sick and through funerals and memorial services, which they value highly because they regard them as a way to honour their ancestors.

The Bible text which I used to work out the subject with the chaplains and which I will discuss in this chapter is 2 Kings 5. I will approach this text from the perspective of pastoral care in order to obtain clues which may enable us to accompany those who are different, whether religious or not or in any other ways that make them 'different' from our understanding of God's people. Mission places us outside these 'limits' and amid new challenges. I thus intend to reflect upon the care-giving aspect. What does care giving mean and how can this enlighten us for our mission? Finally, I would like to share some experiences of this care giving as an aspect of pastoral care in the mission that is taking place in the Cuban Episcopal Church.

Naaman's story: God tends the foreigner

According to Daniel Schipani, pastoral care with people of a different faith from our own raises questions that we must consider. For instance, an interpretative journey through the Old and New Testaments will reveal to us the main biblical sources for the affirmation of God's unlimited grace facing the reality and diversity of human beings, including interreligious situations. All human beings are God's creatures and the object of divine love. Two texts from Leviticus 19.34 and Deuteronomy 10.17–18: 'The alien who resides with you shall be to you as the citizen among you; you shall love the alien as yourself', and 'The Lord…loves the strangers, providing them with food and clothing', show us that taking in, caring for, and tending the alien is a special form of compassion which God urges us to practise. This resonates in times of such great geographical mobility, when borders are blurred by migration, and such people need not only board and lodging, but also that their spiritual needs be taken into account.

Naaman's story can be framed in this way. It is the story of an alien, a military man who is used to commanding rather than obeying. He suffers from leprosy, a physical condition that hinders his duties. Through his wife's maid, a young woman with a profound faith, he hears about a prophet of God in Israel who can heal him.

Nothing else is said about this young woman in the text, even though her role is key in Namaan's decision. She trusts in, claims, and declares the power of the prophet of Israel, which makes her an indirect and alternative evangelist. Yahweh's power is thus incarnated in the prophet and mobilized in the narrative by the young woman who makes his voice heard and takes this man to this foreign land—not as a military commander, but as an alien who needs to be healed. Thus begins the process of visiting the land of Israel. A letter from the King of Syria to the King of Israel states the reason for the visit, and the load of money and clothes that Naaman takes is perhaps the means to 'pay' for the favour.

The Syrian commander is not received by the prophet Elisha in his home. Instead, Elisha sends a messenger to tell him what to do in order to be rid of his disease. Naaman is full of contempt. Being used to commanding, he refuses to comply with the suggestion of a bath in the Jordan. His expectations of what things would be like on his arrival fall apart. There is no warm welcome, no physical examination, no questions. It all comes down to a simple command: 'Go, wash in the Jordan seven times' (2 Kings 5.10). It is not possible to be healed by doing such a simple thing, plunging seven times in that river. He could have done that in the great rivers of his own land. There is, perhaps, a disguised contempt for this land in his words.

Naaman finally sets out on the road towards the healing encounter with the God of Israel, puts his contempt aside, and experiences the healing in his skin. 'Now I know that there is no God in all the earth except in Israel'

(2 Kings 5.15). He acknowledges that life is a gift from God and that it is not possible to make it into an object of exchange. This is confirmed by Elisha when he refuses to accept any of the riches offered by Naaman in gratitude for his healing.

The barriers between the Syrian commander and the prophet are broken down. The contempt towards the foreign country becomes gratitude, which Namaan expresses by acknowledging that there is a God only in Israel and by reverencing the land where he has received healing, which causes him to take some earth back to his country. It is in Israel that he has known God's infinite care and grace, which shows itself beyond Israel's borders, in many different ways and through many different people, providing them with complete healing, salvation, and restoration.

Naaman perceives that he must be honest to Elisha. As one of his duties he must accompany and support his king while he kneels in the temple before the god Rimmon in Syria. The prophet understands him and feels the anguish it causes him to fail the God of Israel, whom he has confessed as the only God. Finally the question arises: what has Naaman found in Yahweh that he has not found in the god Rimmon?

Elisha knows that Naaman will not be the same again. Although he will remain Syrian and a military commander, something in his identity has changed. He is a witness of the power of the God of Israel, and that will endure for ever. Elisha says to him, 'Go in peace' (2 Kings 5.19). He knows that God knows what is in Naaman's heart. Naaman will have to live in Syria grounded in the experience of this restoring and healing encounter in which the God of Israel has been glorified.

Gehazi, the prophet's servant, on the other hand, goes after the Syrian commander and lies to try to gain an advantage from the healing his God has performed. He is condemned by his greed and becomes a leper. Nowadays greed continues to make many people sick: we forget that when Jesus heals us he frees us from all that oppresses and marginalizes his people, as he did with the leper in Mark's Gospel (1.40–45), and that both of these lepers moved out of the small circle in which their disease imprisoned them to witness about their healing and salvation in other lands and to other people.

Naaman's story: clues for the pastoral care of people from other faiths

The term 'care' as Torralba explains it has many meanings which show its conceptual richness. Although care may relate to both objects and living beings, our focus remains on the care of people, and this type of caring action is much more complex as it goes through all the dimensions of human reality. Caring can be seen as compassion for the other, putting yourself in the other's shoes, living through and suffering what they are living through. Caring also allows us to establish a very close relationship where the other's life is integrated in ours; we take part in their thoughts, in their way of feeling, and thus a 'we' is built which transcends the 'I' and the 'you'. It is the vulnerability of the human being, that is, its frailty, which allows care giving, especially when that finite and frail human being experiences highly vulnerable conditions like illness and suffering.

The theologian Leonardo Boff states that in the care-receiving mode of pastoral care ministry, the recipients may demonstrate resistance and anxiety. Nevertheless, these can be overcome with patient perseverance, so that in place of aggression and domination there is mutual affection of two people side by side. It is necessary to develop compassion towards all suffering human and non-human beings, and to obey the logic of the heart rather than the wish to conquer and use things. It is necessary to give up the desire for power, which reduces everything to objects disconnected from human feeling. It is important to reject ever kind of despotism and domination, and to let cold rationality give way to care, so that we can feel in communion with others through the presence of the Spirit who transcends our human limitations and reconnects us with all that is in the universe. We urgently need to rescue our essential humanity in order to avoid the devastation of the biosphere.

Naaman, in his vulnerable condition, received a lesson in humility from God through Elisha. Moreover, as Brueggmann states, this narrative has a great irony, since Syria was Israel's sworn enemy. Notwithstanding this, the main point is that the healing of the Syrian commander in the land of Israel establishes a certain relationship between both nations mediated by a healing act. The commander needed to renounce his wish for power and control of everything in order to see that God does not care about our status but about what our need is, and letting himself be cared for was part of this plan.

The prophet prepares everything for Naaman's visit, and warns the King of Israel that he should not worry, that the commander is coming to visit him as a prophet of his land (which the king seems to ignore). However, Elisha does not want to 'show off' as the person performing the miracle; he knows he is simply God's servant. At last Naaman agrees to be led to the Jordan, and in this act of humility the encounter with God takes place. Being humble implies ridding ourselves of our certainties and viewpoints and letting ourselves be led, allowing the birth of a close relationship where we are integrated into the other's life and feeling.

As Christians we need to be humble; we sin in arrogance when we think of ourselves as better than non-Christians, or better than those who are Christian but in a 'strange' way. We are not called to judge; judgement belongs to God, and in Matthew 25.31–46 it is the lack of care giving that actually condemns us. Often we are not welcome when we visit those who are 'different', perhaps because their experience with other Christians has been negative. There has been too much judgement, a lack of compassion, and a wish to dominate.

We thus forget that evangelism means giving the good news, sharing our faith with others with humility and trust as a gift that shows God's love, grace, and mercy in Christ.

Care giving is an important axis for evangelism. Caring has to go through our eyes: we must look compassionately at those in vulnerable conditions. This was perhaps the young woman's feeling when she found out that her master was suffering from leprosy and witnessed about the power of the prophet from Samaria to heal him. Her unsolicited witness was so convincing as good news of healing and salvation that her master made up his mind to cross the border and go to Israel. God does not believe in borders, and, as Christians, we need to remember that. Evangelism is not taking God to other places, for God is there already.

Caring must go through our hands: we must be willing to uphold and support the weak one, willing to bless, to show affection, to nurture and offer healing actions. Naaman's healing does not make him arrogant; he will not go back to Syria lecturing the king about his experience with the God of Israel. He knows he will have to accompany and support his king, though he does not worship the god Rimmon.

Caring must go through our feet: we must be willing to walk alongside the suffering, walk the way Christ did with the Emmaus walkers, a walk towards the encounter with the Word, not a babble; a walk towards the encounter with the Master, with the table set to celebrate the life that is given when we share the bread.

Our challenge is to renew our commitment, both locally and worldwide, with believers from other religions and cultures in the building of communities of love, peace, and justice, which will become possible only through inter-cultural dialogue and communication, and is impossible with arrogant attitudes. This will be the fruit not only of great worldwide events but also of constant work at the local church. We need to be a healing community where our witness is concrete service to our neighbour, where deep conversations take place every day with all kinds of people everywhere, and bridges and alliances are built through these conversations which favour a culture of peace, based on faith.

Another important point found in the text is that God's grace flows when we are capable of receiving humbly what we have asked for. The prophet knows he has been an instrument of God for Naaman's healing; therefore he does not expect honour or pay, for the glory belongs to God. Nowadays some unscrupulous Christians easily forget that; they make Christian worship into triumphant healing services where the leader is glorified to God's detriment and where false expectations arise. These can be very damaging to people and, in my opinion, become a terrible witness for the church.

In the face of the worry or qualm of conscience that Naaman presents to Elisha about having to go with his king to worship the god Rimmon, the prophet does not give him a doctrinal speech or speak about idolatry; he simply says, 'Go in peace.' We must remember that Elisha was a prophet who spent a long time occupied with tasks which some might describe as 'minor', those related to caring for and accompanying his people in daily situations, but they left a deep mark on these people's lives and their relationship with God. Elisha knows that God has transformed Naaman's life. 'Shalom' is not simply a farewell word. God's shalom has been lived out by Naaman as healing and salvation, as total restoration.

In order to build a pastoral care relationship we must talk less and listen more to people in their need and grief. It is necessary to create a different kind of helping relationship between two cultural universes, where neither of the two parties becomes hostage to the other, a *meta-empathetic* relationship in which, as the theologian Sidnei Vilmar Noé states, participants from different cultures meet in a common space, and which preserves and values the specific cultural elements that each one brings to the encounter. This is increasingly important in a changing world where the Christian outlook is being reconfigured under the influence of the worldwide migration phenomenon.

Another area that the church must strengthen is effective support networks within communities to encourage people to show a genuine interest in one another. Concerns such as crises in families, discontent with employment, unemployment, and so on need to be reaffirmed in the liturgical life of the church. We cannot separate what takes place in the worship place on Sundays from what happens at the workplace or in homes during the rest of the week. I agree with what the theologian Ronaldo Sathler-Rosa suggests in relation to pastoral care being extended to the public domain, and with his call for a 'theology of pastoral action devoted to public life' where pastoral agents, both clergy and laypeople, must be encouraged to carry out their vocation in society and not merely inside their churches. This is our great challenge for our mission as the church, and as ministers we need to remember that the church walls are not a limit for God's action. We need to explore other spaces and other languages, including technology, to bear the good news from this caring perspective.

Pastoral care as respectful and responsible evangelism: two-witness narratives

Rev. Juan Ramón de la Paz[1] states:

> It was a great discovery for me when, in 1956, I read Rev. Dr. Maurice Daily's thesis written in 1951, entitled 'Cuban Spiritualism and Christian Faith: A Study of Some Animistic Elements in Cuban Life with Their Implications for the Christian Movement' when he was studying at the seminary in Matanzas. This paper inspired me to study and enter into dialogue with Cuban religions of African and French origin, their fusion process, as well as their new expressions when getting to the simple people. I have done this throughout my ministry.
>
> In 1993 we met Juan Despaigne, who is Okbbá, and we started a fruitful dialogue with him which included his community and many of his Godchildren. His initial approach was because Juan wanted to read the Bible, get to know about Jesus Christ and he wanted to have someone who could guide him. We started with the reading and study of the New Testament. We had experience exchanges with great respect, he got more interested in getting to know the Episcopal Church better, our beliefs, liturgy, doctrines and symbols. One day, to our surprise, he expressed his desire to get ready for confirmation and always attended the church and the confirmation preparation sessions faithfully. In time, more than 50 believers from that community have been prepared and confirmed in our church. They speak about Christ, the Gospel and its teachings, its ethics and values

> and communicate to us their experiences and blessings. Juan is well loved and popular in several neighborhoods in Havana, visits people in hospitals, and prays for them. To those who ask him about his Afrocuban religion, he preaches and teaches the Gospel of Jesus Christ.[2]

This has been a transformative pilgrimage experience where the church opens up to trans-religious spaces, and the 'God's people' category displaces us from rigid positions and places us as pilgrims on the way together with others. This is where the encounter takes place and where God's people are called to live in relationships of exchange, which implies acknowledgement, dialogue, reciprocity, harmony, and re-creation of all relationships. This exchange is just the manifestation of the Spirit's riches being offered in many ways, including in other religions. Dialogue is here an element of paramount importance for inclusive pastoral care.

Since I was installed in the church of San Felipe el Diácono in Limonar in 2009 I have had several experiences of pastoral care. A female member of the church named Bernarda asked me to visit her godfather Lázaro, who was very sick. He had been baptized as a child in our church but was not an active member. When I got to the old man's house he started to apologize because his house was full of images and symbols related to the saints of the Yoruba religion. With a friendly gesture I took his hand and asked him not to apologize; I was with him in God's name to accompany him and minister to him.

There was a picture with an image of Jesus Christ, and I asked him who Jesus was for him. He said he was number one. Nothing was possible without him. Then I asked him if he wanted me, in Jesus' name, to pray for his healing and read the church's service for the sick. I explained to him what the service was, and that if he so wished, I would anoint him with holy oil and give him communion. First we talked: he told me about his illness (he did not know precisely what he had, but felt very weak) and about his fears, but he also said that 'he had his Father God', and that this encouraged him. I talked to him about the certainty of being God's beloved son and that God cared for him amid everything he was going through, because, as he himself said, 'I do not feel lonely because you all care for me.'

When the service for the sick was over, he felt encouraged, particularly because I had not questioned his other faith, or as he said, 'the things of my religion', and he asked me to return. As the church we supported Lázaro through the sacraments and with pastoral care until his death. This had a deep meaning for the family, the neighbourhood, and the congregation. We performed pastoral care through the church's pastoral rites.

Juan's and Lázaro's stories make us wonder what they found in Christianity that they perhaps did not find in their basic religion. What motivates Juan to keep on witnessing about God's and Jesus' love to his 'disciples' by taking them the good news and inviting them to live a life within an Episcopal community and church?

Some words from the Arusha 'call to discipleship', from the World Council of Churches' Conference on World Mission and Evangelism, provide a fitting conclusion:

> We are called by our baptism to a transformed and transforming discipleship: a life style connected to Christ in a world where many face despair, rejection, loneliness and uselessness.
>
> We are called as disciples to belong together to just and inclusive communities, in our search for unity and in our ecumenical way, in a world based on marginalization and exclusion.
>
> We are called to be faithful witnesses of God's transforming love in dialogue with people from other religions in a world where the politicization of religious identities is a frequent cause of conflict.
>
> We are called to be formed as servant leaders that show the way to Christ in a world that favors power, wealth and money culture.
>
> We are called to pull down barriers and seek justice for people who are dispossessed and displaced from their lands, including migrants, refugees and asylum seekers, and to oppose the new frontiers that separate and kill.

Response

JORDAN HYLDEN (UNITED STATES)

I am deeply grateful to De la Paz Cot for her fine chapter, and for the opportunity to respond to it. Over the past fifty years and more, even before our two churches became separate in 1966, relationships between Anglican brothers and sisters in the United States and Cuba have often been distant at best.

I was moved to read De la Paz Cot's story of the tenacious faith of the women of her church in Limonar, worshippers who continued from Sunday after Sunday to crowd into the sacristy, the only room of their church that remained after a hurricane, to worship the Lord Jesus Christ. It struck me as a beautiful image of the faith and spirit of her country, and of the Christians who worship there. Even in the ruins, there is faith and there is joy, because there is still found there the resurrected Lord Jesus Christ, who is to be worshipped and glorified all the same even if the walls have fallen down around us. I look forward to learning more from such faithful Christians as the bonds that already unite us in baptism knit us more closely together into one church, after so many years apart.

In this brief response I wish to do two things. First, I intend to raise a few questions about De la Paz Cot's exegesis of 2 Kings 5. Second, I will pose a question about her model of 'mission as care', or caring pastoral accompaniment of those of differing religious positions, that I will draw from the great Lesslie Newbigin. In short, I want to suggest that the humble and compassionate care that De la Paz Cot recommends does not need to rule out the call to conversion to the worship of the one true God, the Father of our Lord Jesus Christ, in the power of the Holy Spirit.

First, then, Scripture. Commendably, De la Paz Cot seeks to ground her model in Holy Scripture, taking as her text the story of Naaman's healing of leprosy by the prophet Elisha in 2 Kings 5. Naaman was of course a Syrian, the commander of the army of the King of Aram who set out to Israel to seek a cure for his leprosy. De la Paz Cot draws two key lessons from the story. First, she views Elisha's counsel to Naaman after his healing as a model for how we should accompany others with pastoral care even in the face of religious difference. After Naaman is healed by washing seven times in the river Jordan, as the prophet Elisha has instructed him, he asks pardon from the Lord for something he will need to do upon returning home to the court of the King of Aram. For what does he ask pardon? When the king enters the temple of the god Rimmon, De la Paz Cot writes,

Naaman will be expected to 'accompany and support' his king in his pagan worship. On Elisha's response to Naaman's quandary, she writes that Elisha 'does not give him a doctrinal speech or speak about idolatry; he simply says "Go in peace"'.

Second, De la Paz Cot lifts up the humility and compassionate care that she sees in the story of Naaman and Elisha as an example of what can happen by the grace of God when we lay aside the desire to dominate others and allow ourselves to give and receive care, without a prideful assumption of superiority. Naaman, De la Paz Cot writes, exhibits this humility when he submits to washing in the Jordan, even though at first his pride resists. He renounces his 'wish for power and control', accepting his need for healing. Elisha too exhibits this humility, by not being present at the healing: the washing takes place out of his sight at the river, underscoring that it comes not from his power and status, but from God's grace. De la Paz Cot emphasizes the importance of humility by saying that it is precisely in Naaman's act of humility, in allowing himself to be washed, that 'the encounter with God takes place'. This humility, she goes on to say, 'implies ridding ourselves of our certainties and viewpoints and letting ourselves be led, allowing the birth of a close relationship where we are integrated into the other's life and feeling'.

The lesson for us here, De la Paz Cot writes, is that we must not in arrogance think ourselves better than non-Christians. It is not our place to judge, she writes: that is only the place of God. Rather, in humility, we should join with believers of other religions to build communities of love, peace, and justice, which we will achieve only through dialogue and the daily work of caring service to our neighbours.

Certainly, there is much to value in De la Paz Cot's exegesis. Yet I cannot help but wonder if she has omitted some key features of the biblical text. After Naaman's healing, his first words were: 'Now I know that there is no God in all the earth except in Israel' (2 Kings 5.15). It would seem that this is one of a number of texts in the historical books that underscore that there is only one God, the God of Israel, and that all are called to worship him alone. Elisha, of course, is the protégé of the prophet Elijah, whose confrontation with the prophets of Baal makes this point in a particularly vivid way, not least by killing them after showing their god to be no god at all (1 Kings 18). This approach to dialogue, one might say, is carried on by Jehu, whom Elisha anoints King of Israel, when he kills the remaining priests of Baal and turns their temple into a latrine (2 Kings 10).

Now, I do not mean to recommend this violence as an approach to other religions today. We must view them ultimately through the lens of the King of Kings who is also Prince of Peace. Nevertheless, I see in them as a whole an uncompromising witness that there is only one true God, the God of Israel, a jealous God, who demands that his people may have no other gods but him. I am doubtful, in particular, that Elisha's words to Naaman—'go in peace'—should be read as signifying an approval of pastoral accompaniment of pagan worship as a whole. Rather, it seems likelier that Elisha is recognizing that Naaman is not in fact worshipping the so-called god Rimmon, but is simply supporting the arm of his elderly king. So here then is my first question to De la Paz Cot: does canonical Scripture, viewed as a whole, support the lessons drawn here from 2 Kings? Do these lessons have to depend on a kind of selective reading, instead of wrestling with the canonical witness?

What then should we say, if we do wish to commend the humility and Christ-like care that De la Paz Cot lifts up as crucial for the practice of evangelism? What should we say, if we do wish to reject the cross-cultural arrogance that has too often accompanied the practice of mission? I think De la Paz Cot is completely correct to recommend these virtues, and indeed that Christ-like evangelism and witness require them. But can we have them while also maintaining the zeal for conversion to the worship of the one true God that we find in the prophets Elijah and Elisha? I think we can. In *The Open Secret*, Lesslie Newbigin has this to say about Christ and the religions:

> The church...as it is *in via*, does not face the world as the exclusive possessor of salvation, nor as the fullness of what others have in part, the answer to the questions they ask, or the open revelation of what they are anonymously. The church faces the world, rather, as *arrabon* of that salvation—as sign, first fruit, token, witness of that salvation which God purposes for the whole.... The church is in the world as the place where Jesus, on whom all the fullness of the godhead dwells, is present, but it is not itself that fullness....It must therefore live always in dialogue with the world, bearing its witness to Christ but always in such a way that it is open to receive the riches of God which belong properly to Christ but have to be brought to him.[3]

My second question for De la Paz Cot, then, is whether or not this distinction between Christ and the church might help us both maintain the centrality of witness to Jesus Christ as Lord and saviour of all nations, as Newbigin insisted, while at the same time recognizing that we may always encounter Christ in a fresh way, or be spurred on to fresh obedience, precisely as we bear witness to him to all nations.

We have been given much to reflect on by De la Paz Cot as we consider the difference between the proper enculturation of the Gospel and an improper syncretism. I thank her again for her chapter, and may God bring our two churches and countries ever closer together.

Notes

1 Rev. Juan Ramón de la Paz Cerezo has been a minister in the Episcopal Church of Cuba for more than fifty years, now as a retired clergyman assisting the new Dean of Holy Trinity Cathedral. He is one of the pioneers of interreligious dialogue and respectful evangelization towards people of other faiths. He was Dean of Holy Trinity Cathedral and for many years served as minister of different communities throughout the country, where he deepened his study of popular religiosity, spiritism, and Afro-Cuban religions, participating in national and international events. From 1993 to 2009 he hosted the interreligious dialogue meetings in Holy Trinity Cathedral, in which people from the ecumenical movement also participated.

2 Translated from Marianela de la Paz Cot, 'La Iglesia como comunidad sanadora: desafíos para la Iglesia Episcopal de Cuba', doctoral thesis, Faculdades EST, São Leopoldo, Brazil, 2009, pp. 33–4.

3 Lesslie Newbigin, *The Open Secret* (Grand Rapids, MI: Eerdmans, 1978), pp. 203–4.

Conclusion

STEPHEN SPENCER

This book has revealed a rich diversity of approaches to evangelism and witness in global Anglicanism. In some places the Gospel is communicated through the service of education and medicine (Egypt), or through pastoral care (Cuba). In other places the challenge and invitation of the Gospel needs primarily to be embodied in the life and relationships of the church community (Malaysia, Brazil). In sub-Saharan Africa there is scope for overt evangelism, though this must not ignore the increasingly complex relationship between Christianity and traditional African religion, with many people adhering to both. What is clear is that those who are located in one cultural context, whether it be in the Global North or the Global South, are in no position to decide how evangelism and witness should take place in a different context. Listening to each other, engaging in conversation about these matters, reflecting and praying about them are all necessary, with those who are rooted in a place ultimately being responsible for determining which approach should be taken in that place.

Does this mean we must accept an inherent plurality of approaches and conclude that this is all that can be said about evangelism? Is evangelism endlessly variable, continually reacting to the different contexts in which it takes place? Or is there a common core, an irreducible minimum which needs to be expressed wherever the church is found and which should be placed alongside the other shared elements of the faith, such as the Bible, the creeds, the sacraments, and the orders of ministry?

This book began with words of Hebrews, that Jesus Christ is 'the same yesterday and today and for ever' (Heb 13.8). These imply that evangelism, the telling of the good news about him, must also in some ways be the same yesterday and today and for ever. But we have also seen how the language of such communication, both in words and in other ways, varies from period to period and culture to culture. So the forms of evangelism, broadly understood, will also inevitably vary from context to context and from century to century. The core of evangelism, then, will not be found in the manner of its expression but must be found elsewhere. This means we must look to its content. And what is its content? Hebrews is clear: it is the person of Jesus Christ who is constant and faithful through all time.

Evangelism at its core, then, is about the communication of this person, a living being who reaches out to new believers through the Spirit of God inviting them into an ongoing relationship with him. It is, in other words, always about helping new believers make a connection with Christ and staying in touch with him from that point onwards. As Isabelle Hamley wrote in her response, it is all about 'opening oneself to the otherness of God and, within this dynamic relationship, seeing oneself changing, and participating in the change and transformation of society'.

Finally, as a way of illustrating this, showing how it is taking place in the Anglican Communion today, in one of its churches, the following paragraphs describe an example of evangelism from Tanzania. It is a simple yet inspiring example of what is possible and what can be possible. It expands what was written above about the Mara approach to evangelism.[1] It is presented to encourage readers to embrace and engage in this life-changing activity, and to do so in ways that are appropriate to their own specific contexts. It illustrates a number of the themes in the chapters above.

The example comes from Tarime diocese in the north-west of the country, from an interview I conducted with a parish priest (called there a pastor). A tall and bright-eyed young man, who greeted me with the resonant Swahili phrase 'Karibu' ('You are welcome'), he was enthusiastic about evangelism in his remote parish of subsistence farmers. He described the way he and the people of his church practise it through home visiting. He began by emphasizing the importance of community service provided by the diocese which, as a by-product, prepares the ground for evangelism:

> Often [the people we visit] have heard about the Anglican church and its farm development work. They may have come to the farm development centre for training. This makes the Christian faith more attractive.

He then evocatively described how the Gospel message is communicated to these people. He described a one-to-one encounter used when bringing people to faith, a personal form of evangelism that he undertook most weeks, usually on a Thursday afternoon:

> The plan is to have house-to-house evangelism, going in pairs. We start with visiting the homes of the congregation and then move on to non-believers. When welcomed into a home I first introduce myself as a pastor from the Anglican church and say that we have come to have a discussion about God, Jesus and the Bible. If they say this is OK we might sing a worship song, then sit and pray, and then I will tell them about how God has created the world and that Christians believe in this great God rather than the small gods of pagans. I will tell them the message of John 1, that the Word of God was

> there from the beginning and that nothing has happened without God: so God is the God of all, he is the first and the last, everything is in his hands. I talk about the birth of Jesus, that God has come among us, and of the miracles of Jesus and the difference he makes to our lives.

This is a revealing testimony. It shows that the communication between evangelists and hosts is predicated on the friendliness and vulnerability of the evangelists: they have come into the home of those they are talking to and depend on the welcome and hospitality of that home. The power dynamics of the classroom, where the teacher has power over the students to pass or fail their work, is missing. Instead they come offering a gift in friendship, a gift that can be accepted or refused. Furthermore they offer their teaching only if there is assent from their host: the power lies with the student and not the teacher, as it were. The principle here is not about evangelistic communication having to take place in a home, for in some contexts this is not possible, but about the evangelist being a guest of the host wherever they happen to be meeting.

It is also important to notice how the singing of a worship song and the saying of a prayer consciously bring a third party into the room, which is the presence of God. This means the communication that is taking place is not just the relaying of information from one party to the other. Something more is happening, an engagement with the one who surrounds and dwells within them all. The time together, then, is not only going to point to the Gospel of God; it is going somehow to bring it into effect, a sacramental action.

The pastor's testimony also shows how the content of his teaching mediates between two different realities: the cultural world of the hosts influenced by traditional pagan religion, and Christian faith rooted in the Old and New Testaments. The teaching is a sensitive yet challenging presentation of the latter to the former. What is offered is different and definite, not a simple accommodation to what is there already. This is possible because of the vulnerability of the teachers: they are not imposing what they bring but simply laying it on the table.

The fundamental respect of the relationship between hosts and teachers is again emphasized:

> I always give them the opportunity to choose whether to become a Christian. I offer to come back to continue the conversation. They choose a day which will suit them. If they say they are not sure I will leave them with a Bible verse to read and discuss later. One I often use is Psalm 95.1: 'O come let us sing to the Lord; let us make a joyful noise to the rock of our salvation.' I will write

> it on a piece of paper so that they can meditate on it. If they are old and do not read I will give it to a younger member of the family to read out to them.

This shows the door being opened to active discipleship for the hosts. They can freely choose whether to set out on the path of following Christ, and some words of Scripture are given to encourage them along this path. But note that there is no implied threat of hellfire and damnation. The gift that is being offered is something joyful and life-giving. However, there is an edge to this gift that is relevant to a rural context in which female genital mutilation (FGM) is still practised:

> I will also challenge them about FGM. I will say that in the Bible we are told that all that God created is good —so why harm it? I will challenge them to change their life.

The outcome of this encounter lays a strong and safe foundation for future discipleship:

> If and when they become a Christian they feel they are freed from fear of evil spirits and that demons and devils have been chased away and it is no longer necessary to wear charms. Their protection is now from God.

Note

1 See pp. 142–3. The following paragraphs are based on my book *Growing and Flourishing: The Ecology of Church Growth*, SCM Press (2019), which is an extended analysis and discussion of the Mara approach to church growth.

Index